EMPIRICISM AND EXPERIENCE

Empiricism and Experience

Anil Gupta

OXFORD

UNIVERSITY PRESS

2006

OXFORD

UNIVERSITY PRESS

Oxford University Press, Inc., publishes works that further
Oxford University's objective of excellence
in research, scholarship, and education.

Oxford   New York
Auckland   Cape Town   Dar es Salaam   Hong Kong   Karachi
Kuala Lumpur   Madrid   Melbourne   Mexico City   Nairobi
New Delhi   Shanghai   Taipei   Toronto

With offices in
Argentina   Austria   Brazil   Chile   Czech Republic   France   Greece
Guatemala   Hungary   Italy   Japan   Poland   Portugal   Singapore
South Korea   Switzerland   Thailand   Turkey   Ukraine   Vietnam

Published by Oxford University Press, Inc.
198 Madison Avenue, New York, New York 10016

www.oup.com

Oxford is a registered trademark of Oxford University Press

Library of Congress Cataloging-in-Publication Data
Gupta, Anil
Empiricism and experience / Anil Gupta.
p. cm.
Includes bibliographical references (p.) and index.
ISBN 978-0-19-518958-2
1. Experience. 2. Knowledge, Theory of. 3. Empiricism. I. Title.
B105.E9G87 2006
146'.44—dc22   2005055485

3 5 7 9 8 6 4

Printed in the United States of America
on acid-free paper

To
Mukta
Beloved Friend

PREFACE

My principal concern in this book is to understand the *logical* relationship of experience to knowledge. Experience, it appears, makes *some* contribution to our knowledge of the world. What is this contribution? Say that I look out of my window and see that it is raining. As I look out, I have a visual experience and come thereby to believe that it is raining. My belief is reasonable, and it would appear, it is so in part because of my visual experience. But how does my visual experience contribute to the reasonableness of my belief? This question has no easy answer, and I devote chapter 1 to bringing into clear view the principal obstacle that must be overcome if we are to find a satisfactory answer. It is important to find an answer, for without it, we cannot assess the claims of empiricism.

My approach to the problem of experience and knowledge is shaped by three convictions. The first conviction is that the classical empiricist response to the problem deserves respect. I grant that classical empiricism is unacceptable. However, in the process of throwing away its detailed doctrines, we should take care not to throw away the discipline within which it works and the problems that it addresses. Classical empiricism, as I see it, is founded on genuine constraints and a natural idea. It is not a product of some silly little argument from illusion, or of some pathological preoccupation with skepticism. I argue in chapter 2 that classical empiricism is a powerful—and inevitable—development of a natural idea. Hence, a genuine alternative to classical empiricism cannot be obtained cheaply. It will not be found, for example, by returning to the comfort of common sense, or by browsing the racks of naturalized psychology, or through a refuge in some sort of mythical behaviorism. I argue for all this in chapters 2 and 5. (Especially relevant are §§2E and 5B, where I discuss Willard V. O. Quine's and Wilfrid Sellars's responses to classical empiricism.)

My second conviction is that the problem requires us to take seriously certain interdependencies. In chapter 4, I highlight the relevant interdependencies and go on to develop a proposal about the logical relationship of experience to knowledge. My entire approach here is guided by the work I have done on the logical theory of interdependent definitions. (I provide in chapter 3 a brief introduction to this theory.) This work has made me realize that logical interdependency is not something to be avoided and feared but something to be accepted and exploited. It is a common prejudice that logical interdependency is a source of problems; actually, it is often the route to a solution. The fundamental error in classical empiricism—indeed, in all traditional thinking about knowledge—issues, it seems to me, from its flight from interdependence. The essence of this book can be summed up thus: it is an attempt to address the concerns of the classical empiricists, within the constraints they would insist on, but with a tool they did not possess—the logic of interdependence. It is not a new thought that classical empiricism has elements that deserve to be preserved. And, in contemporary philosophy, logical interdependence is increasingly recognized as legitimate and powerful. The way in which I have put these two ideas together may, I hope, hold some interest.

My third conviction is that this change in logical perspective yields a promising empiricism, an empiricism that does not need to be buttressed by idealism or another form of antirealism. In chapters 5 and 7, I argue that the change of perspective yields an empiricism that is viable. The change provides empiricism with a new tool for dealing with troublesome challenges. In chapters 6 and 8, I argue that the empiricism we obtain is an attractive one. It does not need to make claims that earn it enemies and that embarrass its friends.

These are the convictions that underlie this book. I have argued for them, but I am acutely aware that it is not easy to defend these convictions, much less to prove them. This book is merely a first step toward the defense. I have not cluttered the book with a profusion of 'perhaps', 'maybe', and 'seems to me'. But it should be understood that it is with great tentativeness that I put forward the theory sketched below. The issues are difficult and complex, and in dealing with them, it is particularly easy to mistake illusion for insight. Our subject has known many an arduous program that seemed to its proponents to be insightful—indeed, to provide the only feasible approach—but that was deeply flawed in its very first steps; the entire program looks, in retrospect, quixotic. Hence, it is essential in this subject to scrutinize with the greatest care the first steps before one launches into long and elaborate investigations. I have aimed to provide in this book only such details as are sufficient to determine the structural soundness of the picture I present. I am well aware that a number of elements in the picture—including the notions of view and admissibility—need greater elaboration. The central question is whether these elements *deserve* further elaboration, whether the basic plan of the theory survives a careful first scrutiny. If the theory is deemed quixotic, I wish to have the comfort of knowing that I spared the reader useless and boring complexity.

The book ends with a "Supplement on 'Experience'." Here, I gather together earlier remarks that clarify the concept of experience in play in the book, and I have added some further clarifying comments. Since the supplement presupposes the preceding chapters, I have placed it at the end. But it may be consulted any time the pressure of the question, "What on earth does the author mean by 'experience'?" becomes too great for the reader to bear.

I HAVE BEEN THINKING ABOUT THE PROBLEMS OF EXPERIENCE and knowledge from the very beginning of my philosophical career. These problems were on my mind when I worked in the early months of 1980 on ideas that evolved into the revision theory of truth; my first, inchoate thoughts about the present proposal date from this period. I did not begin to develop these thoughts, however, until the early 1990s. I devoted a part of my stay, in 1998–1999, at the Center for Advanced Studies in the Behavioral Sciences, Stanford, to working out the present proposal. I thank the Center for providing an ideal research environment, and I thank Indiana University and the Andrew W. Mellon Foundation for supporting my stay there. I began serious work on writing this book in early 2001, and before the unsettling events of the fall interrupted my work, I had good drafts of chapters 1, 3, and 4. (I wrote a draft of a part of chapter 2 also but discarded almost all of it.) I wrote much of the rest of the book in the academic year 2003–2004, when I was on a sabbatical leave from the University of Pittsburgh. The leave was supported in part by fellowships from the American Council for Learned Societies and the National Endowment for the Humanities (NEH). I thank these institutions, as well as the University of Pittsburgh, for their generous support. (NEH asks fellowship recipients to include the following disclaimer in their acknowledgments: "Any views, findings, conclusions, or recommendations expressed in this publication do not necessarily reflect those of the National Endowment for the Humanities.")

An essay drawn from this book appears under the title "Experience and Knowledge" in the volume *Perceptual Experience*, edited by Tamar Szabó Gendler and John Hawthorne. I thank the editors and Oxford University Press for permission to use this material here.

I presented some of the ideas developed in this book in seminars and lectures—most recently in my spring 2005 seminar at the University of Pittsburgh and in the lectures I gave at the University of Lethbridge, Smith College, National Taiwan University, and the India International Centre. I benefited from the examination my ideas received on these occasions. I benefited also from the more informal comments and criticisms I received from many friends, students, and colleagues. I thank especially Horacio Arlo-Costa, George Bealer, Nuel Belnap, Bob Brandom, Bill Brewer, Bryson Brown, Joe Camp, Bill Demopoulos, Chris Frey, Kim Frost, Jay Garfield, Tamar Szabó Gendler, John Hawthorne, Katarzyna Kijania-Placek, Hans Kim, Adam Kovach, Byeongdeok Lee, Caleb Liang, John McDowell, José Martínez-Fernández, John Morrison, Karen Neander, Ram Neta, Ted Parent, Nicholas Rescher, Kevin Scharp, Susanna Schellenberg, and Ernest Sosa.

With Chris Hill, I have enjoyed many extended discussions about the metaphysics and epistemology of experience. I learned much from these discussions, and I thank him for the guidance he has given me. With Mark Wilson, I have had over the years many conversations about the philosophy of language, and especially about meaning and truth. His ideas, and his wealth of examples, have enriched my own thinking. I am grateful to Ingo Brigandt, Bosuk Yoon, and the two referees for Oxford for their detailed comments on the book. Anjana Jacob and Christine Young helped me with proofreading, and Endre Begby prepared the first draft of the index. I thank Barbara Edelman and Jessica Ryan for their expert editorial assistance, and Peter Ohlin, senior editor at Oxford, for his keen interest in publishing this book.

My greatest debt is to my wife, Mukta. She brought me light when everything in my life had turned dark. I dedicate this book to her.

CONTENTS

EMPIRICISM AND EXPERIENCE

ONE

TWO TRUISMS

The principal problem addressed in this essay is this: What is the contribution of experience to knowledge? The problem is best appreciated, I think, by reflection on two commonplace ideas about experience and knowledge—ideas that appear to be in some tension with one another. I shall label these ideas the "Insight of Empiricism" and the "Multiple-Factorizability of Experience."

1A. The Insight of Empiricism

According to the first idea, experience is our principal epistemic authority and guide. It is experience that pronounces on the validity of our concepts, conceptions, and theories about the world. And it is experience that guides us to improve our concepts, conceptions, and theories when these prove untenable. Whether we believe that the tides are caused by the motions of two giant turtles in the sea, or whether we accept the more improbable idea that they are caused by the sun and the moon, experience is the final authority on the validity of our beliefs. Whether we believe that there is a merciful God who listens to our prayers or that our lives are shaped by blind forces and chance events, again, it is experience—not some ancient book or sage figure—that is the final authority on the acceptability of these beliefs. Even broad structural ideas about the world, such as those concerning space and time, are under the jurisdiction of experience.[1]

The idea that experience is the principal epistemic authority and guide is a commonplace today, but this should not obscure our appreciation of its power. It is this idea that has shattered false idols and leveled mountains of superstition. And it is this idea that has freed us from enslaving ideologies and institutions. The idea seizes epistemic authority from self-styled sages and cults of pundits, and vests it in experience—experience of the masses. The resulting democratization of knowledge reins in the tyranny that a self-anointed institution would exercise on us. Any such institution is subject to a higher authority: experience.

I will call this idea the *Insight of Empiricism*. The idea, it should be said, is not at the forefront of philosophical debates associated with modern empiricism. These debates are more occupied with psychological and linguistic issues—issues such as whether we have innate concepts, whether the meaning of a sentence can be identified with its verification conditions, and whether there is a philosophically fruitful analytic-synthetic distinction. Nevertheless, the Insight is the most fundamental claim of empiricism. Empiricists would gladly sacrifice their other theses could they but preserve the Insight. Indeed, as we shall see, it is the difficulties that arise in sustaining the Insight that lead empiricists to propound their other, more dubious, theses.

The Insight of Empiricism, I wish to stress, concerns the *normative* role of experience, not its *causal* role. The Insight should not be identified with claims such as that experience is the cause of beliefs or that all true beliefs are causally grounded in experience. These causal claims might be utterly false. We might, for instance, have come into the world with preformed beliefs that are true. Still, this would not diminish the normative force of the Insight: we would remain under an epistemic obligation to test our beliefs

---

1. I will set aside mathematics in this discussion. Note, however, that it is plausible to include mathematical claims within the jurisdiction of experience, insofar as they are *genuinely about the world*. The difficult philosophical questions about mathematics concern the contents of its claims. Are these claims vacuous in the way certain logical claims are? Or are they about broad structural features of the world, or perhaps of language? Or are they about a special Platonic realm that is a genuine part of our world? Whether the jurisdiction of experience extends to mathematics depends on how such questions are answered.

against experience. The issue of the causal origin of our beliefs is quite separate from the issue of their rational grounding.

There is another reason why the causal and normative claims should be sharply distinguished: the former do not readily yield the latter. Suppose that the causal claims are true. How do we derive the injunction that we should test our beliefs against experience? And what does this testing of beliefs against experience come to? The idea cannot be that we should put ourselves in a position so that it is experience that causes beliefs in us. This makes little sense, for the etiology of our beliefs is highly obscure to us. There is, in short, no easy path that connects the causal and normative ideas. It is not surprising, therefore, that philosophers who stress the causal role of experience are often those who deny its normative role—or who despair of making sense of it.[2] It must be admitted that the difficulties one encounters in making sense of the normative role of experience are substantial. Let us now turn to the principal source of these difficulties.

1B. The Multiple-Factorizability of Experience

Experience is a product of the world and of our selves. The subjective character of experience—how things seem to be in experience—is a product of two factors: how things are and our state and position in the world. Further, these factors cannot be recovered from individual experiences. The idea is familiar and is easily illustrated. Some time ago I looked at a wall, light green in color, so large that it occupied my whole view. My visual experience then had a certain subjective character: my whole visual field was filled with the color light green. Plainly, my experience was the result of certain properties of the wall, and of certain properties of my visual system, and of certain relationships that held between the wall and me. The same visual experience—that

---

2. An example is Donald Davidson. In his essay "A Coherence Theory of Truth and Knowledge," Davidson writes, "No doubt meaning and knowledge depend on experience, and experience ultimately on sensation. But this is the 'depend' of causality, not of evidence or justification" (p. 146). John McDowell has rightly stressed, against Davidson, the normative role of experience. See his *Mind and World*, Lecture I.

is, visual experience with the same subjective qualitative character—would have occurred had I looked at a white wall while wearing glasses with a certain greenish tint, or had I instead looked at a blue wall while wearing glasses with a certain yellowish tint.[3] Furthermore, I could have had the same visual experience even with my eyes shut, for certain sorts of direct stimulations of my brain can presumably produce that experience. Finally, in dreams, the same visual experience can perhaps occur without any external stimulation at all.

Let us call a pair of factors that result in experience—that is, a pair consisting of the state of the relevant part of the world and of the state/position of the self—a *world-self combination*. Then the present point is this: any visual experience can result from several different world-self combinations. This feature is not peculiar to visual experience, of course; it applies also to other kinds of experiences (auditory, tactual, olfactory, etc.). For example, I can hear my daughter, Donna, singing in the family room, and I have a certain pleasant auditory experience. The same auditory experience would result if Donna were out of the house but a particular recording of her singing were played in the family room. Further, as before, the same experience could result from a direct stimulation of my brain, and perhaps, it could even occur without any external stimulation at all, as in a dream. The argument plainly generalizes: any auditory and any other kind of experience can result from several different world-self combinations. The point can be strengthened: the same holds of *total* experience at any moment. A total experience, too, can result from several different world-self combinations.

Given two forces that are acting simultaneously on a body, we can calculate the resultant force, but given only the resultant, we cannot recover the two forces. Similarly, given a world-self

---

3. It is sometimes convenient, both here and below, to speak as if experiences with the same subjective qualitative character are identical. I adopt this manner of speaking while remaining neutral on the metaphysics of experience. What is important for present purposes is the relation of "subjective qualitative identity" that obtains between experiences, not how experiences are individuated. We shall later be concerned with certain epistemic properties that subjectively identical experiences share. See the discussion of the Equivalence constraint in §2B. See also the supplement at the end of the book.

combination, we can (in principle) determine the experience, but given only the experience, we cannot recover the world-self combination. No experience carries with it its own genealogy. Any experience can be factored into several different world-self combinations.

This conclusion does not conflict with our ordinary practice of saying that such perceptual judgments as "here is a hand" and "there is an orange coaster" are based on experience. My present experience, as a matter of fact, entitles me perfectly to make these two judgments. But the reason for this is *not* that my present experience cannot be factored into different world-self combinations; it *can* be so factored. Instead, the reason is that I take myself to be entitled to claims such as that my eyes and my perceptual system are functioning properly, that the lighting is normal, and that my friends are not bent on deceiving me. In short, I take myself to be justified in holding a fairly specific conception of myself and my relationship to the world. Given that this conception is justified, my present experience entitles me to the judgments "here is a hand" and "there is an orange coaster." But were I not justified in holding this conception (or another similar conception), my experience would not entitle me to these perceptual judgments. What we call "ordinary judgments of perception" do not issue from experience alone. They are founded in experience *and* conception. Ordinarily, we have no need in our discourse to question or to vary the conception, and we speak as if the justification for perceptual judgments lies solely in experience. The truth is, however, that every experience has multiple factorizations, and no experience *by itself* provides any justification for ordinary judgments of perception.

Let us now consider the width of possible factorizations of any given experience. Consider, for example, the experience I had when I looked at the light green wall under normal conditions. Let us call this experience e. Consider the world-self combinations $\langle w, s \rangle$ into which e can be factored. (Here w represents the state of the relevant part of the world, and s represents the state and the position of the self in the world.) From the causal point of view—that is, when the laws of nature and our own constitutions are taken as fixed—perhaps the range of these world-self combinations is narrow. Our present interest, however, is in the range of factorization from the *normative* point of view. We wish to discover what a rational being can conclude about the self and the world *solely* on the basis of having the experience e.[4] Now, e does not carry information about the nature of the self and its position in the world. For instance, e does not tell me that I am a being who has a body that responds to nearby walls with such and such visual experiences. I may know this about myself, but the basis of this knowledge does not lie solely in e. The subjective character of e is compatible with a wide range of possibilities about my nature and my position in the world. I might be so constituted that I have experiences exactly like e in response to blue walls, or in response to certain kinds of radiated heat from the wall, or in response to sound waves produced by certain waterfalls, or—to be quite wild—in response to the goings on in a distant galaxy. All of these possibilities are compatible with the subjective character of e. A rational being who has the experience e will be unable to rule out any of these possibilities solely on the basis of e. In fact, she will be unable to rule out other possibilities, as well. Consider any state of the world–say, $w^\star$–that does not involve the rational being. We can endow the rational being with a nature and position $s^\star$ such that the world-self combination $\langle w^\star, s^\star \rangle$ yields an experience subjectively identical to e. The world, for all that e reveals to the rational being, might be in the state $w^\star$ and the rational being itself in the state $s^\star$.

Any experience can be factored, then, into a wide range of world-self combinations. It is this idea that I call the *Multiple-Factorizability of Experience*. Let me stress three points about the idea. First, it applies to total experiences also. Second, it concerns epistemic possibilities, not causal possibilities. The idea is addressed to this question: what world-self combinations are compatible with a particular experience from the viewpoint of an ideal rational being? That is, what can the ideal rational being conclude about these combinations on the basis of this particular experience alone? Third, the idea asserts that the range of possible factorizations is wide indeed.

It is important to distinguish the Multiple-Factorizability of Experience from what has been called in the philosophical literature

---

4. Compare the following remark that George Berkeley puts in the mouth of Philonous: "Those things alone are actually and strictly perceived by any sense, which would have been perceived, in case that same sense had then been first conferred on us" (*Three Dialogues between Hylas and Philonous*, p. 204 in the Luce and Jessop edition and p. 90 in the Dancy edition).

the "relativity of sense-perception."[5] The latter refers to the fact that the same object can present different appearances under different perceptual conditions. A white wall, for instance, can appear white under one set of conditions, blue under another set, light green under yet another, and so on. The relativity of sense-perception thus points to the multiplicity of possible experiences for any given *object*. The Multiple-Factorizability idea is different. It points to the multiplicity of possible objects for any given *experience*. The two ideas are logically independent of each other. Objects may generate different appearances, but if, contrary to fact, each experience carried hints of its own genealogy, then Multiple-Factorizability would fail. On the other hand, Multiple-Factorizability could be sustained while perceptual relativity failed. Under this scenario, objects always appear as they are—blue objects, for instance, always appear blue—but Multiple-Factorizability is sustained because any experience has not only ordinary sorts of factorization but also many deviant ones (e.g., there may be subjectively identical dreams and hallucinations). The failure of perceptual relativity would reduce the width of the multiple-factorizability of experience but would not eliminate it altogether.

1C. The Problem of Empiricism and Experience

The Insight of Empiricism assigns to experience a large normative role in adjudicating and shaping our knowledge claims. The Multiple-Factorizability of Experience appears to call into

5. I take this expression from Roderick M. Chisholm, "The Problem of Empiricism." The idea of perceptual relativity is not new with Chisholm, of course. It is one of the pillars on which the skeptics, at least from Aenesidemus on (first century B.C.E.), rested their skeptical conclusions. It is explicitly invoked in Sextus Empiricus' exposition of Aenesidemus' ten modes of skepticism (see Sextus' *Outlines of Scepticism*, written second century C.E.). The idea probably goes back to Pyrrho and the Indian Gymnosophists (fourth century B.C.E.), and perhaps even to earlier thinkers and ascetics. See Julia Annas and Jonathan Barnes, *The Modes of Scepticism*.

The multiple-factorizability of experience is also invoked in the skeptical literature, but not as often. Marcus Tullius Cicero (106–43 B.C.E.) gives in his *Academica* a skeptical argument that relies on multiple factorizability (see fn. 15 of chapter 2). René Descartes's dream argument in the *Meditations on First Philosophy* also appeals to it.

question the capacity of experience to serve this role. Multiple-Factorizability implies that an experience *by itself* does not yield any truths about the world. But if this is so, how can experience play *any* role in adjudicating our knowledge claims? The standard model of adjudication requires us to deduce certain special sorts of statements ("observation statements") from our claims, and to consult experience to determine the truth or falsity of these statements. If experience deems the observation statements to be all true, our claims are confirmed; otherwise, the body of claims from which the statements were deduced stands empirically refuted.[6] Multiple-Factorizability seems to imply that experience does not yield any truths at all, and hence that experience is altogether incapable of pronouncing on the truth or falsity of observation statements. Multiple-Factorizability, it seems, renders experience mute. And a mute experience cannot play any adjudicating role, let alone the large one envisaged in the Insight of Empiricism.

The problem is not overcome by an appeal to a collection of experiences—or even to the totality of all experiences. If individual experiences are mute, then a choir of experiences—no matter how large—is also mute. The problem of understanding the adjudicating role of experience remains.

If we limit the adjudicating authority of experience, if somehow we can establish a priori the truth of a suitable conception of the self and its place in the world—for example, if we can establish a priori that there is a powerful, benevolent, and nondeceiving God who created the self—then there may be a way out of the problem. Experience, when taken in conjunction with this a priori conception, could yield truths and so could serve an adjudicating role in the manner sketched above. However, this way out of the problem comes with a heavy burden and a heavy price. We need to articulate a suitable conception of the self and the world, and we need to provide an a priori argument for it—possibly direct, possibly transcendental. This is a heavy burden. Further, assuming that we could convince ourselves that we had such a conception and such an argument, we would need to remove the conception from the scope of experience. This is a heavy price.

Another way of putting the problem is this. If we could begin our inquiry into the world with a true conception of the self and the

---

6. I mean, of course, that the conjunction of the claims is empirically refuted.

world, then we should have no difficulty deriving truths from experience. On the other hand, if we could derive truths from experience, we could through successive approximations arrive at a true conception.[7] The problem is that at the beginning of our inquiry we have neither: neither a true conception nor a vociferous and truthful experience. Without the guidance of experience, we are unable to arrive at a true conception of the self and the world. Without a true conception, it appears, experience is unable to guide us. The problem is how to break into this circle. As indicated above, one way to do so is to maintain that a true conception is available a priori. But this violates the Insight of Empiricism. Another way is to deny that one needs a conception—or at any rate a rich conception—before one can garner truths from experience. But this violates the Multiple-Factorizability of Experience. Both sorts of moves have found advocates in the history of epistemology. Neither has proved satisfactory.

To summarize: The problem of empiricism and experience is to answer our initial question—what is the contribution of experience to knowledge?—and to answer it in a way that respects the Insight of Empiricism and the Multiple-Factorizability of Experience. It deserves emphasis that our question concerns not the causal role of experience but its rational and logical role.

7. Assuming that the truths yielded by experience are rich enough.

TWO

SOME VIRTUES OF CLASSICAL

EMPIRICISM

Classical empiricism offers a striking approach to the problem of empiricism and experience—an approach that occupied center stage in epistemology for about 300 years but which has been the subject of incessant attacks since about the middle of the twentieth century.[1] In my discussion below, I shall acknowledge the problems that classical empiricism faces. These problems are serious and seem to me insoluble within the confines of classical assumptions. I willingly grant, therefore, that classical empiricism is fundamentally flawed. Nevertheless, my aim in this chapter is to highlight some of its virtues.

2A. A Cartesian Conception of Experience

Classical empiricism is founded on a radical and seductive conception of experience and the self. The immediate object of experience, according to this conception, is not the familiar world—things in public space and time—but a special, sensory world. This general conception assumes a number of specific forms in classical empiricism, of which perhaps the most important is the

1. The approach still attracts adherents, however. See, for instance, Howard Robinson's *Perception*, Evan Fales's *Defense of the Given*, and Richard A. Fumerton's *Metaphysical and Epistemological Problems of Perception*.

sense-datum theory. This theory is best introduced via an example. Consider my present situation. I am sitting before my computer. I can hear the soft whirring sound of the hard drive. And I can see on my right a round and orange coaster that lies next to a square, yellow one. Now, according to the sense-datum theory, the immediate objects of my experience are not the hard drive and the two coasters but certain fleeting sense-data.[2] These sense-data include a whirring auditory sense-datum, and an oval-shaped patch of orange next to a diamond-shaped patch of yellow in the right part of my visual field.[3] I am distracted by a knock on the door, and I turn my head. The coasters are no longer in my field of vision, and for a moment, I lose awareness of the noise of the hard drive. The three sense-data have ceased to exist.

According to the sense-datum theory, my position relative to my present sense-data is absolute. I do not view my sense-data from a point of view. I do not, for example, occupy a place in the visual field, the field that contains my visual sense-data (e.g., the orange oval and the yellow diamond). It makes no sense to ask, for instance, how the oval sense-datum would appear had I experienced it from the position of the diamond-shaped one. (This would be like asking how the number 7 would appear were I to look at it from the position of the number 2.) The space of my visual field is not the space of physical objects. My visual field is subjective; it is peculiar to me. The space of physical objects is objective; it is shared by many. I cannot—*logically* cannot—occupy any position in the visual field. By my very nature, I necessarily exist outside this field—and here 'outside' is not meant literally. There is no space, objective or subjective, that contains both me and my sense-data.

According to the sense-datum theory, the self is directly and immediately aware of its sense-data. The self's relationship to its sense-data is not mediated by any process that might affect its apprehension. In particular, none of the various factors that distort our perceptions of ordinary things is present here. The relationship

---

2. David Hume called sense-data "impressions." John Locke and George Berkeley called them "ideas," but their use of this term was broader (and also suffered from ambiguity).

3. These are not the only sense-data present in my experience. A complete enumeration would certainly be tedious, perhaps impossible.

of a self to its sense-data is transparent, direct, and unmediated. The sense-data are just what they seem to be.

What we ordinarily call 'experience of physical objects' is, according to the sense-datum theory, a complex of experience proper (also called 'immediate experience'), which is *of* sense-data, and a judgment, implicitly based on this experience, about physical objects.[4] In ordinary language, we report our experience by saying such things as "I see that this is an orange coaster." But according to the sense-datum theory, such reports invariably go beyond what is truly given in experience. What is truly given is a collection of sense-data with their properties, and we implicitly infer claims about physical objects (e.g., the coaster) from the sense-data we directly apprehend. It is as if sense-data are the shadows cast in our minds by external objects, and these shadows provide the only clues available to us about the existence and nature of external objects. (This metaphor would not be accepted by all proponents of sense-data, for not all think that external objects are distinct from sense-data.)

The sense-datum theory respects the Multiple-Factorizability of Experience (§1B) on the objective realm. It holds that an experience taken by itself does not reveal anything about objective things. But it insists that experience reveals much about the subjective. The theory thus denies Multiple-Factorizability on the subjective realm. It maintains that there is a unique factorization of experience into sense-data and the transparent self: the subjective character of experience fixes the characteristics of the apprehended sense-data.

The sense-datum theory preserves an element of the naive picture that in experience we make a direct perceptual contact with public, physical objects and with (some of) their properties and relations. The theory retains the idea of direct perceptual contact but introduces new subjective entities—sense-data—to be the objects of this contact.

The sense-datum theory is a descendent of Descartes's view that the foundations of our knowledge lie in the subjective realm, that is, in the knowledge the mind has about itself and its own "ideas." In the *Meditations*, Descartes says this about sensory awareness:

---

4. The notion of "immediate experience" goes under various names, including 'direct awareness', 'direct apprehension', 'sensing', and 'acquaintance' (Bertrand Russell).

And outside me, besides the extension, shapes and movements of bodies, I also had sensations of their hardness and heat, and of the other tactile qualities. In addition, I had sensations of light, colours, smells, tastes and sounds. . . . Considering the ideas of all these qualities which presented themselves to my thought, although *the ideas were, strictly speaking, the only immediate objects of my sensory awareness.*[5]

Hume, though he differs greatly from Descartes on the nature of ideas, is in fundamental agreement with him that the immediate objects of sensory awareness are subjective. These are internal impressions, not external objects:

Nothing can ever be present to the mind but an image or perception, and . . . the senses are only the inlets, through which these images are conveyed, without being able to produce any immediate intercourse between the mind and the object.

Every impression, external and internal, passions, affections, sensations, pains and pleasures, are originally on the same footing; and . . . whatever other differences we may observe among them, they appear, all of them, in their true colours, as impressions or perceptions. . . . For since all actions and sensations of the mind are known to us by consciousness, they must necessarily appear in every particular what they are, and be what they appear. Every thing that enters the mind, being in *reality* a perception, 'tis impossible any thing shou'd to *feeling* appear different. This were to suppose, that even where we are most intimately conscious, we might be mistaken.[6]

---

5. "Sixth Meditation," p. 52 in the Cottingham, Stoothoff, and Murdoch edition and p. 75 in the Adam and Tannery edition; emphasis added.

6. The first extract is from *Enquiry Concerning Human Understanding*, 12.1, and the second is from *Treatise of Human Nature*, I.4.2. The basic Cartesian assumption is accepted by Locke and numerous philosophers after him, empiricists and non-empiricists alike. Locke opens book IV of his *Essay Concerning Human Understanding* with these famous words:

Since *the Mind*, in all its Thoughts and Reasonings, hath no other immediate Object but its own *Ideas*, which it alone does or can contemplate, it is evident, that our Knowledge is only conversant about them. (IV.1.1)

And near the end of book IV, he writes:

For since the Things, the Mind contemplates, are none of them, besides it self, present to the Understanding, 'tis necessary that something else, as a Sign or Representation of the thing it considers, should be present to it: And these are *Ideas*. And . . . the Scene of *Ideas* that makes one Man's

The view that experience informs us primarily about subjective entities has, since Descartes, been accepted by a large range of philosophers. There have been disagreements, however, over the nature of these subjective entities. In the last extract above, taken from *Treatise*, Hume says that the objects of direct awareness "must necessarily appear in every particular what they are, and be what they appear." This points to one source of disagreement. All proponents of Cartesian conceptions accept the second part of Hume's claim, that the objects of awareness are what they appear to be. But many reject the first part, that they "appear in every particular what they are." Another issue that has provoked controversy is whether the objects of direct awareness are all universals, such as orange, white, and soft, or whether they include particulars, such as an oval instantiation of orange. Yet another point of contention is whether the self is an object of direct awareness.[7] That is, can the reports of immediate experience take the form of, for example, "I sense an orange oval sense-datum"? Or must these reports be of the form "Lo! An orange oval sense-datum," which excludes all mention of the self? Even deeper disagreements have arisen. Some philosophers who advocate a Cartesian view reject the whole idea that in immediate experience there is an awareness of *things*. The objects of immediate experience, in their view, are *states* of the self, and reports of immediate experience take the form exemplified by "I am appeared to orangely." Here 'orangely' serves to characterize the state that I am in or the process of perception, not a thing that I immediately experience. According to these philosophers, I can be appeared to orangely, though absolutely nothing in the world—not even a sense-datum—is orange. There are other points of disagreement, as well.[8]

Fortunately for our purposes, we need do no more than notice the internecine battles among Cartesian conceptions of experience. More important for us is to mark their shared characteristics. These conceptions contain a notion of "direct awareness." In direct awareness, the self has transparent and immediate access to a special

---

Thoughts, cannot be laid open to the immediate view of another. (IV.21.4)

7. Russell expresses uncertainty on this issue in *Problems of Philosophy*.

8. See essays in part II of Robert J. Swartz's *Perceiving, Sensing, and Knowing*. Robinson's *Perception* contains an extended defense of the sense-datum theory against its competitors, as well as against major objections.

realm of facts, distinct from the realm of familiar public facts (e.g., "there is an orange coaster on my right"). The facts revealed in direct awareness are subjective and internal; familiar public facts, on the other hand, are objective and external. The gulf between the subjective truths revealed in direct awareness and the objective truths that constitute our commonsense conception of the world is thus wide. And, consequently, the problem of justifying our knowledge of the external world is acute in Cartesian conceptions of experience.[9] Classical empiricists have displayed their greatest ingenuity—Berkeley being perhaps the most ingenious—in response to this problem.

In the discussion below, I shall take the sense-datum theory as my model of a Cartesian conception of experience. My argument will not rest, however, on any special features of this particular theory. It will apply to Cartesian conceptions in general.

2B. Constraints on an Account of Experience

Cartesian conceptions of experience are radical. They are far removed from our commonsense view that in experience we have a direct awareness of public objects and their properties. And, it must be admitted, Cartesian conceptions generate formidable epistemological problems. Nevertheless, despite a clear appreciation of the ensuing difficulties, classical empiricists have repeatedly reaffirmed these conceptions. Critics of classical empiricism have seen the reaffirmations as rooted in some vice: a neurotic preoccupation with skepticism, a simple logical error in an argument from illusion, and even a forgetfulness about linguistic usage. I want to suggest, however, that the reaffirmations are rooted in some virtues: the respect for genuine constraints and the acceptance of a natural idea. Cartesian conceptions, I shall argue, are natural consequences of

9. I am following the common practice of calling such conceptions 'Cartesian', thus recognizing the importance they gained with the work of Descartes. The conceptions themselves are much older. J. L. Austin writes in *Sense and Sensibilia* that they "were already quite ancient in Plato's time" (p. 2). A. D. Smith cites the Cyrenaic doctrine "only sense-impressions are apprehensible" (*Problem of Perception*, p. 3), which probably dates from the time of Plato. In his *Perception*, Bimal Krishna Matilal draws attention to Buddhist phenomenalism and, in particular, to Vasubandhu's "Illusionism" (circa 400 C.E.), which also anticipate Cartesian conceptions.

genuine constraints on any account of experience. The wish to escape from these conceptions and their problems is understandable. It is important to recognize, however, that the escape cannot be gained cheaply; it requires the rejection of a natural idea. Let me begin by spelling out and motivating the constraints I have in mind—they are four in number. I shall then turn, in §2C, to the argument for Cartesian conceptions.

THE FIRST CONSTRAINT AFFIRMS THAT EXPERIENCE PLAYS A rational role in shaping our knowledge. Let us understand the *given* in an experience to be the total rational contribution of that experience.[10] Then, the first constraint can be formulated as follows.

> *Existence* (*existence of the given*): Something is given in each experience; that is, each individual experience makes a rational contribution to knowledge.

This constraint is weak. It says nothing about the magnitude of the rational contribution of any experience (or of all experiences taken together). It allows that the contribution may be virtually nil. The constraint should therefore be acceptable to most nonempiricists. All that the constraint concedes to the empiricists is that they are not making a category mistake: they are not wrong to think that experience does have a rational bearing on our beliefs.[11]

There is a familiar distinction between a particular *state* of belief and an abstract something associated with it—its *content*—by virtue of which the state enters into logical relations with, for example, other beliefs. Similarly, the Existence constraint implies that there is a distinction between a particular occurrent experience and an

---

10. Sometimes the expression 'the given in experience' is used in a more narrow and philosophically loaded way. It is used to talk about the immediate contents of experience—things such as ideas, impressions, and sense-data—and the immediately available propositions about them. See Alan H. Goldman's "The Given." One can deny the existence of the given in this narrow sense (as I wish to) and yet insist (as I shall) that experience makes a rational contribution to knowledge.

11. It may be objected that the constraint is too strong. For, it may be said, some experiences are so thin and fleeting that they make no contribution to knowledge. Now, as far as the argument below for sense-data is concerned, this objection can be accepted and the constraint suitably weakened. My own preference, however, is to accept the unrestricted version of the constraint and to deal with thin and fleeting experiences by assigning them thin and fleeting givens (the given may even be as bare as "I exist now").

abstract something—I am calling it 'the given'—by virtue of which the experience enters into logical relations with, for example, beliefs. But there is a need to exercise a little caution here. Some philosophers think that experience is like belief in that it, too, has a propositional content.[12] If this is right, then experience can certainly enter into logical relations with beliefs (and other propositional attitudes). But the content that these philosophers associate with an experience is not necessarily the given in that experience. The given, by definition, is supposed to capture the *input* of an experience to the rational cognitive "mechanism," and this may well differ from the propositional content associated with the experience. A mental state—for example, a supposition—may carry a hefty content but may provide little input. Of course, a theorist may choose to identify the propositional content that she associates with an experience with the given in that experience. The present point is that this should be recognized to be a substantive thesis, not a tautology.

The Existence constraint is neutral not only on the logical weightiness of the given but also on the logical character of the given. It allows that the given may be an object, a property, a proposition, or something altogether different. Consider the experience, *e*, that I had when I looked at the orange coaster. One account of the given in *e* may hold that it contains the proposition that the coaster is orange. Another account may hold that the given contains the proposition that the oval sense-datum in my visual field is orange. Such propositional accounts of the given are certainly the most natural, but they are not the only ones permitted by the Existence constraint. The constraint does not rule out, for example, the following kind of story: The contribution of experience to knowledge is like that of a materials supplier to a builder. Experience supplies the bricks and mortar, and some other "bricklaying" rational faculty builds up judgments and the rest of the edifice of knowledge from them. In one version of the story, the materials supplied by experience are sense-data and their properties. (So, the given in my experience *e* would contain a particular visual sense-datum and the property of being an orange sense-datum.) In another version, the materials may be ordinary objects and their properties. (Now the given in *e* would contain the coaster itself and the physical property

---

12. One such philosopher is Wilfrid Sellars. I discuss Sellars's account of experience in §5B.

of being orange.) In either version of the story, experience fails to yield propositions, but its contribution to knowledge is nonetheless significant. Let me hasten to add that I mention this possibility not to recommend it but only to illustrate the latitude allowed by the Existence constraint. Elements of the bricks-and-mortar model of experience are definitely to be found in the writings of the classical empiricists. And antiempiricists have rightly cast a cold, skeptical eye on them.

The terminology of 'the given' allows me to formulate a little more precisely an empiricist thesis that shall concern us: *the given in experience can logically force our knowledge of the world*. I use the less specific 'logically force' here, instead of 'logically imply', because I want to allow for the possibility that the given is nonpropositional. And I formulate the thesis modally to ensure that it concerns the logical power of experience in general. It does not make a claim about the specific experiences that we have, as a matter of fact, suffered.

The present thesis should be sharply distinguished from the other theses that sometimes go under the label of 'empiricism'. It is completely independent of, for instance, the *psychological* thesis that our concepts and our states of knowledge have causal origins in our experiences. It is independent also of the *methodological* theses that, in particular domains of inquiry (e.g., sociology), empirical collection of data is more fruitful than the construction of theoretical models. Our thesis affirms a *logical* relationship between experience and knowledge. It says nothing of the psychological relationship between the two. And it does not have, when taken in isolation, any implications for the methodology of the special disciplines. One can accept the logical thesis but reject the psychological and methodological claims, and one can accept the latter while rejecting the former. The empiricism we shall be concerned with affirms only the logical thesis, for it is the logical thesis that is needed to fully sustain the Insight of Empiricism, not the psychological and methodological theses.[13]

---

13. I do not mean to suggest that philosophers generally regarded as empiricists subscribe to the logical thesis. Hume and Russell, in particular, did not accept it. The thesis captures something empiricists wish for, not something that empiricists think they can sustain.

For a brief but instructive history of the term 'empiricism', see appendix B in Bas C. van Fraassen's *Empirical Stance*.

THE SECOND CONSTRAINT IS THIS:

> *Equivalence (epistemic equivalence of subjectively identical experiences):*
> Subjectively identical experiences make identical epistemic contri-
> butions. More precisely, if *e* and *e'* are subjectively identical expe-
> riences of an individual, then the given in *e* is identical to the given
> in *e'*.

This constraint says nothing about the *nature* of subjectively
identical experiences. It allows that such experiences may vary
radically in their makeup. My visual perception of the orange
coaster may be subjectively identical to an earlier visual hallucination. Yet the nature of the two—what the two are in reality—
may be quite different: one may be an exemplification of a complex
relationship between me and the coaster, and the other may involve nothing distinct from me. The Equivalence constraint allows
all this. It places a restriction only on the epistemology of experience, not on its metaphysics.[14]

The Equivalence constraint is reasonable because "the given"
aims to capture the contribution of experience from the viewpoint
of the *experiencing subject*. We want to understand the enrichment
that a particular experience entails (or should entail) in the cognitive life of the experiencing subject—not in the cognitive life of
an external observer prying into the subject. And we want to
understand this enrichment from the internal viewpoint of the
subject. Imagine a being who suffers a series of veridical experiences and arrives at some beliefs about the world. Now, consider a
slight variant of this scenario in which one of the experiences *e*—
for instance, the glimpse of the subject's cat racing across the
room—is replaced by a subjectively identical hallucinatory experience *e'*. From the external, objective point of view, *e* and *e'* are
substantially different: one is veridical and the other hallucinatory.
And this difference affects one kind of assessment that we can make
of the subject's beliefs, namely, the assessment of their truth or
falsity. In the first scenario, the beliefs may all be true; in the

---

14. The constraint is therefore consistent with the "disjunctive" accounts of
perception favored by J. M. Hinton, John McDowell, Paul Snowdon, and others.
See Hinton's "Experiences," McDowell's "Criteria, Defeasibility, and Knowledge," and Snowdon's "Objects of Perceptual Experience."

second, some of them will be false. However, there is also an internal, subjective point of view from which we can assess the subject's beliefs: we can assess whether the beliefs are rational, given the subject's situation and the resources available to the subject. For this assessment, the differences between *e* and *e'* are totally irrelevant. If the subject's beliefs in the first scenario are rational, then they must also be rational in the second scenario, and conversely, if they are rational in the second, they must be rational in the first. The impact of subjectively identical experiences on the rational evolution of a subject's beliefs must be the same.[15]

It may be asked whether subjectively identical experiences must yield the same given for *different* experiencing subjects. I have formulated the Equivalence constraint so as to remain neutral on this issue.[16] Nevertheless, I think that a positive answer is plausible here. Suppose we modify the example just given and let two subjects, similarly endowed, undergo a series of subjectively identical experiences; that is, each experience in the series of one subject is

---

15. The intuition underlying the Equivalence constraint has been on the epistemological scene since ancient times. Cicero gives in his *Academica* (2.83) the following skeptical argument against the Stoic notion of "cognitive impression"— an argument he attributes to the New Academy of Arcesilaus (315–240 B.C.E.).

There are four headings to prove there is nothing which can be known, cognized or grasped, which is the subject of this whole controversy. The first of these is that some false impression does exist. The second, that it is not cognitive. The third, that *impressions between which there is no difference cannot be such that some are cognitive and others not*. The fourth, that no true impression arises from sensation which does not have alongside it another impression no different from it which is not cognitive. Everyone accepts the second and third of these headings. (A. A. Long and D. N. Sedley, *Hellenistic Philosophers*, vol. I, 40J; emphasis added)

The third "heading," italicized above, is a neighbor of the Equivalence constraint.

The widely discussed Argument from Illusion also draws on the same intuition. See §2C for a brief discussion. Smith's *Problem of Perception* contains an excellent and remarkably thorough examination of this argument.

16. Note that this neutrality requires either that we relativize the given to an experiencing subject and speak of "the given in an experience *e* for a subject *X*," or that we so individuate experiences that the subject is built into the identity conditions for an experience. I favor the latter option, for it permits the briefer locution "the given in *e*." I shall understand an experience as a particular occurrence or process, narrowly individuated. It will therefore make sense to speak of the subject of an experience, its time of occurrence, its context, and so on. If *e* and *e'* are experiences of distinct subjects, then, by definition, *e* is not identical to *e'*.

subjectively identical to its counterpart in the series of the other subject. We expect the cognitive lives of the two subjects to run parallel to each other. Furthermore, our evaluation of the rationality of the corresponding beliefs of the two subjects will be the same, irrespective of the external situation. (One of the subjects may be in a normal environment, and the other may be a brain in a vat.)

Subjectively identical experiences can, I acknowledge, prompt subjects to rationally arrive at different beliefs. A mature astronomer looking at the southern sky on a summer night might have an experience subjectively identical to the one that he had as a mere boy. But the mature adult may rationally arrive at conclusions quite different from those of his youth. The lesson to draw from this example is not that the Equivalence constraint is doubtful. The lesson is that the given in the astronomer's experience does not contain the different conclusions he reaches as a youth and as an adult. The given is supposed to capture the distinctive rational contribution of experience and experience *alone*—not of experience together with the other factors in play in the formation of perceptually based rational belief. The fact that the mature astronomer is entitled to draw different conclusions is to be explained by the different antecedent beliefs that he brings to bear on the experience. It is not to be explained by any differences between his mature and youthful experiences, and hence not by any differences in the given in these experiences.

The Equivalence constraint is subjectivist in orientation—it is concerned with the perspective of the experiencing subject—but it does not require the given to be subjective. The constraint allows that the given in my perception of, for example, the orange coaster may contain the objective proposition that an orange coaster exists. But if this is so, then the constraint requires that the proposition is in the given of each of my experiences that is subjectively identical to my perception. The Equivalence constraint, despite its subjectivist orientation, does not force us into positing subjectivist foundations for knowledge.

It is important to mark the distinction between the subjectivist project—that of understanding experience and knowledge from the subject's point of view—and the idea of subjectivist foundations. One can abandon the latter but embrace the former. We are in the process of reviewing an argument that aims to connect the subjectivist project with subjectivist foundations. The argument, as I have noted, is highly natural. But it is not rock solid, and the importance of the distinction remains.[17]

The Equivalence constraint allows ordinary judgments of perception to be in the given in an experience, but it is necessary to exercise a little care here. Consider two subjectively identical experiences e and e' of seeing a ripe tomato. Suppose that in the experience e, the object seen is Tomato One, and in e', it is Tomato Two. Now, the propositional contents expressed in the two cases by the judgment "that tomato is red" are plainly different. In the first case, the propositional content is that Tomato One is red; in the second, it is that Tomato Two is red. According to the Equivalence constraint, these propositional contents cannot belong to the givens of the respective experiences. Still, there is something closely related to the propositional contents that can belong to these givens. This something is the *schematized proposition* expressed by the judgment "that tomato is red," roughly:

---

17. Though our concerns here are decidedly internalist, we can stay neutral on an issue that occupies center stage in the current internalism-externalism debate in epistemology. Let us follow Alvin Plantinga and define "warrant" to be the difference between knowledge and true belief (Plantinga's *Warrant*, p. 1). Then the issue is this: whether warrant should be understood in purely internal terms (e.g., reasons and justification possessed by the subject) or purely external terms (e.g., reliability of the belief-producing mechanism), or perhaps a mixture of the two. The debate here centers on our knowledge *attributions*. And it is rendered difficult by the fact that these attributions, like much else in our ordinary talk, display a bewildering complexity. Fortunately, our concerns allow us to sidestep this debate. Our goal is to gain an understanding of the given in experience and of its relationship to our commonsense view of the world. This goal does not require us to provide a theory of knowledge attributions. And it does not commit us to an internalism about warrant. Even if externalism about warrant is right, no shadow is cast on our project. (For a discussion of another dimension of externalism, see §2E, where I take up Quine's "Naturalized Empiricism." I discuss the notion of justification in §6A.)

For the internalism-externalism debate, see especially essays 8 and 9 in William P. Alston, *Epistemic Justification*; Kent Bach, "A Rationale for Reliabilism"; Michael Bergmann, "A Dilemma for Internalism"; Laurence BonJour, "Externalist Theories of Empirical Knowledge"; Earl Conee and Richard Feldman, "Internalism Defended"; Richard Foley, "What Am I to Believe?"; Carl Ginet, *Knowledge, Perception, and Memory*; Alvin Goldman, "Internalism Exposed"; and John Pollock, "A Plethora of Epistemological Theories." James Pryor provides a very helpful overview of the debate in his "Highlights of Recent Epistemology."

That tomato—the one manifested in such-and-such a way in *this experience*—is red.

Here, "*this experience*" functions as a variable, and the schematized proposition yields ordinary propositional contents—for example, that Tomato One is red—once certain values are specified for this variable.[18] The ordinary propositional contents can now be seen as belonging to the given at one remove: they are recoverable from the schematized propositions in the given. For ease of exposition, I shall speak of the given as *yielding* or *entailing* an ordinary propositional content. This should be understood as meaning that the content belongs to the given directly or at one remove.[19] I shall also speak about the given as yielding a perceptual judgment. This should be understood as meaning that the propositional content

---

18. An exact modeling of schematized propositions is not needed for the purposes of this essay. Nevertheless, let me briefly address this issue. I think of ordinary propositions (e.g., that Tomato One is red) as structured entities that fix truth conditions. And I think of schematized propositions as ordinary propositions from which certain constituents have been extracted—thus leaving holes—together with restrictions on how the holes may be filled. Thus, the schematized proposition expressed by the perceptual judgment "that is red" may be viewed as a pair ⟨"( ) is red," R⟩, where the first part is a proposition with a hole and the second part, R, states a restriction on how the object filling the hole must be related to the variable experience. For a discussion of propositions with holes, see James Hardy's *Instantial Reasoning, Arbitrary Objects, and Holey Propositions*.

19. The technique of schematization can be used, of course, with other context-sensitive elements in perceptual judgments, e.g., 'now', 'here', and 'that'. It can also be used with certain empirical predicates—e.g., 'water'—whose interpretation depends upon contextual factors.

Note that the sense-datum theory, as ordinarily formulated, does not bypass the need for schematization, for propositions about *particular* sense-data can belong to the given only at one remove. Still, it is possible to so formulate the sense-datum theory that schematization becomes dispensable. Instead of saying that the given in an experience contains a proposition such as

Sense-Datum One is orange, and Sense-Datum Two is yellow and is to the right of Sense-Datum One,

we can say that it contains the proposition

there are sense-data x and y such that x is orange & y is yellow & y is to the right of x.

In this variant formulation, the given is weaker, but the loss of strength may be of little consequence; the same objective propositions may still be derivable.

expressed by the judgment belongs in the given either directly or at one remove.[20]

Finally, let me note some ways of strengthening the Equivalence constraint. (i) The constraint may be strengthened, as I have already indicated, to encompass subjectively identical experiences of different subjects. (ii) It may be strengthened to apply not just to experiences that are subjectively *identical* but also to those that are subjectively *similar*. The constraint would now require that relevantly similar experiences yield relevantly similar givens. The idea here is hard to make precise, but the intuition is fairly robust. The experience of seeing a tomato against a white background is in some respects subjectively similar to the experience of seeing the same tomato against a yellow background. This similarity demands, according to the strengthened constraint, that there be a corresponding similarity in the givens yielded by the two experiences. For example, if the given in one experience yields the proposition that there is a tomato, then the given in the other should also yield this proposition. (iii) The constraint may be strengthened to encompass possible experiences. I have never dreamt of a tomato against a yellow background. But, presumably, this dream experience is one that I might have had. The strengthened constraint says that if the experience is indeed possible, then the given in it must be identical to that in all other possible experiences that are subjectively identical. (iv) These ways of strengthening may be combined with each other to yield yet further variants of the Equivalence constraint.

THE THIRD CONSTRAINT IS PERHAPS THE MOST IMPORTANT. It imposes a considerable discipline on a theory of the given and makes the theory nontrivial (and thus interesting). I consider it a great virtue of classical empiricism that it respects this constraint.

> *Reliability (reliability of all experience)*: The given in an experience does not yield anything false or erroneous; in particular, it does not yield a false proposition.[21]

---

20. The idea of schematization may be applied to items in other logical categories, e.g., objects and properties. And the terminology of "yields" and "entails" extends to these categories in a parallel way.

21. Also, if a schematic proposition *P* belongs to the given in an experience *e*, then the propositional content expressed by *P* relative to *e* must not be false.

Note that this constraint places a restriction only on the rational contribution of experience, not on its causal contributions. The constraint is perfectly compatible with the idea that often—even always—experience plays a critical role in the genesis of false belief. Furthermore, the constraint does not, by itself, imply any restrictions on the content of experience (assuming that there is such a thing). Of course, if the content is identified with the given, then Reliability translates into a constraint on content. But, as we saw above, this identification is a substantive theoretical claim; so it should not be read into the constraint. Notice also that the constraint is negative in character. It requires that false propositions, for example, be excluded from the given; it imposes no requirement that some true propositions be included in it.[22]

The principal doubt that attaches to the Reliability constraint is that it is just too strong, that it cannot be met in any plausible way. This doubt can be dispelled only by a positive theory of experience, one that is plausible and that satisfies the constraint. This is the burden of the constructive part of the present essay. Let me for now gesture in the direction of two motivating considerations in favor of the constraint.

The first consideration is that experience is passive, and it is always a good policy not to assign fault to the passive. If, during a walk in a forest, I bump my head on a low branch of a tree, it is better that I assume responsibility (and change my ways) than that I pin the blame on the tree. The tree is passive. It is bound to be the way it is, given the circumstances, and it is useless to blame it for my sore head. Similarly, if, having suffered an experience, I acquire a false perceptual belief, it is better that I assume responsibility (and change my manner of "reading" experience) than that I pin the blame on the experience. The experience is bound to be the way it is, given the circumstances, and it is useless to blame it for my false belief. The best remedy for false perceptual beliefs is to change *oneself*, not to hope that experience will change its ways.

---

22. Observe that the constraint remains powerful even if the given is not propositional. Whatever its logical category, the given must not be erroneous. So, if the given yields an object, the object must be present in an appropriate relation to the subject. If the given is a property, the property must be instantiated in an appropriate way relative to the subject. And so on.

When I have what is called a 'misleading' experience, experience has *done* nothing to mislead me. The fault, if any, lies with *me* and *my* beliefs—beliefs for which *I* am responsible. When on a foggy day I mistake a pillar for a man, it is not my visual experience that tells me there is a man before me; the experience is ill-equipped to do such a thing. *I* form the belief that there is a man. *I* read the experience as indicating the presence of a man. I could have the same visual experience but without the disposition to falsely conclude that there is a man. And here it is not as if I have to resist the prodding of experience that tells me that there is a man before me. A misleading experience is not like a liar. It is not even like an innocent misinformer. Liars and misinformers *say* things, and their lies and misinformation cast doubt on their character. Misleading experiences do not cast any doubt on the character of experience. In a misleading experience, I am misled, but it is not experience that does the misleading. Experience remains innocent.

The second consideration in favor of the Reliability constraint is this: only skeptics and rationalists can comfortably abandon it, but not empiricists, who view experience as vested with the highest epistemic authority. If experience sometimes lies, if the given in experience sometimes yields false propositions, how does one correct the resulting error? Skeptics can comfortably hold that no way exists of correcting the error. Rationalists can comfortably appeal to one of the substantive constraints that they deem to be truths supplied by reason. But what can empiricists say? That the error is corrected through considerations of coherence, the coherence of the totality of experiential judgments? The notion of coherence invoked here cannot be purely logical, since, from the logical point of view, even false judgments yield coherent wholes; they even yield coherent wholes that are maximal.[23] But if coherence is substantive, whence does it derive its authority?[24] The empiricists are in danger of positing a

---

23. I am assuming that a proposition given in an experience is never self-contradictory.

24. It seems to me that coherence is substantive only if an antecedent conception of the world is in play, and the richer this conception, the richer the ensuing notion of coherence. Plainly, in everyday assessments of the coherence of theories, stories, and excuses offered us, we bring to bear a rich conception of how things are. Without such a conception, I do not see what coherence can amount to apart from logical and conceptual consistency.

sixth sense, the sense of coherence, as the ultimate seat of epistemic authority. And their differences from the rationalists now appear to be merely verbal: rationalists call this sixth sense *reason.*[25]

LET US OBSERVE THAT THE THREE CONSTRAINTS CONSIDERED above are all independent: any two can be accepted and the third denied. Furthermore, the constraints do not imply a Cartesian conception of experience. Suppose, for instance, that each experience is assigned as its given only the proposition "Earth's core is, was, or will be hot." Then the contribution of each experience is fully objective, yet all the constraints are met. This "theory" of the given, sufficient though it may be to make a logical point, is of course absurd. It makes the given completely independent of the character of experience. We should also impose a fourth constraint:

> *Manifestation (manifestation of the given)*: The given in an experience must be manifested in that experience; that is, it must depend systematically upon the subjective character of the experience.

FINALLY, LET ME EMPHASIZE THAT I DO NOT REGARD THE constraints introduced above as absolute. I regard them as good *initial* constraints on an account of experience. But I allow that at a more mature stage of inquiry, when we better understand the epistemology and metaphysics of experience, we may have reasons

---

25. The Reliability constraint, too, has an established position in the history of epistemology. It is, for instance, a crucial ingredient in Berkeley's argument for his claim that only ideas are immediately perceived by sense. This argument, which receives an extended treatment in *Three Dialogues between Hylas and Philonous*, is an ancestor of the Argument from Illusion. Note that a version of the Reliability constraint is explicitly invoked by Philonous in his speech on page 238 of the Luce and Jessop edition of the *Dialogues* (p. 121 in the Dancy edition).

It is a tempting thought that one can avoid Cartesian conceptions by rejecting the Reliability constraint. However, as we shall see below, the argument for Cartesian conceptions can bypass the constraint altogether (see §2C and, in particular, fns. 27 and 28). The Reliability constraint renders the argument for Cartesian conceptions particularly clear and straightforward, but the constraint is not essential to the argument.

to relax, and even to abandon, these constraints. Until that distant day, however, we should work within the bounds set by them.

2C. The Argument from the Propositional Given

It is a natural idea that the function of experience is to reveal some facts about the world. Suppose that I walk into a room and see that Fred is wearing a red tie. It is a natural thought that my experience reveals to me the color of Fred's tie, that it entitles me to the perceptual judgment that Fred's tie is red. Faced with a skeptical inquiry, I have no better justification for my perceptual judgment than to draw attention to my experience. Our ordinary judgments of perception seem to be the epistemological rock bottom of our knowledge. If they are called into question—or if the dialectical situation somehow forbids an appeal to them—then we do not know how to begin to justify any of our substantive empirical claims. Ordinary judgments of perception seem to be the starting points, supplied by experience, of all our more sophisticated inquiries into the world.

There is truth in these simple reflections. But a naive incorporation of them into an epistemological theory results in a gross error. Let *Naive Epistemological Realism* be the thesis that the given in an experience yields ordinary judgments of perception.[26] Then it is easily seen that Naive Epistemological Realism is false. Let e be the experience I had when I saw Fred and his tie, and let e' be a subjectively identical dream experience (or a subjectively identical hallucination or . . .). If the given in e yields ordinary judgments of perception—for example, "that man is Fred" and "that man is wearing a red tie"—then, by the Equivalence constraint, the given in e' must also yield these judgments. But now the given in e' violates the Reliability constraint. It follows that the given in e does

---

26. 'Naive realism' is sometimes used as a name for the position that things are as they appear to be. So, if Fred's tie looks red, then it is red; if the stick looks bent, then it is bent; and so on. This position has little to be said in its favor and is better dubbed 'incredibly naive realism'. What I am calling 'Naive Epistemological Realism' is not this simple-minded position. Naive Epistemological Realism is a natural starting point for an inquiry into the epistemology of experience; the position called 'naive realism' is not.

not yield ordinary judgments of perception, and Naive Epistemological Realism is therefore false.[27]

This is the first stage of our argument for sense-data. It uses the
Equivalence and Reliability constraints to undermine a simple way
of thinking about the given. The second stage of the argument is

---

27. This conclusion can be gained without any appeal to the Reliability constraint. Suppose that a judgment such as "that man is wearing a red tie" belongs to
the given in *e*. Then, Equivalence dictates that the judgment also belongs to the
given in all subjectively identical experiences. Now, the given in an experience is
supposed to capture its rational contribution. So, if a judgment *P* belongs to the
given in an experience, then the subject of the experience is rationally obligated to
adjust his view in light of *P*. It is plain, however, that I can undergo an experience
subjectively identical to *e* even when I have no concept of "tie" (or even that of
"man"). For instance, I might have had such an experience—say, *e'*—when I was a
small child and had no concept of "tie." I would not then have had any rational
obligation to adjust my view in light of the judgment "that man is wearing a red tie."
Consequently, this judgment belongs neither to the given in *e'* nor that of *e*.

It may be objected that concepts are essential to an experience, that the experience *e* of seeing Fred and his red tie could not have occurred in the absence of the
concept "tie." However, even if the premiss of the objection is true, the objection has
no force. The above argument makes no assumptions about the conditions under
which *e* may or may not occur. The argument claims only that an experience
subjectively identical to e can occur even though the concept of "tie" is not in play.
Visually, it can be exactly the same for me when I undergo *e'* as when I undergo *e*,
even though on the first occasion I have no concept "tie." (The fact that I have
different thoughts on the two occasions is irrelevant, for this has no bearing on the
visual character of the two experiences.) It may be objected that a concept can affect
the visual character of an experience. However, this may well be true, but it does not
follow that the concept is a *prerequisite* for the subjective visual character of the
experience. For example, an acquaintance with rabbits may enable a subject to have
the visual experience of seeing the duck-rabbit figure as that of a rabbit. But it does
not follow that an acquaintance with rabbits is a prerequisite—much less that the
concept of rabbit is a prerequisite—for a subjectively identical visual experience. Such
an experience is possible even if there were no rabbits in the world but the experiencing subject had acquaintance with, e.g., rabbit-like replicas or rabbit pictures.

The present argument is bolstered by a reflection on the phenomenology of visual
experience. When I consider my visual experience *e* of Fred and his red tie, I find
nothing in it that entitles me to the judgment that it is a *tie* that is before me. Ties are
pieces of clothing, not sensory organs of the wearer; they have a volume; they persist
through time; and so on. But nothing in my visual experience tells me that the object
before me is not an unusual sort of tongue, or that it is not a mere three-dimensional
surface, or that it did not come into being at the moment of my perception. We need
to exercise care when constructing an account of the given. We must not put into the
given elements whose source is not experience. Ordinary perceptual judgments are
shaped, in part, by our beliefs and concepts, and they do not belong in the given.

constructive. It begins with the Existence and Manifestation constraints (that the given exists and is manifested in experience). And it accepts the natural idea, present in the simple account, of the *propositional given*: the idea that the given must be propositional in form. The argument for sense-data now proceeds as follows. Consider again my experience *e* of Fred and his tie. Our premisses imply that some propositions are given in *e*. The Manifestation constraint and the phenomenology of experience make it plausible that the most basic of these propositions are of the forms "this K is F," "this K bears R to that K'," and so on, for ternary and perhaps for some higher-place predicates. The objects denoted by "this K" and "that K'" in these propositions depend, in part, on the subjective characteristics of the experience. Now, by the argument of the first stage, the sort K cannot be "man," "tie," or "surface of a tie" (and the same goes for the sort K'). Indeed, it cannot be any sort pertaining to external objects. What then might K be? By the Equivalence and Reliability constraints, K must be such that the perceptual judgment "that K is F" is true with respect to *e* and also with respect to any subjectively identical experience e'. The K, then, must exist and be F even when e' is a dream or a hallucination. Objects of this special sort—objects that exist whether or not experience is veridical or hallucinatory, objects for which the experientially tied demonstratives "this K" and "that K" always denote—are known as *sense-data*.[28] If the given is propositional, sense-data must exist.[29]

When I had the experience *e*, I was prepared—and was entitled—to make the perceptual judgments "that tie is red," "that

28. The appeal to Reliability is eliminable here also. The sort K must be such that the perceptual judgment "that K is F" is rationally forced on the subject when he undergoes *e*, and also when he undergoes any subjectively identical experience e'. Hence, the mere subjective character of experience must make the concept K available to the subject, and it must entitle the subject to judgments about Ks. Objects that fall under such special Ks are known as *sense-data*.

29. *Objection*: The existence of sense-data is not proved. This is because it is possible that the given consists of propositions of the sort "if the circumstances are normal, then the tie is red," not of plain unconditional propositions such as "the tie is red."

Reply: The possibility envisaged should be rejected. First, it makes the given too weak. It is only on the basis of experience that one can determine whether circumstances are normal. But under the envisaged possibility, this is impossible. In order to use the given to arrive at a substantive conclusion (e.g., that the tie is red), one already needs the premiss that the circumstances are normal. Hence, the given cannot help us to reach the

man is wearing that red tie," and so on. The first stage of the argument showed that, while the entitlement may be genuine, it does not issue solely from my experience *e*. The second stage of the argument shows that *e* yields entitlement only to such judgments as "that sense-datum is red" and "that man-shaped visual sense-datum bears such-and-such spatial relation to that red sense-datum." These latter judgments are bound to have the same status with respect to all experiences subjectively identical to *e*. Phenomenologically, experience seems to present us with external objects and their properties and relations: the red tie vividly before me in *e* seems to be a part of my consciousness. The second stage preserves the idea that experience presents us with some objects and their properties and relations. But it teaches that the red thing so vividly before me in *e* is not really the tie itself but a sense-datum.

The first two stages establish that the given in *some* experiences, such as *e*, concerns sense-data. The next and final stage of the argument aims to generalize this conclusion to *all* experiences. The simplest way here is to push through the earlier argument for each experience. This requires, however, an acceptance of a strong existence claim: that sufficiently varied subjectively identical, but nonveridical, experiences always exist.[30] Such strong claims are sometimes made in the epistemological literature. Cicero takes it as a premiss in the skeptical argument cited above that "no true impression arises from sensation which does not have alongside it another impression no different from

---

conclusion that the circumstances are normal. Second, despite the weakness of the proposed given, there is no assurance that the Reliability constraint will be met. Our concept of red, for instance, may embody a confusion or misconception. If it does, then the above example of the given fails to satisfy Reliability: circumstances may well be normal, but the consequent claim that the tie is red will be erroneous. It will not do to gain Reliability by defining 'red' as applying to those physical objects that under normal circumstances cause "red" experiences. This move simply returns us to a Cartesian conception of experience, because now experience reveals its own character, and what is most fundamentally given is the subjective. Third, the proposal is phenomenologically odd. It has experience informing us about normal circumstances, which may well be nonactual. But this has no grounding in the phenomenology of ordinary experiences. Ordinary experiences do not acquaint us with the concept of normal circumstance, nor do they contain any reference to normal circumstances.

30. The claim is even stronger than it may seem: the subjectively identical experiences must be of the same subject. This is required by our formulation of the Equivalence constraint.

it which is not cognitive."[31] Fortunately, the desired generalization can be gained in other ways. One can trade in the strong existence assumption in favor of stronger versions of the Equivalence and Reliability constraints.[32] For example, if we strengthen these constraints to apply to all possible experiences, then we can gain the generalization from a weak (and plausible) existence assumption, namely, that a subjectively identical dream experience *can* exist. For another example, suppose we strengthen the Equivalence constraint to say that relevantly similar experiences yield relevantly similar givens; then we can gain the generalization with a considerably weaker existence assumption, while avoiding all appeal to possible experiences. (The exact nature of the existence assumption will depend upon the reading given to 'similar experience'.)

We conclude that the given in all experiences concerns sense-data. If the notion of direct awareness is understood epistemologically—that is, if "direct awareness of X" is understood to imply that experience, by itself, entitles us to perceptual judgments about X—then we can say that there is never a direct awareness of external objects. The objects of direct awareness are invariably sense-data.

I will call the above argument for sense-data the *Argument from the Propositional Given*, thereby highlighting the key assumption in it. I do not regard the argument as a *proof* of the sense-datum theory. But I do think the argument shows this theory to be entirely natural. Once we accept the informant model of experience—that is, once we accept the idea that the epistemological role of experience is to reveal facts about the world—we commit ourselves to the propositional given. And this commitment inexorably drives us, in light of the phenomenological features of experience, to the sense-datum theory.

Let me make a couple of observations about the above argument. First, it does not fully settle the nature of sense-data. It does not settle their precise identity conditions, or whether they have properties other than those perceived, or whether unsensed sense-data exist. It is understandable, therefore, that disputes should arise among the

31. This is the fourth "heading" in the quote from Cicero in fn. 15. Note that Cicero suggests by his remark that "everyone accepts the second and third of these headings" that not everyone accepts the fourth. Indeed, a little later in the same speech, Cicero says that "the entire battle" between the skeptical Academics and the Stoics [in the then current context] is over the fourth heading.

32. The Reliability constraint is dispensable in the manner indicated in fns. 27 and 28.

proponents of sense-data on just these points. Second, the argument helps in understanding the viewpoint of some of the opponents of sense-data—for example, those who hold an "adverbial" theory of sensing. These philosophers reject the idea that the given contains perceptual judgments of such forms as "this K is F" and "this K bears R to that K'." They maintain that the propositions in the given have a different form—for example, the form "I am sensing G-ly." This maneuver allows one to bypass a commitment to sense-data while holding on to the informant model of experience. It must be said, however, that the maneuver pays a high phenomenological price. Sense-datum theory remains phenomenologically the more compelling.

In summary, then, the propositional given forces one to a Cartesian conception of experience.[33] It forces one to hold that the given is about the subjective realm and that a logical gulf exists between ordinary judgments of perception and the given in experience. Since there is little reason not to admit the propositional given once one accepts a Cartesian conception, we can formulate our conclusion thus: *Cartesian conceptions are equivalent to the propositional given.* More precisely, the acceptance of a propositional given goes hand in hand with the acceptance of a Cartesian conception. The sense-datum theory, as I see it, rests on these two pillars: a natural logical idea (the propositional given) and the phenomenology of experience. Once one accepts the logical idea, one must accept a Cartesian conception; when in addition one respects the phenomenology, one is forced to accept sense-data.[34]

33. Note that Cartesian conceptions cannot be avoided simply by shifting to the idea that the given consists of objects or of properties (or relations). The three-stage argument above can be reformulated to show that the objects in the given must be sense-data and that the properties must be properties of sense-data.

34. In his important book *Mind and World*, John McDowell arrives, after traversing some rugged Kantian and Hegelian terrain, at a commonsense conception of experience: "experience as openness to the layout of reality" (p. 26). Experience, according to McDowell, has conceptual content and can therefore provide a rational constraint on empirical thought. Furthermore, the constraint is substantial because, in McDowell's view, the conceptual content of experience is rich: "In a particular experience in which one is not misled, what one takes in is *that things are thus and so*. . . . But *that things are thus and so* is also, if one is not misled, an aspect of the layout of the world" (p. 26; emphasis original). Experience can have a rich conceptual content because, McDowell holds, following Kant, that in experience, both receptivity and spontaneity (i.e., conceptual capacities) are in play. Consequently, our beliefs, our worldview, shape the contents of our experiences (pp. 29–34).

THE ARGUMENT FROM THE PROPOSITIONAL GIVEN IS SIMILAR to the much maligned Argument from Illusion. (I had the latter argument very much in mind as I formulated the former.) The Argument from Illusion goes, in outline, as follows. It begins with the familiar examples of illusions and hallucinations (stage 1). For concreteness, let us work with the old favorite of the stick that looks bent in water. The conclusion is now drawn (stage 2) that there must be something bent that is directly perceived. This something cannot be the stick, for the stick by hypothesis is straight. Nor can it be any other ordinary object. It must therefore be a special kind of object, a sense-datum. The rule of inference invoked in this stage has been dubbed the "sense-datum inference." The rule allows one to derive "there is something *F* that is directly perceived" from "there looks to be something *F*." (At least, it allows this transition for certain readings of 'looks' and for certain predicates *F*.) Finally, the conclusion of stage 2—that the objects of direct awareness in illusions and hallucinations are sense-data—is generalized to all experiences, including veridical perceptions (stage 3). The consideration appealed to here is the similarity of illusions and hallucinations to veridical perceptions. H. H. Price puts the point this way in his *Perception*:

> The abnormal crooked sense-datum of a straight stick standing in water is qualitatively indistinguishable from a normal sense-datum of a crooked stick.... Is it not incredible that two entities so similar in all these qualities should really be so utterly different: that the one should be a real constituent of a material object, wholly independent of the observer's mind and organism, while the other is merely the fleeting product of his cerebral processes? (pp. 31–32)

There is much that is attractive in McDowell's picture: it preserves the commonsense view of experience, it assigns experience a rational role in shaping empirical knowledge, it frees the idea of "the given" from mythical elements, and much else. But these gains are obtained at a high price. McDowell's account is bound to violate either the Equivalence or the Reliability constraint. If an illusory experience has a conceptual content different from a subjectively identical veridical experience, then Equivalence is violated. If, on the other hand, the contents of the two experiences are the same, then Reliability is violated. McDowell's picture accepts the propositional given. And with this idea in place, there is no way of preserving the constraints other than via a Cartesian conception. We are forced to think of experience as openness to the layout of a *subjective* reality.

The objects of direct awareness, it is thus concluded, are invariably sense-data.[35]

The Argument from Illusion has attracted much criticism and even scorn. Austin calls the argument itself an "illusion" and suggests that it arises from a "happy style of blinkering philosophical English." Jackson says that this "notorious" argument "proves nothing." Even Ayer, whose philosophical position should make him sympathetic to the argument, distances himself from it.[36] It must be acknowledged that the criticism (and even the scorn) is not entirely unwarranted. The sense-datum inference, invoked at stage 2, seems patently invalid. The generalization move of stage 3 is also questionable: why can't a veridical perception and a hallucination, for example, be of radically different kinds of objects and still be subjectively identical? My present concern, however, is neither to criticize nor to defend the Argument from Illusion. My concern is to highlight some differences between this argument and the Argument from the Propositional Given. Even if one rejects the former as plainly fallacious, I want to suggest, one should see the latter as resting on a natural and highly plausible idea (the informant model of experience). And if this is so, then one should also see the Cartesian conceptions (and classical empiricism) as entirely natural.[37]

The two arguments, Illusion and Propositional Given, proceed in parallel ways. Both reach a conclusion about the existence of sense-data in certain special cases. And both then generalize this conclusion to all experiences and, in particular, to all veridical perceptions. The Illusion argument reaches a conclusion about the existence of sense-data in illusions and hallucinations and then generalizes this to

35. Expositions of the Argument from Illusion along the above lines may be found in, among other texts, A. J. Ayer, *Foundations of Empirical Knowledge* and *Problem of Knowledge*; C. D. Broad, "Some Elementary Reflexions on Sense-Perception"; Frank Jackson, *Perception*; H. H. Price, *Perception*; and Smith, *Problem of Perception*. (Smith divides the argument into two parts, one of which appeals to illusions and the other to hallucinations. However, both arguments run parallel to the argument sketched above.)

36. Austin, *Sense and Sensibilia*, p. 4; Jackson, *Perception*, p. 107; and Ayer, *Foundations of Empirical Knowledge*, chapter 1.

37. *Pace* Austin, who declares that such conceptions are attributable to "an obsession with a few particular words, the uses of which are over-simplified, not really understood" and to "an obsession with a few ... half-studied 'facts'" (*Sense and Sensibilia*, p. 3). This declaration is all the more astonishing given Austin's statement that these conceptions are "at least as old as Heraclitus" (p. 1).

all veridical perceptions. The Propositional Given argument, on the other hand, reaches a conclusion about the existence of sense-data in some *veridical perceptions* and then generalizes this conclusion to all other veridical perceptions. The differences here are important. Doubts attaching to the generalization step in the Illusion argument have no bearing on the Propositional Given argument. The possibility of subjectively identical dreams, for example, can fully guarantee the generalization step in the latter argument but not in the former. So even if one rejects the generalization step in the Illusion argument, one should find the generalization step in the Propositional Given argument to be compelling.

A further, more important, difference is that the Propositional Given argument makes no appeal to the sense-datum inference. The Illusion argument invokes this rule to derive the conclusion that, in the illusory experience of the stick in the water, there is something bent that is directly perceived. At the corresponding stage, the Propositional Given argument works with a veridical experience and concludes that some propositions in the given are of the forms "this K is F," "this K bears R to that K'," and so on. It then shows why K and K' must stand for the sort "sense-datum" (and not any sorts pertaining to external objects). There is no appeal in any of this to the sense-datum inference.[38] If the Propositional Given argument is sound, then this inference rule is indeed valid. The argument can therefore justify the rule, but it does not rely on the rule.

The final difference between the two arguments to which I wish to draw attention is this: If one rejects the Cartesian conceptions, then one will take away only something banal from the Illusion argument (e.g., that the sense-datum inference is invalid—something we had suspected all along). However, from the Propositional Given argument, one should take away something substantive, namely, that a Cartesian conception of experience is forced by the Propositional Given. The argument thus teaches the cost of denying Cartesian conceptions: one must give up the informant model of experience; one must give up the idea that

---

38. The appeal to the sense-datum inference gives the Illusion argument a metaphysical flavor. It seems to be directed to the metaphysical nature of experience. The Propositional Given argument, on the other hand, is fully centered on the epistemology of experience.

experience reveals to us some facts about the world. The resistance one feels to giving up the informant model should equal the attraction one feels toward Cartesian conceptions.

2D. Classical Empiricism and Skepticism

Cartesian conceptions of experience are, from a historical point of view, closely tied to an engagement with skepticism. Descartes thought that his method of radical doubt would lead to increased clarity and certainty in all our theoretical knowledge, and he bequeathed to posterity his bewitching conception of mind and its ideas. The empiricists who followed him abandoned the hope of finding theoretical knowledge that is absolutely certain (or even nearly certain) and contented themselves with discovering secure foundations for empirical knowledge. This quest led them to the sense-datum theory and to other Cartesian conceptions. The project of the classical empiricists, if successfully completed, would answer the skeptic. It would provide, for any bit of knowledge K, a justification that would begin with absolutely certain propositions and would show, on the basis of these propositions, that belief in K was warranted. The project envisions the justification as being gained in several stages. Sense-datum judgments belonging to the self would constitute the foundations. Then the existence and properties of material objects would be established on this solipsistic basis. Next, the distinctive behavior of certain bodies would be used to establish the existence (and characteristics) of other minds. At this stage, knowledge of language would gain a grounding in behavioral evidence. Having thus regained the basic features of our commonsense conception of the world, further domains of knowledge (in particular, theoretical knowledge) would be justified in familiar ways. The projected justification is lengthy but, if constructed, should silence the skeptic. The "if" here, it must be said, is a big one. The empiricist project encounters great—perhaps even insurmountable—difficulties at all stages of its execution.

The figure of the skeptic looms large in epistemology. Russell once declared that "the whole subject is a product of Cartesian doubt."[39] The suggestion is thus inevitable that if the skeptic can

---

39. Bertrand Russell, *Inquiry into Meaning and Truth*, p. 16.

legitimately be told to "get lost,"[40] we shall rid ourselves of Cartesian conceptions and, indeed, of a wide swath of traditional epistemology. It is therefore important to observe that the above argument for Cartesian conceptions is entirely independent of one's attitude toward skepticism. One may think that Descartes's method of doubt is a theoretical dead end. One may think that the skeptic's persistent demands for justification are illegitimate. One may think that any doubt about the existence of the external world is pathological. Still, one can—and should—find the Argument from the Propositional Given to be natural and powerful. What motivates this argument is not a quest for certainty or a wish to answer the skeptic but a desire to understand the logical relationship of experience to knowledge. We can be interested in the question "how much load do these columns carry?" even though we have no concern that the building will collapse into a heap of rubble. In the same way, we can be interested in the question "what logical contribution does experience make to knowledge?" even though we have no concern that knowledge will collapse into mere opinion. A concern to answer the skeptic actually impedes progress with our question, for it encourages the assumption that the contribution of experience must be propositional in form. This forces us to accept a Cartesian conception and leaves us no options but to follow one of the well-trodden paths of traditional epistemology.

THE ARGUMENT FROM THE PROPOSITIONAL GIVEN, THOUGH not motivated by skepticism, does provide material assistance to the skeptic, for if the given in experience is solely about sense-data, it becomes difficult to see how we could be entitled to any judgments about the external world, including ordinary judgments of perception. Let us quickly review the main strategies we might follow to gain this entitlement. First, we might hope for some help from a causal principle. We might hope, for example, that a causal principle would enable us to infer the existence of a red tomato from the existence of a particular red and round sense-datum. We would be disappointed, however, for there is no known causal principle that links the two; moreover, even if there were such a principle, its status would be at least as

---

40. Richard Rorty's expression, cited by Davidson on p. 156 of *Subjective, Intersubjective, Objective*.

problematic as the claim it is being used to justify.[41] Second, we might try holding that the relationship between the external world and sense-data is similar to that between theoretical posits and observed phenomena. The hypothesis that there is an external world, the thought goes, is justified because it provides the best explanation of our sense-data.[42] But a decisive objection to this strategy was given by Berkeley:

> Though we give the materialists their external bodies, they by their own confession are never the nearer knowing how our ideas are produced: since they own themselves unable to comprehend in what manner body can act upon spirit, or how it is possible it should imprint any idea in the mind. Hence it is evident the production of ideas or sensations in our minds, can be no reason why we should suppose matter or corporeal substances, since that is acknowledged to remain equally inexplicable with, or without this supposition.[43]

The assumption of external bodies provides us with no *explanation* of the existence and nature of sense-data. Hence, an appeal to "inference to the best explanation" will not yield the desired justification.[44]

The third strategy is due to Berkeley, and it is historically the most important.[45] Berkeley observed that the philosophical conception that the objects of direct awareness are sense-data (or, in

---

41. The problems with the causal strategy were laid out with great clarity by Hume. See the *Enquiry*, §§4, 7, and 12.

42. This idea was embraced by a number of philosophers, including Ayer in his *Central Questions of Philosophy*

43. Berkeley, *Treatise Concerning the Principles of Human Knowledge*, part I, §19.

44. For another important criticism, see P. F. Strawson, "Perception and Its Objects."

45. Berkeley's own motive was not so much to sustain classical empiricism as to convert "sceptics and infidels" using only "the most rigid laws of reasoning" (Preface, *Three Dialogues*; p. 168 in Luce and Jessop and p. 56 in Dancy). Berkeley thought he could provide a new and completely convincing proof for the existence of God. Berkeley's argument begins with the premise that we have knowledge of ordinary, objective things and concludes, on the basis of this premise, that God must exist. Berkeley is not interested in showing how knowledge of ordinary things can be founded on knowledge of sense-data (or, in his terminology, "ideas"). Indeed, such a program runs counter to his argument for the existence of God. The point of his argument is precisely that we can gain objective knowledge on the basis of sense-data only via the mediation of God. Nonetheless, Berkeley's suggestions, though made with a different end in view, have had a powerful influence on classical empiricism.

Berkeley's terminology, "ideas") is perfectly compatible with the commonsense conception that the objects of direct awareness are ordinary things (e.g., tomatoes). We can accept both, Berkeley argued, if we recognize the truth of *idealism*: that ordinary things *are* sense-data. (In Berkeley's terminology, "things are ideas.") This move allows us to reject as illusory the seeming gulf between subjective sense-data and the objective world external to us. Russell sharpened Berkeley's dictum to say that things are "logical constructions" out of sense-data.[46] The point here is that, while it may be impossible to identify a thing (e.g., a tomato) with a particular sense-datum (or a collection of sense-data), the content of any claim about external objects can be specified entirely in terms of sense-data.[47] This is the thesis of *phenomenalism*, and it brings the issues about content and meaning to the center of the debate about empiricism. In the first half of the twentieth century, the whole debate about empiricism centered on the question of whether the *meaning* (and, more specifically, the *cognitive content*) of our ordinary and theoretical claims about the external world could be reduced to sense-datum terms. C. I. Lewis, Ayer, and others partial to classical empiricism attempted to spell out the reduction, while critics—of whom the most important were Roderick Chisholm and W. V. Quine—pointed out important difficulties in their way.[48] The basic difficulty is straightforward: any plausible attempt to spell out the content of an ordinary judgment (e.g., "that is a tomato") in terms of sense-data renders it necessary to appeal to some objective concepts (e.g., "light being normal" and "touching

---

The same kind of point can be made for other philosophers that loom large in the history of classical empiricism (Locke, Hume, Russell, and others). They all had a diversity of concerns, interests, and views. Consequently, their relationship to the various elements of classical empiricism is complex (and open to debate). The fact that these philosophers made a large contribution to classical empiricism should not be taken to suggest that classical empiricism was their predominant concern, or even that they subscribed to it.

46. There are anticipations of this sharpening in Berkeley's own writings.

47. Example: the content of the perceptual judgment "that is a red tomato" might be "that is a red and tomato-shaped sense-datum *and* if I were to form such and such volitions [in objective terms: to reach out to the tomato to touch it], then I would experience a smooth tactile sense-datum *and*. . . ."

48. The titles of Chisholm's and Quine's most influential papers—respectively, "The Problem of Empiricism" and "Two Dogmas of Empiricism"—show how closely empiricism was identified with reductive phenomenalism in this period.

the tomato"). Further, any attempt to reduce these concepts brings to the fore yet further objective concepts. One thus finds oneself with a regress of reductions, each containing various objective concepts and none exhibiting the purity one seeks. Quine diagnosed the problem as arising from verification holism: "our statements about the external world face the tribunal of sense experience not individually but only as a corporate body."[49] In other words, our statements about the external world imply basic sense-datum statements only when taken together, not when taken in isolation. Empirical content can be assigned, Quine argued, only to our theory when it is taken as a whole. It cannot be distributed on a statement-by-statement basis. I will not say that we have proof here that phenomenalistic reductions must fail, for Quine's holism can be— and has been—questioned.[50] Nevertheless, only the most optimistic of philosophers retain any hope that such reductions are feasible.[51]

Hume argued that classical empiricism makes skepticism about the external world inevitable. Indeed, he went further and declared that here "the profounder and more philosophical sceptics will always triumph, when they endeavour to introduce an universal doubt into all subjects of human knowledge and enquiry" (*Enquiry*, 12.1). Two different, though connected, skeptical arguments occur in Hume. One argument, which occurs in §12 of the *Enquiry*, proceeds via a Cartesian conception and has in effect been reviewed earlier in this section. The other argument occurs in §4 of the *Enquiry*, and we should take a brief look at it. This argument draws a skeptical conclusion *directly from the propositional given*, without invoking

---

49. "Two Dogmas of Empiricism," §5, p. 41.

50. Furthermore, verification holism does not by itself imply that phenomenalistic reductions are impossible. It implies that objective statements such as "that is a tomato" cannot be assigned, e.g., a packet of falsifying experiences. Still, this does not establish the impossibility of phenomenalistic reductions. The following possibility remains open, for example: Experiences can directly falsify only atomic sense-datum statements, and objective statements are invariably reduced to compounds of sense-datum statements. Furthermore, these compounds do not imply any atomic statements when taken in isolation (they are, say, disjunctions); they do so only when they are taken in conjunction with certain other compounds. We can even preserve holism along these lines: when the reductions of *all* the statements in a theory are taken together, then and only then can we deduce atomic sense-datum statements.

51. See §5A for some further remarks on phenomenalism.

a Cartesian conception. The following famous passage contains the core idea of the argument:

> As to past *Experience*, it can be allowed to give *direct* and *certain* information of those precise objects only, and that precise period of time, which fell under its cognizance: But why this experience should be extended to future times, and to other objects, which, for aught we know, may be only in appearance similar; this is the main question on which I would insist. (*Enquiry*, 4.2)

Let P be the conjunction of all the truths revealed by the totality of our past experiences. P concerns, as Hume says, some "precise objects only" and some "precise period of time." Let Q be a proposition that concerns some other objects or some other period of time (e.g., the proposition "the sun will rise tomorrow"). Hume is asking how we might be entitled to Q. We would be entitled to Q if we were somehow entitled to the conditional proposition $P \rightarrow Q$. But, by hypothesis, experience does not yield this entitlement. Further, reason cannot do so, either, because the conditional is contingent and synthetic. It does not express, in Hume's terminology, a mere "relation of ideas." How, then, might we be entitled to Q? This question—the "main question" on which Hume insists—has not received, as far as I know, a satisfactory answer from the proponents of the propositional given.

WHAT CONCLUSION SHOULD WE DRAW FROM ALL THIS? Certainly not the Pyrrhonian conclusion that we should suspend our ordinary beliefs, nor the conclusion that we should abandon empiricism and seek an authority more potent than experience,[52] nor that we should abandon the project of understanding experience and knowledge from the viewpoint of the experiencing subject. (I argue for this last point in §2E.) The proper conclusion is a modest one: we do not fully understand the logical relationship of experience to knowledge. It will readily be granted by all that we do not fully understand the causal mechanisms underlying our cognition of the world. It will also readily be granted that we do not fully understand the relationship of the causal domain to the logical

---

52. Some authors, e.g., Pierre-Daniel Huet (1630–1721), used skepticism as a stepping stone to an extreme fideism. See Richard H. Popkin, "The High Road to Pyrrhonism."

domain. What we are now being asked to recognize is not all that surprising: that we do not fully understand the logical domain. The final outcome of our reflections on classical empiricism is thus only moderately skeptical.

2E. Quine's Naturalized Empiricism

Quine's influential reaction to classical empiricism is not moderate but radical. Quine rejects the entire project of traditional epistemology, which he takes to be that of providing a justification for the claims and concepts of science. Quine thinks that this project is bound to fail. "The Humean predicament," he quips, "is the human predicament."[53] There is no viewpoint above or apart from science from which the claims and concepts of science can be adjudicated; there is no "First Philosophy." The proper aim of epistemology, as Quine sees it, should be to help us understand our knowledge from within the perspective of our best account of the world. As he says in his last book, *From Stimulus to Science*, "Unlike the old epistemologists, we seek no firmer basis for science than science itself; so we are free to use the very fruits of science in investigating its roots" (p. 16). This investigation would show how, given the impacts on our sensory surfaces, we have managed to arrive at our successful theories of the world. Epistemology thus becomes, in Quine's conception, a chapter of psychology. Quine leaves no room for the subject-centered *logical* project of traditional empiricism—the project of showing how it might be reasonable for a being to arrive at our view of the world, given that it suffers experiences similar to ours.

In Quine's hands, then, the project of epistemology undergoes a radical transformation. Nevertheless, curiously, Quine takes over much of the substance of classical empiricism in his own positive account. He declares in "Epistemology Naturalized" that

> two cardinal tenets of empiricism remained unassailable ... and so remain to this day. One is that whatever evidence there *is* for science *is* sensory evidence. The other ... is that all inculcation of meanings of words must rest ultimately on sensory evidence. (p. 75)

---

53. "Epistemology Naturalized" (henceforth EN), p. 72.

Quine offers us an empiricism that, structurally, is just a liberalized version of phenomenalism.[54] Quine has a notion of "observation sentence" and assigns to it essentially a traditional role. Observation sentences are the "intersubjective tribunal" by which scientific hypotheses are tested; they are "the repository of evidence for scientific hypotheses" (EN, p. 88). Furthermore, observation sentences are fundamental to semantics; on them "meaning is firmest" (p. 89). Unlike a theoretical sentence, an observation sentence "has an empirical content all its own and wears it on its sleeve" (p. 89). What Quine rejects in phenomenalism is only the idea that empirical content can be assigned to theoretical sentences taken individually.[55] Quine does not abandon the fundamental equation of meaning with empirical content.[56] Indeed, this equation is crucial to the argument for his distinctive claim that theoretical sentences fail to have determinate meanings. In the realm of the theoretical, the carrier of meaning, Quine thinks, is not the individual sentence but the whole of science.

The novelty in Quine's positive view is to be found in his explanation of "observation sentence." Quine does not understand this notion as capturing the given in experience, or as picking out sentences that are somehow justified by experience. He understands the notion naturalistically. In "Epistemology Naturalized," he defines "observation sentence" as "one on which all speakers of the language give the same verdict when given the same concurrent

54. Quine himself draws attention to his indebtedness to phenomenalism. Referring to his new, naturalized conception of epistemology, Quine writes, "Despite this radical shift in orientation and goal, we can imitate the phenomenalistic groundwork of Carnap's *Aufbau* in our new setting" (*From Stimulus to Science*, p. 16). Note that Quine's reading of the *Aufbau* has been called into question by Michael Friedman, Alan Richardson, and Werner Sauer. See Friedman's *Reconsidering Logical Positivism*, Richardson's "Conceiving, Experiencing, and Conceiving Experiencing," and Sauer's "On the Kantian Background of Neopositivism."

55. It is thus that Quine obtains what he calls "an empiricism without the two dogmas"—the "dogmas" of the analytic-synthetic distinction and of sentence-by-sentence reductionism. See §6C for a brief discussion of the relationship of empiricism to the analytic-synthetic distinction.

56. Quine writes, "epistemology remains centered as always on evidence, and meaning remains centered as always on verification; and evidence is verification" (EN, p. 89). He notes that these ideas are in perfect accord with the "preconceptions of old Vienna."

stimulation" (pp. 86-87).[57] Quine tells us in *Pursuit of Truth* that "by the stimulation undergone by a subject on a given occasion I just mean the temporally ordered set of all those of his exteroceptors that are triggered on that occasion" (p. 2). Quine's concept of "observation sentence" uses, therefore, a substantive element of our scientific view of ourselves. This would be completely unacceptable if our goal were the traditional one, to justify the claims and concepts of science. But given Quine's new conception of epistemology, one that makes epistemology a part of science, the use of scientific concepts is unobjectionable.

Despite his transformation of the epistemological project, Quine retains a keen interest in such traditional topics as evidence and the testing of theories. Indeed, he thinks that his notion of "observation sentence" enables an improvement over earlier accounts. Unlike sense-datum statements, observation sentences are not confined to being about the subjective. The sentence 'that is a rabbit' no less plausibly satisfies Quine's conditions on "observation sentence" than does the subjective 'I seem to be seeing something red'. Another advantage is that Quine's notion is entirely independent of the distinction between observation and theoretical *terms*; one can reject the latter distinction as unfounded and yet retain Quine's notion. Quine's account allows both 'that is red' and 'that is an X-ray machine' to

---

57. In *Word and Object* (1960) and in *Pursuit of Truth* (1992), Quine imposes the further requirement that an observation sentence must also be an "occasion sentence": true on some occasions and false on others. (So, 'this is red' is an occasion sentence, but 'gold is malleable' is not.) With the addition of this requirement—and its omission, I think, is simply an oversight—the definition in "Epistemology Naturalized" (1969), quoted above, is essentially a crisper version of the definition Quine gave in *Word and Object*.

In *Pursuit of Truth*, however, Quine's definition of "observation sentence" is radically different. In the 1980s, Quine became dissatisfied with his earlier definitions of "observation sentence" and sought alternatives. The main source of his dissatisfaction was the use in the earlier definitions of the notion of sameness of stimulus across individuals. Quine came to feel that this notion may make no empirical sense, for perhaps there is no similarity of structure in the nerve endings of different individuals (see *Pursuit of Truth*, §15). Quine's later efforts to free himself of this notion were not, in my opinion, successful. (In *Pursuit of Truth*, he is reduced to relying on the thoroughly non-Quinean notion of "witnessing of an occasion.") In any case, I want to set aside the issue of the structure of nerve endings, and shall therefore work with Quine's earlier, crisper definition.

qualify as observation sentences.[58] Admittedly, this last example probably fails to be a Quinean observation sentence. But Quine points out that the notion of observation sentence can usefully be relativized to subcommunities. Relative to the community of all English speakers, the sentence 'that is an X-ray machine' probably fails to be observational, but relative to the subcommunity of radiologists, for example, it probably does so qualify. This kind of relativity is in accord with our commonsense conception of what is observable.

QUINE'S PHILOSOPHY IS THE RESULT OF HIS SYNTHESIS OF naturalism and empiricism. In this synthesis, naturalism has a subservient role: it serves to buttress Quine's empiricism. And the shape of Quine's naturalism is dictated by his empiricism. Considered apart from his empiricism, Quine's naturalistic account has little motivation, for there is little independent reason to think that a naturalism that operates at the level of sensory stimulations will have much use for the notion of "giving a positive verdict" or even for the notion of sentence. (Compare: an account of the computer that works at the level of the flow of electrical charges may have little use for the notion "delete the next sentence.") Quine's naturalistic account makes sense only when viewed as an adjunct to his empiricism. In Quine's philosophy, empiricism does not serve naturalism. (Indeed, I think it distorts naturalism.) It is naturalism that serves—or is meant to serve—empiricism.

Quine relies on naturalism to address the central weakness of classical empiricism, namely, its lightweight foundations. Quine's naturalistic notion of "observation sentence" is weightier, but as far as I can see, it is completely unsuitable for empiricism: it cannot do the required epistemological work. In particular, Quine's observation sentences cannot be "the repository of evidence for scientific hypotheses." Nothing can be evidence that is not antecedently reasonable or, in the terminology I prefer, rational. If my belief that *P* is rational, then it can count as my evidence for some of my further beliefs. But it cannot so count if my belief is not rational. One may possess a logically valid argument for an outrageous belief

Q, but if one's belief in its premises is not rational, then one has no *evidence* for Q. Quine's observation sentences cannot constitute the evidentiary base for science because their acceptance is not assured to be antecedently rational.[59] In the Quinean picture, the assent to an observation sentence occurs as a result of the stimulation of the subject's sensory surfaces. The relationship between stimulation and assent is *causal*. Nothing in this relationship provides assurance that the assent will be rational: irrational assents, too, are often prompted by sensory stimulations. The problem is not overcome by the requirement that the connections between sensory stimulus and assent be uniform across the linguistic community. Again, this requirement does not gain us rationality: irrationality that extends across the linguistic community is neither inconceivable nor all that rare.[60]

Quine's notion of observation sentence differs fundamentally from the ordinary notion of perceptual judgment and also from the classical empiricist notion of sense-datum statement. The latter two are intimately linked to *entitlement* and *rationality*; not so for the Quinean notion. Suppose a normal individual, Fred, makes the perceptual judgment "that's a rabbit" as he looks across his lawn. The very fact that the judgment is perceptual means that Fred is

---

59. In fact, the assent is sometimes not antecedently rational. Suppose that O is a Quinean observation sentence (e.g., "that is a rabbit") and T is a theoretical sentence that expresses a deeply entrenched bit of common knowledge in the linguistic community (e.g., "Earth is round"). Then the sentence O & T also counts as a Quinean observation sentence: since speakers give the same verdict on O when given the same concurrent stimulation, the same will hold for O & T. (And, of course, O & T is an occasion sentence.) But O & T cannot be cited as observational evidence for a claim. In a well-educated community, T might be the conjunction of the community's entire scientific theory. But we would not want to say that the community had in O & T an observational *proof* of their theory. Quine himself subscribes to the traditional idea that observations can at best refute a theory, not prove it (*Pursuit of Truth*, pp. 12–13).

Note also that, while members of a community may agree on an observation sentence X, their agreement is not necessarily grounded in the fact that X is an observation sentence. 'X is an observation sentence' is not itself an observation sentence. In fact, agreement on X may occur even when no member of the community knows that X is an observation sentence.

60. If, in the example of n. 59, the communitywide belief in T is irrational, then O & T is a Quinean observation sentence assent to which is irrational across the linguistic community. (Note that the point I am making requires irrationality across the linguistic community only on *some* sentences. It does not require the community to be through and through irrational.)

entitled to it; Fred is not irrational when he adjusts his beliefs in light of the judgment. There is, as we have seen, a problem to be solved here. The rationality of Fred's perceptual judgment issues somehow from Fred's experience. But the relationship between the two is not simple: Fred's judgment is not rendered rational simply by virtue of belonging to the given in his experience (for it does not belong to the given). We are faced, therefore, with the problem of explaining the rationality of Fred's perceptual judgment. It is a virtue of classical empiricism that it at least addresses this problem and does so with the right concepts at hand: experience and justification. Quine seems to be working with the wrong concepts— stimulation and causation—and he seems bent on evading the problem rather than addressing it.[61] The problem cannot be evaded, however. We cannot understand our epistemic practices unless we understand the rationality of our perceptual judgments.

The problem of perceptual judgments—that is, the problem of understanding the rationality of perceptual judgments—does not require us to subscribe to First Philosophy. The problem is completely independent of the Cartesian project of gaining certainty.[62] It is independent also of the more moderate project of using epistemology to improve the sciences. We can, and should, follow Quine in rejecting First Philosophy. But the rejection does not entail a dismissal of the problem of perceptual judgments. It is true

61. Some readers of Quine—e.g., Rorty and Davidson—have recognized this point and have responded to it in somewhat different ways. Rorty rejects the entire enterprise of epistemology. According to him, there is no interesting story to be told about the rationality of our beliefs, perceptual or otherwise; the only story worth telling is the causal story. In "Realism, Antirealism, and Pragmatism," Rorty writes, "If you forget about representational relations between mind and world and stick to causal relations between organisms and environments, as Davidson does, it is not clear that you will want, or can get, a theory of knowledge" (p. 149). And it is plain that Rorty accepts the antecedent of this conditional.

Davidson himself is a little less radical. According to him, there is a story to be told about the rationality of perceptual belief. But experience does not figure in the story, for the relationship of experience to belief is purely causal. Perceptual beliefs, like other beliefs, are rational, Davidson holds, in virtue of their relationships to other beliefs. Davidson thus ends up with a coherence theory, which he bolsters via his celebrated claim that belief is intrinsically veridical. In §6C, I briefly take up Davidson's argument for this claim.

62. Quine writes, "The Cartesian quest for certainty had been the remote motivation of epistemology, both on its conceptual and its doctrinal side; but that quest was seen as a lost cause" (EN, p. 74).

that if we solve the problem of perceptual judgments, we improve (in a sense) all of our empirical knowledge, for we become clearer about our entitlement to empirical judgments, and consequently, we can meet certain kinds of challenges to them. However, this kind of improvement does not in any way threaten the authority and the autonomy of the sciences. There is no return to First Philosophy here, no dictating to the sciences from the pulpit of philosophy.

Naturalism does not provide the only available strategy for solving the problem of perceptual judgments. We can accept Quine's claim that the sciences provide our best account of ourselves and the world. Still, we can reject the idea that the only way to address the problem of perceptual judgments is through a naturalistic account of ourselves, an account that makes free use of all of the results of the sciences. The special status of the sciences does not rule out the *logical* approach to the problem. In this approach, we take experience as providing a given, and we seek to understand the nature of this given and of its relationship to the contents of our perceptual judgments. The logical approach can accept the authority of the sciences, but it will not allow free use of the results of the sciences in "deriving" perceptual judgments from the given.[63] The special status of the sciences provides a desideratum for the logical approach: the approach must validate the rationality of the claims of the sciences. The special status does not exclude the logical approach.

It deserves emphasis that Quine has not refuted the logical approach. Quine has reasonable complaints against classical empiricism. But classical empiricism is only one particular development of the logical approach. Even if Quine's complaints constitute a refutation of classical empiricism, they leave the broader approach untouched.[64]

63. A simple and familiar analogy: We can undertake to examine the logical structure of arithmetic while fully aware that arithmetical texts contain our best account of number. In this inquiry, we would seek to derive even the simplest theorems from the narrow base of explicitly stated axioms, and we would abstain from free use of arithmetical theorems. A similar abstinence is proper in the logical approach to the problem of perceptual judgments.

64. Quine's main argument against classical empiricism is that it leads to skepticism. This is a strong reason to view classical empiricism with suspicion. But it is not a strong reason for casting aside the whole logical approach; much less is it a reason for casting aside the problem of perceptual judgments. The Humean predicament had better not be the human predicament. Our perceptual judgments *are* rational, and we need to work at an explanation of this fact. (Quine is able to be generous with the skeptics only because he does not take them and their concerns seriously.)

Quine's naturalism, with its skepticism about meaning and with its behaviorism, provides an unpromising environment for solving the problem of perceptual judgments. We want to understand how it is that, in perception, a subject is rational in taking the world to be a certain way. We want to answer this question: what is it that the subject's experience contributes that makes the judgment rational? In Quine's naturalism we have merely the husk: disposition to assent to a sentence. The substance—that is, the subject's taking the world to be a certain way—is lost altogether.

More generally, it is not obvious that *any* naturalistic approach, with its emphasis on description, can provide a solution to the problem of perceptual judgments. But even if there were a naturalistic solution, the need for the logical approach would remain. Suppose that at some future time we manage to construct a rich naturalistic theory T of ourselves, a theory that provides a reductive account of the notions of rationality and perceptual judgment. The theory T, we can imagine, will yield a deep explanation of the rationality of perceptual judgments. Still, this explanation will not serve all of our needs. It will not help us to understand the rationality of perceptual judgments from the perspective of subjects who do not accept T; it will not help us to understand *their* reasons for accepting perceptual judgments. Consider this parallel: T may provide a reductive explanation of why an acceptance of T is rational. But this explanation, no matter how deep, carries little rational force. It cannot be *our* reason for the acceptance of T. Even a highly superstitious view can contain an internal "proof" of its own rationality, but such a "proof" does not compel acceptance.

We may distinguish two sorts of explanations of rationality. One sort (e.g., the naturalistic one) uses hefty theoretical resources, while the other sort (the logical one) does not. The naturalistic approach may well provide deep insights, but because of its use of hefty resources, it cannot be expected to capture the *subjects'*

Quine's response to classical empiricism has this merit, however: it does not fall into the trap of abandoning classical empiricism while at the same time preserving the propositional given. Quine has an analog of the propositional given in his observation sentences. But these sentences are tied to stimulus, not experience. And an assent to an observation sentence is caused by a stimulus; it is not rendered rational by the stimulus. Unlike the responses of many other critics of classical empiricism, the package offered by Quine, though radical, has an internal coherence.

reasons for their judgments or views. The logical approach, if it could be carried through, would fill this need—at least in an idealized setting. It would explain how a rational being, one who has not already reached the lofty perspective of the naturalistic theory, could arrive at such a perspective.[65] Naturalism may be the present queen of metaphysics, but it cannot anoint itself the queen. Its legitimacy, if it can claim any, must be grounded in experience.

Naturalism does not provide a feasible strategy—at least not at present—for solving the problem of perceptual judgments. The project of constructing a naturalistic account of rationality and of perceptual judgment is, at the present stage of inquiry, nothing but quixotic. Not only do we not possess an advanced enough understanding of our bodies, but also we do not understand well enough the relationship between the concepts of science and normative concepts such as rationality. The naturalistic approach to the problem is akin to the following: in order to understand the rationality of some arithmetical judgments, we propose working on a particular subsection in Quine's projected psychology book, the subsection devoted to naturalized arithmetic. Such a proposal is so unfeasible as to be absurd.[66]

IN CONCLUSION: QUINE PRESERVES THE DETAILS OF CLASSICAL empiricism (e.g., the verification theory of meaning) while

---

65. *Objection*: The naturalistic story will contain analogs of experiences the subjects suffer, of the subjects' rational perceptual judgments, and of their evolving views. Hence, the naturalistic explanation can be expected to subsume the logical explanation.

Reply: First, the premise of the objection is doubtful. The naturalistic explanation may well bypass the subject's viewpoint and, with it, the logical account. Second, even if the premise is allowed, it does not follow that the logical explanation is dispensable or less fundamental. The logical explanation, too, will subsume the naturalistic explanation. The naturalistic story, with its analog of the logical story mirrored within it, would appear as one stage among many in the rational evolution of our view in light of experience. Thus, in their idealized forms, the logical and the naturalistic explanations would reflect each other ad infinitum.

66. I intend this criticism of naturalism to be narrow. Naturalistic and, more generally, externalist programs about knowledge—e.g., those recommended by Fred Dretske, Alvin Goldman, Hilary Kornblith, Alvin Plantinga, and others—are undoubtedly valuable. I wish to question only the idea that such programs have the resources to adequately address *all* the traditional epistemological problems (as Kornblith claims in his "Naturalistic Epistemology and Its Critics"). My aim here is to make room for the logical approach, not to undermine naturalism in general.

rejecting its broad framework (e.g., its goals and the constraints within which it works). I am suggesting that we should do the very opposite. We should preserve the broad framework of classical empiricism and reject those detailed doctrines that fail to serve it. The motivations for the framework remain even when the details are discarded, but the motivations for the details disappear once we abandon the framework. The verification theory of meaning, for instance, has a strong motivation within a Cartesian conception of experience. For, as Berkeley pointed out, idealism is the most defensible way of avoiding skeptical consequences of such conceptions. However, once the Cartesian conceptions are abandoned, little motivation remains for the verification theory. Within a naturalistic setting, in particular, there is little reason for understanding meaning in terms of sensory stimulations—little reason, that is, to cast aside the entire animal and its environment when attempting to understand meaning.[67]

2F. Passage to a Nonclassical Alternative

Classical empiricism builds a model of experience and knowledge on a natural idea, the idea that the logical function of experience is to provide us with some truths about the world. Classical empiricism denies, as a consequence, the universal validity of the Multiple-Factorizability of Experience (§1B). It maintains that, in experience, the self transparently takes in a range of subjective facts: here the contribution of the self is null, and it is trivially factored away. Thus, experience can serve as an informant, albeit only of a special subjective realm.

The resulting Cartesian model of experience and knowledge is decidedly radical. But, I have argued, it is forced upon us by the propositional given. It is a virtue of classical empiricism that it

---

67. Indeed, Quine himself is led to a peculiar kind of linguistic idealism because of his allegiance to the verification theory of meaning (see §6C). He writes in "Reply to Stroud,"

> I have depicted a barren scene. The furniture of our world, the people and sticks and stones along with the electrons and molecules, have dwindled to manners of speaking. Any other purported objects would serve as well, and may as well be said already to be doing so. (p. 474)

This consequence, one is inclined to think, should be utterly unpalatable to a proponent of naturalism.

recognizes the close linkages between the propositional given, the Cartesian conceptions, and the denial of Multiple-Factorizability. Under plausible assumptions, these three ideas are equivalent. If we wish to deny Multiple-Factorizability, then the only remotely plausible way to do so is via a Cartesian conception, and this provides us with a propositional given. And we have already seen the converse: the acceptance of a propositional given entails the acceptance of a Cartesian conception, and this leads to a denial of Multiple-Factorizability. Thus, the three ideas—the propositional given, the Cartesian conceptions, and the denial of Multiple-Factorizability—stand and fall together. However much we may criticize classical empiricism and Cartesian conceptions, they will continue to entice and haunt us unless we are armed with a better model of experience and knowledge. And we have no hope of constructing such a model unless we recognize, with classical empiricism, the equivalence of the above three ideas.

Classical empiricism fails to preserve the Insight of Empiricism (§1A). It gives experience a voice, but the voice turns out to be feeble. It makes experience unfit to be the supreme epistemic authority. Experience can command little respect as an adjudicator of the far-reaching claims of religion and science, when it has difficulty reaching a decisive verdict on the most ordinary of the claims— claims that a child can settle easily and correctly. As we have seen, classical empiricism leads to either skepticism or idealism. In the former case, it is plain that the Insight is not preserved. The same holds in the latter case also, though this can be masked by phenomenalist constructions. If our talk of the public world is a mere shorthand for complexes of statements about subjective entities, if nothing independent of our minds is knowable, then why would exploration and experiment—or, more accurately, their phenomenal counterparts—be especially important in improving our theories, conceptions, and concepts? If the world is not independent of the self, little motivation remains for the Insight. Analogy: One can gain knowledge about a real ball by experimenting with it, but not about a dreamed up ball (or a hallucinated ball). Experimentation in a dream reveals nothing about the ball. At best, it reveals something about the dreaming self, and that, too, because we have a moderately realistic conception of the dreamer. The underlying motivation for the Insight comes from a moderately realist attitude toward the world. Once one accepts idealism, the Insight loses all motivation.

We noticed in chapter 1 that the Insight of Empiricism stands in apparent tension with the Multiple-Factorizability of Experience. It seemed that Multiple-Factorizability forces a denial of the propositional given and, consequently, renders experience mute. It seemed, therefore, that experience cannot pronounce on our theories and conceptions, and hence that the Insight is undermined. The examination of classical empiricism here reveals, however, that it is the propositional given that actually comes into conflict with the Insight. The propositional given lands us in a Cartesian conception of experience, thereby landing us in idealism or skepticism. Either way, we fail to sustain the Insight.

We are thus led to conclude that perhaps there is no real tension between the Insight and Multiple-Factorizability. Indeed, perhaps the proper way to sustain the Insight is by embracing Multiple-Factorizability, not by denying it. This conclusion has, on the one hand, some intuitive appeal. It is because experience is a product of the world and the self, and because neither of these factors can readily be recovered from individual experiences, that we need to put ourselves in different situations to obtain a full and adequate view of the world. Hence arises the fallibility of our theories and conceptions, and the consequent importance of testing them against a wide range of experiences. On the other hand, the conclusion raises considerable difficulties. The intuitive thought linking Multiple-Factorizability to the Insight rests on a moderately realist attitude toward the world. The denial of Multiple-Factorizability, we have seen, does not help us to sustain such a realism. But it is difficult to see how an affirmation of Multiple-Factorizability improves matters. More fundamentally, if we affirm Multiple-Factorizability—and so deny the propositional given— what are we to say about the contribution of experience to knowledge? What form does it take? The answers to these questions are not obvious. But part of the path that we must follow is clear enough. Whereas classical empiricism holds fast to the interconnected ideas of the propositional given, Cartesian conceptions, and the denial of Multiple-Factorizability, we need to abandon all three of these ideas.[68] Hence, we must abandon the idea of a transparent self taking in an unobstructed view of the

---

68. In chapter 5, I trace the fundamental error of classical empiricism to its denial of Multiple-Factorizability. See §5D.

layout of reality. We must hold firm to the fact that our understanding of the world is interdependent with our understanding of the self, and we must work out an account of the given that fully respects this interdependence. But how should we proceed to construct such an account? How does experience contribute to knowledge if not by revealing some truths about the world? We shall gain an important clue in our search for answers if we study the phenomenon of interdependence in a simple setting. This is the goal of chapter 3.

꒰◯꒱

THREE

INTERDEPENDENT DEFINITIONS:
AN INTRODUCTION

꒰◯꒱ Mutually dependent definitions provide a simple setting
in which to study the phenomenon of interdependence.
A brief exploration of them will provide us with conceptual tools
useful for understanding the logical relationship of experience to
knowledge. (Readers already comfortable with the logical phenomenon of interdependence, or impatient to get on with the main
business, may skip this chapter.)

3A. Revision Rules

Imagine that you have a conversation with a friend, say, about
arithmetic. Imagine that in the course of the conversation your
friend stipulates the following definition of a new general term G.

(1) x is $G =_{Df} x$ is an even number and x is H.

Here '$=_{Df}$' is the sign of definitional equivalence. On the left-hand
side of this sign occurs the *definiendum*, that which is to be defined.
On the right-hand side occurs the *definiens*, that which serves to
define the definiendum. Suppose, for simplicity, that your conversation has a narrow focus: it is concerned only with the natural
numbers between 0 and 6. In other words, your *domain of discourse* is
the set of numbers $\{1, 2, 3, 4, 5\}$. Your friend needs to give you a
definition of H to complete the definition of G, but let us imagine

that your conversation is interrupted and the friend has to leave before he can give you this definition.

Now, because of the unfortunate interruption, you do not know the meaning of G, nor do you know the objects in the domain of discourse of which G is true. You have, nonetheless, some significant information about G. For example, you know that if H is true of nothing, then G is also true of nothing, for now the definiens of (1) is not true of anything. For another example, you know that if H is true precisely of 1 and 2, then G is true precisely of 2. It will be convenient to express this bit of your knowledge in the following way: if the *antecedent extension* of H is $\{1, 2\}$, then the *consequent extension* of G is $\{2\}$. The first example can now be expressed in this way: if the antecedent extension of H is $\{\}$ ("null"), then the consequent extension of G is also $\{\}$. The general point that these examples illustrate is this: even though you do not know what G is true of—you do not know what the actual extension of G is—still you can figure out the consequent extension of G once you are given an antecedent extension of H. You know how the consequent extension of G varies as the antecedent extension of H is varied. This knowledge can be represented as in table 3.1. Note that the table is incomplete. It does not show the consequent extension of G under all possible antecedent extensions of H. A complete table would have 32 rows.

The general point we have observed about (1) holds also for other incomplete definitions. Imagine, for example, a situation like the one above but in which your friend leaves you with the following incomplete definition of H.

(2) x is $H =_{Df} x > 3$ or x is not G.

As before, you can calculate the consequent extension of H, given any antecedent extension of G. For instance, if the antecedent

Table 3.1

Antecedent Extension of H	Consequent Extension of G
$\{\}$	$\{\}$
$\{1\}$	$\{\}$
$\{1, 2\}$	$\{2\}$
$\{1, 2, 3\}$	$\{2\}$
$\{2, 3, 4, 5\}$	$\{2, 4\}$
$\{1, 2, 3, 4, 5\}$	$\{2, 4\}$

extension of G is $\{\}$, then the definiens of (2) is true of every object in the domain of discourse. So the consequent extension of H is $\{1, 2, 3, 4, 5\}$. Table 3.2 displays the results of this and of some other similar calculations. Again, the table is incomplete.

Let us now put (1) and (2) together to obtain a system of interdependent definitions:

> (3) x is $G =_{\mathrm{Df}} x$ is an even number and x is H;
> x is $H =_{\mathrm{Df}} x > 3$ or x is not G.

The first clause of this system makes the meaning of G dependent upon the meaning of H, and the second clause makes the meaning of H dependent upon the meaning of G. One may well have doubts whether this sort of thing is legitimate. Let us for the moment put aside these doubts and reflect on the system of definitions before us. The first point to observe is that the information we had when we considered the two clauses of the system in isolation is still with us. It is not lost somehow when we put the two clauses together. Given an antecedent extension of G, we can still use the second clause to calculate the consequent extension of H. And, given an antecedent extension of H, we can use the first clause to calculate the consequent extension of G. Indeed, we can put the two calculations together: given antecedent extensions for both G and H, we can use the system of definitions (3) to calculate the consequent extensions for G and H. An example: Let the antecedent extensions for G and H both be $\{\}$. Then, the first clause of the system tells us that the consequent extension of G is $\{\}$. (See the first row of table 3.1.) And the second clause tells us that the consequent extension of H is $\{1, 2, 3, 4, 5\}$. (See the first row of table 3.2.) Let us sum up these results thus: given the pair $\langle \{\}, \{\} \rangle$ of antecedent extensions for G and H, the system of definitions (3) yields the pair of consequent extensions $\langle \{\}, \{1, 2, 3, 4, 5\} \rangle$.

Table 3.2

Antecedent Extension of G	Consequent Extension of H
$\{\}$	$\{1, 2, 3, 4, 5\}$
$\{1\}$	$\{2, 3, 4, 5\}$
$\{2\}$	$\{1, 3, 4, 5\}$
$\{1, 2\}$	$\{3, 4, 5\}$
$\{1, 2, 5\}$	$\{3, 4, 5\}$
$\{1, 2, 3, 4\}$	$\{4, 5\}$

(Note that the first entry X in a pair $\langle X, Y \rangle$ corresponds to G and the second entry Y to H.) This sort of calculation can be carried out for any pair of antecedent extensions. The results of some of these calculations are displayed in table 3.3. Observe that this table is obtained by weaving together tables 3.1 and 3.2. Observe also that it is even more incomplete than the two earlier tables. A complete table would have 32×32 ($= 1{,}024$) rows.

In general, systems of definitions fix how consequent extensions of their definienda depend upon antecedent extensions. Suppose we have a system that contains interdependent definitions of three predicates G, H, and K. Then, given a triple of antecedent extensions for G, H, and K, the system yields a triple of consequent extensions for the three predicates. Suppose, for another example, we have a system that defines just one predicate G and does so using G itself—so the system consists of a *circular* definition of G. Then, given an antecedent extension of G, the system yields a consequent extension of G. Here is an illustration: Let the domain of discourse be $\{0, 1\}$, and let the system consist of the following definition.

(4) x is $G =_{Df} x = 0$ and something is G, or $x = 1$ and nothing is G.

Let the antecedent extension of G be $\{\}$. Then the definiens is true precisely of 1, and so the consequent extension of G is $\{1\}$. The results of this and other similar calculations are exhibited in table 3.4, and now the table is complete.

Here are two variant examples that will prove useful. The first system consists of

(5) x is $G =_{Df} x = 0$ and nothing is G.

Table 3.3

Pair of Antecedent Extensions for G and H	Pair of Consequent Extensions for G and H
$\langle \{\}, \{\} \rangle$	$\langle \{\}, \{1, 2, 3, 4, 5\} \rangle$
$\langle \{1\}, \{\} \rangle$	$\langle \{\}, \{2, 3, 4, 5\} \rangle$
$\langle \{\}, \{1\} \rangle$	$\langle \{\}, \{1, 2, 3, 4, 5\} \rangle$
$\langle \{\}, \{1, 2\} \rangle$	$\langle \{2\}, \{1, 2, 3, 4, 5\} \rangle$
$\langle \{1, 2, 5\}, \{1, 2, 3\} \rangle$	$\langle \{2\}, \{3, 4, 5\} \rangle$
$\langle \{1, 2, 3, 4\}, \{1, 2, 3, 4, 5\} \rangle$	$\langle \{2, 4\}, \{4, 5\} \rangle$

Table 3.4

Antecedent Extension of G	Consequent Extension of G
{}	{1}
{0}	{0}
{1}	{0}
{0, 1}	{0}

This yields table 3.5.

The second system consists of

(6) x is $G =_{Df} x = 0$ and something is G.

This yields table 3.6.

When terms belong to a system of interdependent definitions, we are unable to determine in any direct way the objects of which they are true. With the system (3), for example, to determine the objects of which G is true, we need to know the objects of which H is true; and to determine the objects of which H is true, we need to know that which we are trying to determine in the first place—namely, the objects of which G is true. We are caught in a circle. Interdependent definitions get us entangled in circles such as these. They also yield, however, vital information—information that

Table 3.5

Antecedent Extension of G	Consequent Extension of G
{}	{0}
{0}	{}
{1}	{}
{0, 1}	{}

Table 3.6

Antecedent Extension of G	Consequent Extension of G
{}	{}
{0}	{0}
{1}	{0}
{0, 1}	{0}

allows us to exploit the circles in which we find ourselves. As we have seen above, given antecedent extensions of the definienda, interdependent definitions allow us to figure out consequent extensions. This is *the* vital information that these definitions give us. And the proper way of exploiting this information, I suggest, is to treat the transition from antecedent extensions to consequent extensions as a *rule of revision*: the consequent extensions are better hypotheses for the interpretation of the definienda than are the antecedent extensions—or at least they are as good as the antecedent ones.[1] For example, we have seen that, given the pair of antecedent extensions $\langle \{\}, \{\} \rangle$ for G and H, the system (3) yields the pair of consequent extensions $\langle \{\}, \{1, 2, 3, 4, 5\} \rangle$. The suggestion I am making is that we should view $\langle \{\}, \{1, 2, 3, 4, 5\} \rangle$ as a better proposal for the interpretation of G and H than $\langle \{\}, \{\} \rangle$.[2]

When definitions form an interdependent system, we cannot, in general, determine the extension of any definiendum in isolation. The definitions do not provide a rule for carving the domain of discourse into a part containing objects of which a definiendum is true and a part containing objects of which the definiendum is false. The definitions provide instead a rule of revision: a rule for improving any hypotheses about the extensions of the definienda. The definitions do not confer (at least directly) a categorical meaning on the definienda. They confer only a hypothetical meaning: they tell us what the extensions of the definienda should be relative to a hypothesis. The vital information that interdependent definitions give about their definienda is captured by their rule of revision.

Whenever we aim to understand a phenomenon that contains interdependencies, we should seek out, I suggest, the underlying rule of revision. If our conception of ourselves depends upon our conception of the world, and if our conception of the world, in turn, depends upon our conception of ourselves—if neither can be determined in isolation from the other—we are caught in an epistemic circle. The way out is to look for an underlying rule of revision. But, it will be asked, how will this rule of revision, even if we can find it,

---

1. From now on I shall suppress this qualification. 'Better' should be read as 'better or equally good'.

2. Note that it is the first *pair* of extensions that is a better proposal than the second pair. This does not imply that the first component, for instance, of the one is better than that of the second. The "better than" relation is claimed to hold between total hypotheses, not their components.

help? And where will the rule come from, anyhow? Let us tackle the first question first. We shall see in §3B how revision rules, though hypothetical in character, can yield categorical information. This will provide useful hints for making sense of our epistemic situation. The second question will be addressed in chapter 4.

3B. Revision Processes

A revision rule ρ enables us to improve any given hypothesis h: the rule ρ applied to h yields a hypothesis, $\rho(h)$, that is better than h.[3] An obvious and natural way of using a revision rule is this: Pick an arbitrary hypothesis h. Apply the revision rule ρ to obtain a better hypothesis $\rho(h)$. Now $\rho(h)$, though better than h, may itself be amenable to improvement. We can apply ρ to $\rho(h)$ to obtain a still better hypothesis $\rho(\rho(h))$. Another application of ρ yields a yet better hypothesis $\rho(\rho(\rho(h)))$. The process can be repeated indefinitely to yield a *revision sequence*,

$$h, \rho(h), \rho(\rho(h)), \rho(\rho(\rho(h))), \dots .$$

It will be useful to speak of the *stages* of a revision sequence. At the zeroth stage in the above revision sequence we have the hypothesis h, at the first stage we have $\rho(h)$, at the second $\rho(\rho(h))$, and so on.

Consider the system (4) and its revision rule—call the revision rule δ. This rule is summed up in table 3.4. Suppose we begin with the hypothesis that the extension of G is $\{\}$. We can improve this hypothesis by applying the revision rule δ to it. Table 3.4 tells us that

$$\delta(\{\}) = \{1\}.$$

So, at the first stage of revision, we obtain a new and improved hypothesis $\{1\}$ $[=\delta(\{\})]$. We can improve this new hypothesis by another application of δ. Table 3.4 tells us that

$$\delta(\{1\}) = \{0\}.$$

So at the second stage we obtain a further improved hypothesis $\{0\}$ $[=\delta(\{1\})]$. Now we can try to improve $\{0\}$ with yet another application of δ. Since

$$\delta(\{0\}) = \{0\},$$

---

3. Again, I understand 'improves' weakly: improves or yields an equally good hypothesis.

we obtain {0} [$=\delta(\{0\})$] again at the third stage of revision. Plainly, we shall obtain {0} at all subsequent stages. Observe that the rule yields a strictly better hypothesis up until the second stage of revision. From the third stage on, however, the rule yields a hypothesis that is not strictly better but only as good as the preceding one. The rule is unable to effect any strict improvement in the hypothesis {0}; it keeps repeating {0} over and over again.[4] This means that, according to δ, {0} is one of the *best* hypotheses for the interpretation of G.

We have seen that if we begin with the hypothesis that the extension of G is {}, then the rule δ yields the following revision sequence $\mathcal{S}^{\star}$:

$$\{\}, \{1\}, \{0\}, \{0\}, \{0\}....$$

Consider the behavior of the number 0 in this sequence. Observe that there is a stage of revision—namely, the second—after which 0 always belongs to the revised extensions. I shall express this by saying that 0 is *stably in* the revised extensions of G in $\mathcal{S}^{\star}$. Similarly, there is a stage after which the number 1 always falls outside the revised extensions: I shall say that 1 is *stably outside* the revised extensions of G in $\mathcal{S}^{\star}$. I shall also express these facts as follows: 0 is stably G and 1 is stably non-G in $\mathcal{S}^{\star}$. I shall also say that 0 and 1 are *stable* in $\mathcal{S}^{\star}$.[5]

---

4. A hypothesis h is a *fixed point* of a rule ρ iff $\rho(h) = h$. (Here and below, 'iff' abbreviates 'if and only if'.) If a fixed point h occurs at any stage of a revision sequence $\mathcal{S}$, then h recurs at all higher stages of $\mathcal{S}$.

5. Let $\mathcal{S}$ be a sequence of revised extensions of G. Let $\mathcal{S}_n$ be the nth stage of $\mathcal{S}$. Then an object d in the domain of discourse is *stably G* iff there is a number n such that, for all numbers $m \geq n$, d belongs to $\mathcal{S}_m$. And d is *stably non-G* iff there is a number n such that, for all numbers $m \geq n$, d falls outside $\mathcal{S}_m$. Finally, d is *stable* in $\mathcal{S}$ iff d is either stably G or stably non-G in $\mathcal{S}$; d is *unstable* otherwise.

Here and below, I am concerned only with systems of first-order definitions that are *finite*, where a system of definitions is finite iff its revision process invariably requires only finitely many stages. (For a more precise characterization, see my "Finite Circular Definitions.") Maricarmen Martinez has shown that a first-order definition of a monadic predicate is finite if, with the exception of identity, all resources in its definiens are monadic (see her essay "Some Closure Properties of Finite Definitions"). It can be shown that, in a countable language, finite definitions are recursively enumerable but they are not in general recursive; i.e., there is no effective method for separating finite definitions from nonfinite ones (see "Finite Circular Definitions").

A *general* theory of definitions cannot confine itself to finite revision processes. It has to take into account transfinite applications of revision rules. For these, see Nuel Belnap's and my *Revision Theory of Truth*.

So far, we have considered only the results of applying the revision rule δ to the initial hypothesis $\{\}$. We should consider what happens when the initial hypothesis is varied. If we begin with $\{0, 1\}$, we obtain the following revision sequence:

$$\{0, 1\}, \{0\}, \{0\}, \{0\}, \{0\}....$$

There are two further hypotheses to consider, $\{0\}$ and $\{1\}$. These yield the following sequences:

$$\{0\}, \{0\}, \{0\}, \{0\}, \{0\}...$$
$$\{1\}, \{0\}, \{0\}, \{0\}, \{0\}....$$

The totality of the revision sequences that a rule generates is the *(full) revision process* for the rule.[6] The revision process for δ consists, then, of the above four sequences. Observe that 0 is stably G in all four sequences and that 1 is stably non-G in them. I shall express this by saying that 0 is *categorically G* and 1 is *categorically non-G* in the revision process. I shall also say that 0 and 1 are *categorical* and, alternatively, that the revision process *yields a categorical verdict* on 0 and 1.[7]

The rule δ behaves in an ideal way. It stabilizes at and converges to a unique extension. No matter where we begin the revision process, it lands us in the hypothesis that the extension of G is $\{0\}$. The process dictates that $\{0\}$ is *the* best hypothesis about the extension of G. Here we have an instance of the general fact that revision rules, even though hypothetical in character, sometimes result in unique categorical extensions for the definienda.

This ideal behavior does not always obtain. Consider the system (5) and its rule of revision, which is displayed in table 3.5. The revision process for this rule consists of the following four sequences:

6. Some applications require restricted revision processes, i.e., processes that contain revision sequences with a specific character. For finite definitions, however, we can work with full processes. I shall drop the qualification "full" in the exposition below and speak simply of "revision processes."

7. An object *d* in the domain of discourse is *categorically G* in a revision process iff *d* is stably G in all revision sequences in the process. It is *categorically non-G* iff it is stably non-G in all these sequences. And it is *categorical* in the process iff it is either categorically G or categorically non-G in the process. We say that *d* is *categorically G* (*categorically non-G, etc.) for* a revision rule ρ iff *d* is categorically G (categorically non-G, etc.) in the revision process generated by ρ.

$\{\}, \{o\}, \{\}, \{o\},\dots$
$\{o\}, \{\}, \{o\}, \{\},\dots$
$\{1\}, \{\}, \{o\}, \{\},\dots$
$\{o, 1\}, \{\}, \{o\}, \{\},\dots.$

The process yields a categorical verdict on 1: 1 is stably non-G in all four sequences. But it does not yield a categorical verdict on o: o flip-flops in and out of the revised extensions in all four sequences. It is as if the process cannot "make up its mind" about the status of o. It declares o to be G at one stage and at a later stage reverses itself and declares o not to be G. Objects on which the revision process does not yield a categorical verdict will be called *pathological*. Objects that display the specific behavior of o here—that is, flip-flopping in all revision sequences—will be called *paradoxical*.[8] Note that the peculiar behavior of o reflects an interdependence imposed by definition (5). If o is supposed to be G, then the definiens of (5) turns out not to be satisfied by o and the definition dictates that o is not G. But if o is supposed to be non-G, then the definiens *is* satisfied by o (since the definition dictates that nothing other than o is G) and we are led to conclude that o is G. It is this interdependence of "o is G" and "o is not G," imposed by the definition, that is reflected in the behavior of o in the revision process.

Contrast the behavior of (5) with that of (6). The rule for (6), displayed in table 3.6, generates a revision process consisting of the following four sequences:

$\{\}, \{\}, \{\}, \{\},\dots$
$\{o\}, \{o\}, \{o\}, \{o\}, \{o\},\dots$
$\{1\}, \{o\}, \{o\}, \{o\}, \{o\},\dots$
$\{o, 1\}, \{o\}, \{o\}, \{o\}, \{o\}.\dots$

---

8. An object in the domain of discourse is *pathological* in a revision process iff it is not categorical in the process; it is *paradoxical* iff it is unstable in all revision sequences in the process. All paradoxical objects are pathological, but not conversely.

Note that there is nothing genuinely problematic about paradoxical objects or their behavior. I call these objects 'paradoxical' because, first, they exhibit behavior characteristic of certain entities that have been regarded as paradoxical (e.g., the Liar statement and the Russell class). Second, these objects show that the system of definitions violates the traditional logical laws of definitions. This is not genuinely paradoxical because the traditional laws are correct and appropriate only for "straight" definitions, not for circular definitions or for systems of interdependent definitions.

There is nothing bad or diseased about pathological objects. I am using the terms 'pathological' and 'paradoxical' without any negative logical or emotional connotations.

Here, the number 1 exhibits the same behavior as before: it is categorically non-G. The number 0 exhibits new behavior, however. It is stable in each sequence, but the revision process fails to yield a categorical verdict on it. The process fails to *converge* with respect to 0: revisions of initial hypotheses do not all yield the same judgment about 0. Under some revision sequences, 0 is declared to be G; under others, it is declared to be non-G. Again, the behavior of 0 here reflects an interdependence imposed by the definition. Definition (6) makes the status of "0 is G" depend in part on itself. That is why the supposition that 0 is G confirms itself in the course of revision.

Let us say that d is *convergent* in a revision process for G iff d behaves the same way—that is, it is stably G or it is stably non-G or it is unstable—in all sequences in the process; otherwise, let us say that d is *divergent*. Further, let us say that a process is *convergent* iff every object in the domain of discourse is convergent in it; otherwise, the process is *divergent*. Now the difference between the revision processes of (5) and (6) can be expressed as follows: The revision process for (6) is *stable*—in the sense that on every sequence in the process every object stabilizes—but it is not convergent.[9] The revision process for (5), on the other hand, is convergent but not stable. Observe that all divergent objects are pathological and non-paradoxical. The number 0 is divergent in the revision process of (6); it is an example of an object that is pathological but not paradoxical.

Let us now return to the system of definitions (3). The revision rule for this system, as we have seen, applies to pairs of extensions for the definienda G and H, and yields revised pairs of extensions. Let D be the domain of discourse ($= \{1, 2, 3, 4, 5\}$). Then, it is easily verified that the rule when applied to a pair of extensions $\langle X, Y \rangle$ yields the pair $\langle U, V \rangle$ such that

$U =$ the set of even numbers in Y

and

$V =$ the set containing 4 and 5 and those members of D that are not in X.

---

9. An object is *stable* in a revision process iff it is stable in every sequence in the process. A revision process is *stable* iff every object in the domain of discourse is stable in the process; otherwise, the process is *unstable*.

There are several distinct notions of stability (and of convergence) of revision processes. I am here highlighting just one of these notions.

Observe that this accords with the preceding calculations. For example, $\langle \{\}, \{\} \rangle$ is revised to $\langle \{\}, \{1, 2, 3, 4, 5\} \rangle$. Now, since the revision rule operates on pairs of extensions, the revision process consists of sequences of such pairs. That is, the revision process is a compound one: it contains simultaneous revisions of the extensions of G and H.[10] This is inevitable because of the interdependence of G and H. Nevertheless, we can recover from the compound process individual revision processes for the two predicates. For G, we simply take the first components of the ordered pairs in the revision sequences, and for H, we take the second components. The definitions of "categorically G," and other notions can then be carried over without modification. For example, the compound revision process for (3) contains the following revision sequence:

$$\langle \{2, 4\}, D \rangle, \langle \{2, 4\}, \{1, 3, 4, 5\} \rangle, \langle \{4\}, \{1, 3, 4, 5\} \rangle, \langle \{4\}, D \rangle,$$
$$\langle \{2, 4\}, D \rangle, \ldots .$$

The derivative process for G will contain the sequence

$$\{2, 4\}, \{2, 4\}, \{4\}, \{4\}, \{2, 4\}, \ldots$$

consisting of first components of the pairs. And the process for H will contain the sequence

$$D, \{1, 3, 4, 5\}, \{1, 3, 4, 5\}, D, D, \ldots$$

consisting of the second components. A little calculation shows that the derivative processes for G and H yield categorical verdicts on all objects except 2, which is paradoxical in both processes. All numbers except 2 are categorically H; 4 is categorically G; and 1, 3, and 5 are categorically non-G.

REVISION PROCESSES ENABLE US TO EXTRACT CATEGORICAL information from hypothetical revision rules. They thus enable us to make semantic sense of interdependent definitions. Furthermore, they yield a notion of logical validity, which, it can be shown, is captured by a sound and complete logical calculus.[11]

---

10. In general, the rule of revision for a system with n definienda operates on n-tuples of extensions. And the revision process consists of sequences of n-tuples.

11. For the logical calculus and the definition of validity, see my "Finite Circular Definitions." Philip Kremer has proved that there cannot be a complete calculus when

Interdependent definitions, and the concepts they define, do not fit within the boundaries set by traditional semantics and logic. But this provides, Belnap and I have argued, a reason for stretching out these boundaries, not for ruling such definitions and concepts to be illegitimate. Some of our ordinary concepts, it can be shown, are in fact circular. Belnap and I have argued at length that this is so for the concept of truth.[12] And parallel arguments establish the circularity of reference, necessity, and knowledge. Francesco Orilia, André Chapuis, and Byeongdeok Lee have respectively made it plausible that predication, rational choice, and certain concepts of belief are fruitfully viewed as circular.[13] It is interesting that with all these concepts, even the nonideal behavior of the revision process serves an explanatory function. As is well known, these concepts sometimes exhibit logically puzzling behavior (e.g., truth exhibits puzzling behavior in the Liar sentence, "this very sentence is not true"). The nonideal elements of the revision process prove to be helpful in predicting and explaining this behavior. The puzzling behavior turns out to be rooted in the circularity inherent in these concepts.

It is important when thinking about interdependency to keep in mind the possibility that the revision process exhibits some pathology. Even this dimension of the process can illuminate features of the phenomenon under investigation.

---

the theory is extended to include nonfinite definitions, i.e., definitions whose revision processes extend into the transfinite. Such definitions can greatly enrich the expressive power of language, with the concomitant Gödelian result that the set of validities is not recursively enumerable. See Kremer's "The Gupta–Belnap Systems $S^\#$ and $S\star$ Are Not Axiomatisable."

12. See *Revision Theory of Truth*. A briefer, more accessible argument can be found in my "Remarks on Definitions and the Concept of Truth." The argument builds on the seminal work of Alfred Tarski and Saul Kripke. It is also indebted to the work of Robert L. Martin, Peter Woodruff, and Hans Herzberger. For an overview of this work, see my survey article "Truth." Tarski's seminal paper appears as chapter 8 of his *Logic, Semantics, Metamathematics*. The papers of Kripke, of Martin and Woodruff, and of Herzberger are reprinted in Martin's *Recent Essays on Truth and the Liar Paradox*.

13. See Orilia's "Property Theory and the Revision Theory of Definitions" and *Predication, Analysis and Reference*; Chapuis's "Rationality and Circularity"; and Lee's "The Paradox of Belief Instability and a Revision Theory of Belief." See also my "On Circular Concepts."

3C. A Summary of Main Points

The following points about interdependent definitions deserve emphasis.

1. A system of interdependent definitions yields a *rule of revision.*[14] This rule, when applied to a *hypothesis* about the extensions of the definienda, yields a *better* hypothesis about the definienda.

2. Repeated applications of a revision rule ρ to an initial hypothesis yield a *revision sequence.* The totality of revision sequences—one revision sequence for each initial hypothesis—constitutes the *revision process* generated by ρ.[15] Revision processes have breadth; that is, they contain the results of revision of many initial hypotheses. They also have depth: they contain the results of iterated applications of the revision rule.

3. In general, the revision process gives a definite verdict on some elements, but not all. Whether the process gives a verdict—and what this verdict is—depends upon the behavior of the element across both the depth and the breadth of the revision process.

4. The process gives a definite verdict on those elements whose behavior is both *stable* and *convergent.* If, in the course of a revision sequence, an object d eventually belongs to all the subsequent revised extensions of a predicate G, and if d behaves in the same way in all revision sequences, then the process yields a definite verdict that d is G. Similarly, if in all revision sequences there is a stage after which d falls outside all the subsequent extensions, then the revision process yields the definite verdict that d is not G.

5. The revision process does not give a definite verdict on those elements whose behavior is unstable or divergent or both. Different types of failure of stability and convergence correspond to different types of *pathological* behavior. It is a characteristic feature of interdependent definitions that under certain circumstances they display such behavior.

---

14. The expressions italicized in this section are given a precise and, sometimes, specialized sense in the theory of definitions. I have given an informal explanation of these expressions in my exposition above.

15. As noted above, some applications require restricted revision processes—i.e., processes that contain revision sequences with specific characteristics.

Revision rules and revision processes are fundamental tools for dealing with phenomena containing interdependencies. The precise definitions of these rules and processes vary from application to application. Nevertheless, the general structure sketched above is found to persist. We shall see in chapter 4 that this is so with the epistemological interdependencies that concern us here.

FOUR

A MODEL OF EXPERIENCE

AND KNOWLEDGE

I wish to develop an account of experience and knowledge that takes seriously the interdependence of our conceptions of the self and the world. Without an adequate conception of the world, we cannot have an adequate conception of the self. And, conversely, without an adequate conception of the self, we cannot have an adequate conception of the world. The two are interdependent. We do not begin our inquiry with adequate conceptions of the self and the world; it is rather the goal of inquiry to furnish us with such conceptions. I want to develop an account of experience and knowledge that respects these facts.

Classical empiricism is founded on the Cartesian view that we begin, or ought to begin, our inquiry with a true and adequate conception of the self: the self has direct awareness of its sensations, sense-data, ideas, and so on. I have argued that this view rests on a logical thesis, namely, that the contribution of experience to knowledge is propositional in form. Indeed, once the logical thesis is accepted, some form of Cartesianism becomes inevitable (see chapter 2). Hence, we can do justice to the interdependence of our conceptions of the self and the world only if we are willing to abandon the logical thesis. I argue in §4A that the contribution of experience to knowledge falls in a new logical category—not the familiar categories of object, concept, and proposition. This raises an immediate question: if the contribution is not propositional, how can it be substantial? In §4B, I sketch an idealized picture of knowledge that addresses this question. The picture sketched, though highly incomplete, shows how it is possible for experience to exercise a substantial rational constraint even when its contribution ("the given") is not propositional in form. Legitimate objections can be raised against the picture, and I draw attention to them in §4C. I address the most serious of these objections in chapter 5.

4A. The Given in Experience

Consider an ordinary, everyday type of situation. Say I am walking along a street, I turn a corner, and I am surprised to find myself in front of a large wall, light green in color. I have a certain type of experience and I take myself to know a few things that I did not know before. I am prepared to assert—and I take myself to be entitled to assert—that there is a wall before me, that it is light green in color, that it lies around the corner from such-and-such a street, and so on. Only a fool or a philosopher would question my entitlement—the former for poor and silly reasons, the latter for deep and subtle ones. The latter insists that my entitlement does not lie solely in the experience itself. An ideal rational being subjected only to a subjectively identical experience would not be in a position to make the assertions that I am prepared to make. This is a fair point. Still, the following is beyond doubt: *given* my concepts, conceptions, and beliefs—in short, given my *view*—at the time of the experience, I am perfectly entitled to perceptual judgments such as "there is a light green wall before me." The entitlement claimed here is only hypothetical: assuming that I am justified in my view, I am justified in my perceptual judgments. This is perfectly compatible with the philosopher's point that my experience by itself does not provide any justification for my perceptual judgments, for the experience by itself does not provide a justification for the view I bring to bear on it. The philosopher is not questioning the idea of conditional entitlement: given that I have the experience and given that I am entitled to my view, it follows that I am entitled to my perceptual judgments. This is something that only a fool would question. The philosopher's point is that the move from the conditional entitlement to a categorical entitlement requires a *prior* entitlement to my view. And here there is a serious problem: how can I be entitled to a view if my only entitlement to perceptual judgments is thus conditional?

Let us leave this troublesome problem to one side for the moment and focus on the point of agreement, which we may represent schematically thus:

(1) View + Experience ⇒ Perceptual Judgments.

In the above example, when I turned the corner and was confronted by the wall, I had a certain view—that is, I had certain concepts such as "wall" and "light green," I had the ordinary conception of street corners and walls, and I had certain beliefs such as that my eyes are functioning properly, the lighting is normal, and so on. Once I bring this view to my experience, I am entitled to certain perceptual judgments—judgments such as "there is a light green wall before me." Now, I can take the same experience and consider it under a different view. I can, for example, consider it under a view like the one just described but with the belief that a certain disease has tinged my eye lenses yellow and that things that look green to me are actually blue. Considered under this view, the experience entitles me not to the perceptual judgment "there is a light green wall before me" but to the contrary judgment "there is a blue wall before me." So, the same experience when conjoined with different views can yield different perceptual judgments.

Let us observe that an experience and a view may entitle me to false perceptual judgments. In the preceding example, my belief about my eye lenses may be false—my eyes may be perfectly fine— and I may in fact be standing before a light green wall. Nevertheless, given my view, I am entitled to the false judgment "there is a blue wall before me." Furthermore, the perceptual judgments can even be radically false: the same view, the same experience, but I am dreaming. I remain entitled to judge that the wall I am seeing is blue, but now there is no such wall. Similar examples show that perceptual judgments can also be vague and confused. The general point is that perceptual judgments are liable to reflect the defects of the views we bring to bear on experience. They are not pristine truths built from clear and distinct concepts.

Experience yields judgments even when conjoined with extraordinary views. Consider a *Cartesian view*: I am a mind that has direct awareness of itself and its own sense-data, concepts, and thoughts; it does not have direct awareness of physical objects such as walls—these are mere logical constructions or posits from sense-data.[1] When I conjoin my experience with the Cartesian view, I am entitled to perceptual judgments such as "a light green sense-datum fills my entire visual field," "I sense a colored sense-datum," and so on. A variant of the Cartesian view is the *neutral-monist* view.[2] This view holds that we are directly aware of sense-data and their properties, but not of the self. The self is as much a logical construct or posit as are physical objects. Under the neutral-monist view, my experience yields judgments such as "Lo! A light green sense-datum."

Experience yields judgments even when conjoined with views that are crazy, wild, and utterly false. Let me try to cook up such a view now. The view will be intermediate between Cartesianism and Naive Epistemological Realism (§2C), and I will call it the *surfective* view. According to this view, I am a self that with other selves occupies positions in space. Further, I have direct, unmediated knowledge of the color, shape, and motion/rest of certain things called *surface-perspectives* or, more briefly, *surfectives*. Roughly, a sur-fective is a surface of an object as it is viewed *from a particular position in space*. As I look at the round, orange coaster on my desk, I am directly aware, according to this view, of a special object—a surfective—that is oval in shape and orange in color. The surfective is not identical to the orange coaster or to its surface, for neither the coaster nor the surface is oval. In this respect, surfectives are like sense-data: they are distinct from physical objects and their parts. But, in another respect, surfectives are like physical objects and unlike sense-data: they are objective entities. They exist in public space, and the same surfective can be the object of direct awareness of another perceiver. The orange oval surfective of which I am aware is also the object of direct awareness of a perceiver who looks at the orange coaster from my present position. The surfective view goes on to claim that we arrive at our knowledge of physical objects through some sort of inference from our knowledge of surfectives and other objects of direct awareness. (Surfectives are meant to

---

1. This description provides only a hint of the contents of the Cartesian view. It should not be treated as a complete description. If it were a complete description, the view would not yield any judgments under any experience.

2. See William James, *Essays in Radical Empiricism*; and Russell, *The Philosophy of Logical Atomism*.

account only for visual data; new objects will have to be made up for auditory and other types of data, as well.) The view obviously requires much elaboration, but I hope what I have said is enough to give the reader a rough idea of what I have in mind. The point I mean to illustrate with this example is that experience yields judgments even when conjoined with such a wild and crazy view about the self and the world. The surfective view, when it is brought to bear on the experience I had when I faced the wall, yields judgments such as "there is a light green surfective before me."

In summary, an experience when combined with a view yields judgments. The view may be ordinary or extraordinary; it may be clear or confused; it may be true or utterly false—in each case, experience yields judgments. These judgments themselves can be of varying character, ranging from ordinary, clear, and true to extraordinary, confused, and utterly false. The character of the judgment depends in part on experience and in part on the view that is brought to bear on it. This observation would not, I think, be disputed by philosophers, no matter how skeptical their disposition.

Now one strategy—the classical strategy—for extracting the contribution of experience from this observation is through a process of filtration: filter out all views and judgments that are in any way doubtful or uncertain. The pure residue, consisting of absolutely certain propositions, is what experience contributes to knowledge; this is what is given in experience. I have noted that this strategy is forced upon us if we insist that the given is propositional in form. If, however, we are willing to abandon the idea of a propositional given, then a natural alternative presents itself. We can forgo the process of filtration and say simply that the contribution of experience is conditional in character: it yields judgments only when conjoined with a view. The logical category of the contribution of experience is not that of proposition but that of *function*. Let e be an experience and let Γ_e be the logical contribution of e— the *given* in e. Then the suggestion is that Γ_e is a function that takes views v as input and yields classes of judgments $\Gamma_e(v)$ as output.[3]

---

3. Strictly speaking, I should let $\Gamma_e(v)$ be a vague class, since it can be indeterminate whether a judgment belongs to $\Gamma_e(v)$. E.g., the experience one sometimes has of the sky around the setting sun can leave it indeterminate whether one is entitled to the judgment "the part of the sky over there by the sun is orange." Furthermore, I should let $\Gamma_e(v)$ carry information about the degrees of confidence that one is entitled to have in perceptual judgments. An experience and a view may

More precisely, $\Gamma_e(v)$ is a class of schematized propositions (see §2B).[4] Propositional contents expressed by perceptual judgments are recoverable from schematized propositions once the value of the experiential variable e is fixed (again, see §2B). For much of the exposition below, the distinction between schematized propositions and propositional contents can be neglected, and I shall continue to speak of $\Gamma_e(v)$ as yielding perceptual judgments.

Experience does not yield, then, an absolute entitlement to any judgments. It yields at best only conditional entitlements: given such-and-such a view, one is entitled to such-and-such judgments. An experience taken in isolation does not pronounce on how things are. It tells us only how to fill out a view—any view. It adds just a little bit of color and a little bit of detail to the view.

THE CHARACTER OF THE GIVEN IN EXPERIENCE IS IN SOME respects parallel to that of an argument-form (e.g., *modus ponens*). An argument-form draws a connection between premisses and conclusions. Similarly, the given draws a connection between views and perceptual judgments. Suppose the argument-form rules that

$$P_1, \ldots, P_n, \text{ therefore, } C$$

is valid. Then, it imposes a rational constraint on an individual who believes the premisses $P_1, \ldots, P_n$. In most cases, the constraint is met simply by adding the conclusion C to the individual's beliefs, but not in all cases. Sometimes the constraint requires that one modify one's attitude toward the premisses—for example, when

---

entitle one to have greater confidence in some perceptual judgments than in others. These complications are best neglected, I think, at this stage of our inquiry. I shall continue to think of $\Gamma_e(v)$ as a class of judgments.

4. The need for schematization is reduced under the present proposal. We can allow schematized propositions to contain external constituents, e.g., the kind *tomato*, as long as the view also contains these constituents in a suitable way. E.g., if the commonsense view is interpreted as being directed, in part, to the kind *tomato* (as opposed to the kind *to which such-and-such things belong*), then the perceptual judgment "that is a tomato" can also be interpreted as being about the kind *tomato*. Externalist individuation of views and perceptual judgments is permitted as long as it is uniform. Of course, externalist individuation is not forced on the present proposal; we can schematize, if we wish, all references to the external world. It is the conditional character of the given that makes possible this desirable flexibility.

one is shown that one's premisses are logically incoherent.[5] The situation is similar with the rational constraint imposed by experience. Suppose that an experience e yields, when conjoined with a view v, a class of judgments that contains Q. Let us represent this as follows:

(2) $Q \in \Gamma_e(v)$.

Suppose further that we have a rational being who holds the view v and suffers the experience e. This being has to cope with the rational constraint expressed in (2). In most cases, the constraint is met simply by accepting Q, but in some cases this may require a modification of the view v. I shall sometimes read (2) as saying that the experience e and the view v *entail* the judgment Q.[6] The present point, then, is that the character of this entailment is similar to that of logical entailment: it does not always yield entitlement. A rational being that holds the view v and suffers the experience e is not automatically entitled by (2) to the perceptual judgment Q. Constraint (2) forces the rational being to adjust its view v *in light of* Q (and the other judgments in $\Gamma_e(v)$). Most often this is achieved simply by adding Q to v. But sometimes it requires a substantial revision of the original view v to a new view v'. It is possible that v' does not sustain the judgment Q—it may even be that e and v' entail the negation of Q. In such a case, the total effect of e and v precludes entitlement to Q. I shall provide some illustrations of this point in §4B.[7]

The given in experience establishes, then, rational linkages between views and perceptual judgments. It deserves emphasis that the rational linkages obtain whether or not the subject entertains the judgments. A glimpse of a crowded parking lot may yield, relative to the commonsense view, a large range of perceptual judgments of the form "there are at least n cars in the lot," even though the subject does not bother to consciously entertain any of them. This is similar to what we find with valid argument-forms.

5. Gilbert Harman has stressed this point.
6. If the view v is clear from the context, I shall sometimes say that e entails Q. Similarly, I shall sometimes suppress the variable e and say that v entails Q. Another reading of (2) that I shall use—and have used—is "e and v yield Q."
7. The terminology 'perceptual judgment' suggests entitlement, and the suggestion is harmless in most situations. But it is important to stress that there is not always an entitlement to perceptual judgments—at least in the understanding of 'perceptual judgment' that I adopt in this book.

The rational linkages represented in the argument-forms obtain whether or not any individual makes the transition from the premises to the conclusions.

There are, of course, important differences between argument-forms and the given in experience. First, an argument-form has no new information to add to the premises: the content of the conclusion of a valid argument is already contained in that of the premises. The situation with experience is radically different: the content of perceptual judgments is not already to be found in the view. Perceptual judgments extend and, sometimes, disturb the view. A view v may be coherent and yet may become incoherent when the judgments $\Gamma_e(v)$ entailed by e are added to it.

Second, valid argument-forms do not yield conclusions for all possible premises. *Modus ponens*, for instance, does not yield any conclusion if it is fed the premises "P or Q" and P. Experience, on the other hand, yields perceptual judgments for *all* views. I shall not consider anything to be a view unless it yields at least some perceptual judgments for each and every experience. This constraint is weak, since "I hear something," "something is happening," and "Lo! Blue!" count as perceptual judgments.

Third, with argument-forms, the premises and the conclusions belong to the same logical category, namely, proposition. Not so with the given in experience. A view is not a proposition or a judgment. A view contains judgments (e.g., "I am wearing glasses that are tinted yellow"). But it cannot be identified with a conjunction (or other complex) built out of judgments. Having a view is not the same thing as having an attitude of belief (or acceptance) toward a complex of judgments. No belief, no matter how complex, can by itself prompt me to respond—or make it rational for me to respond—to *this particular* experience that I am having right now with the judgment "there is a beige monitor before me." Even if I have a belief such as "experiences having *these* qualities signal the presence of beige monitors," there is still a gap to be bridged before I can judge "there is a beige monitor before me." I need to judge of *this particular* experience that it has *these* qualities. And belief alone cannot prompt me—or make it rational for me—to do so.

It is a form of Cartesianism to insist that our judgments about the external world must be mediated by (implicit) beliefs of the form "experiences having *these* qualities signal the presence of such-and-such objects." This is to suppose that perceptual judgments are primarily about the character of experience—a supposition that is plainly false. A glance entitles a craftsman to judge that a flange is one-eighth of an inch thick. Does the craftsman have any better description of his visual experience than the one that relies on his perceptual judgment? The craftsman makes the perceptual judgment "right off." He does not need a prior description of his experience in order to reach his judgment. Rather, it is the other way around. It is the perceptual judgment that provides him with a good description of his experience: "the flange *looks* one-eighth of an inch thick."[8]

A view may license a substantive and fully objective transition from experiences to perceptual judgments. These transitions cannot be recovered from the constituent judgments in the view. Indeed, a view may be poor in judgments but rich in the perceptual transitions it permits—the views of young children being perhaps an example. Schema (1) is therefore best reformulated as follows:

(3) View v ⇒ (Experience e ⇒ Perceptual Judgments $\Gamma_e(v)$).

This makes explicit the fact that a view yields a function that captures the dependence of perceptual judgments on experiences.

Evaluative concepts that we apply to judgments—for example, the concepts "true" and "false"—can also be applied to views, since views have judgments as their constituents. A view may be said to be *true* relative to a subject S at a moment m iff all the constituent judgments in it are true at m relative to S;[9] it may be said to be *false* otherwise. But these concepts are not fully adequate because they neglect the perceptual transitions licensed by views. A fuller evaluative notion, which I shall dub 'correctness', may be defined as follows:

A view v is *correct* for a subject S at a moment m iff v is true for S at m and, for any experience e that S has at m, the judgments $\Gamma_e(v)$ are also true for S at m.

---

8. This point is stressed by Strawson; see his "Perception and Its Objects."

9. Here and below, 'iff' abbreviates 'if and only if'. I have made truth relative to the subject S and the moment m because the view will contain, among its constituents, judgments such as "I am thirsty," which require for their evaluation a specification of the subject and of the moment of evaluation. I am assuming that the values of the other contextual parameters can be recovered from the values of S and m. If necessary, this assumption can be weakened and further relativization can be allowed in the definition of truth.

For example, my commonsense view is correct at the present moment iff its constituent judgments are all true and the perceptual judgments it yields for my present experience are also all true. What matters for correctness is the contingent experience that I happen to have, not the merely possible experiences that I might have had. The perceptual judgments that a possible hallucination yields are most likely untrue, but this does not affect the actual correctness of my view.

THE ACCOUNT OF THE GIVEN IN EXPERIENCE THAT I AM proposing is built on scheme (3). I have noted that perceptual judgments do not bring with them entitlement. A rational being that holds a view v and suffers an experience e is not always entitled to affirm the judgments $\Gamma_e(v)$. There is another point about perceptual judgments that is important to note: the demarcation of judgments that are perceptual is not absolute. The demarcation can shift as one shifts one's view. The shift can be large, for example, when we shift from our ordinary, commonsense view to a sense-datum view. Under the former view, judgments such as "there is a light green wall before me" count as perceptual, whereas under the latter view, only judgments such as "I am presented with a light green sense-datum" do so. The shift can be small and subtle, for example, when we shift from one ordinary view to another. My judgment "I saw Fred enter the bank" may count as perceptual in the context of an inquiry from Fred's son about Fred's whereabouts but may fail to count as perceptual in the context of an inquiry from Fred's lawyer at Fred's trial. This shift will occur if the views in play in the two situations are relevantly different. Suppose, for example, that Fred's lawyer has established that at the time in question someone else entered the bank and that this person can easily be mistaken for Fred. Now, with this information at hand, I can no longer insist that my judgment "I saw Fred enter the bank" is perceptual. On the other hand, in the context of the inquiry from Fred's son, where the information provided by Fred's lawyer is unavailable, my judgment counts as perceptual. The shifting demarcation of the perceptual from the nonperceptual is not a problem for our account of the given. The account does not rest on a prior, absolute demarcation of the perceptual. It needs only a *relative* demarcation, a demarcation that may shift with view. Scheme (3) should be understood thus:

(4) View $v \Rightarrow$ (Experience $e \Rightarrow$ Judgments $\Gamma_e(v)$ that are deemed
    perceptual by the view v).

The precise way a view demarcates the perceptual is often—though not always—a matter of little importance. Let us think of an experience e as a (rational) force that impinges on a view v and changes it to a different view v'. Then, we can think of the judgments $\Gamma_e(v)$ as being a measure of the rational force that e brings to bear on v. Now, in most cases, the effect of e is simply to add new content to v. This content consists of the perceptual judgments e entails and of the consequences of these judgments in light of v. Plainly, in such cases, it makes little difference whether we take $\Gamma_e(v)$ to be the class of judgments strictly deemed perceptual by v, or we take it to include also some of their consequences. Either way, $\Gamma_e(v)$ has the same effect—it represents the same rational force. Still, as I have noted, the demarcation of the perceptual from the nonperceptual *is* of importance in some situations. When experience entails a significant revision in the original view, the character of the revision is guided in part by how the perceptual is demarcated from the nonperceptual. The fact that such situations are relatively rare may explain why the demarcation of the perceptual is so flexible in ordinary life. Often a rigid demarcation has little work to do.

Let us note that the present account of the given presupposes no relations of "direct awareness," "acquaintance," and the like posited in classical empiricism. It presupposes nothing about the nature of the self and its relation to the world. Such presuppositions are proper to *views* and are confined to them. They do not sully the given.

THE PRESENT PROPOSAL HAS LITTLE DIFFICULTY IN accommodating the four constraints laid down on an account of experience in §2B. The Existence constraint ("existence of the given") is obviously met because every experience e imposes a rational requirement: a rational being holding a view v must adjust v in light of $\Gamma_e(v)$. The Manifestation constraint ("manifestation of the given") also poses little difficulty. The given, in the present proposal, definitely depends on the subjective character of experience. The perceptual judgments yielded by, for instance, the ordinary commonsense view and the sense-datum view are plainly so dependent. More generally, we should read Manifestation as providing a constraint on views: the perceptual judgments that a view yields must be tied to the subjective character of experience. (This does not mean, of course, that the judgments must be *about* the subjective character.)

The Equivalence constraint ("epistemic equivalence of subjectively identical experiences") can be met by imposing the following natural requirement on Γ_e. If e and e' are subjectively identical experiences, then Γ_e and $\Gamma_{e'}$ are identical. This requirement implies something that we have already noted: a dream experience yields the same schematized propositions as a subjectively identical waking experience.[10] The present account allows us to go further and impose the following stronger requirement on the given: for any experiences e and e', $\Gamma_e = \Gamma_{e'}$ iff e and e' are subjectively identical. That is, the sameness of the given implies, and is implied by, the subjective identity of experiences. A particular view may fail to register, in the entailed perceptual judgments, a subjective difference between two experiences. But for any such difference, there is a view that attaches epistemic significance to the difference and, thus, yields different perceptual judgments. It follows that the givens in the two experiences are bound to be distinct.

To see that the Reliability constraint ("reliability of all experience") is met, it is helpful to return to the parallel between argument-form and the given in experience. A valid argument-form is perfectly reliable in the sense that, if the premises are true, then the conclusion is bound to be true. To object that the form is not reliable because the conclusions are sometimes false is to misunderstand the nature of argument-forms. Similarly, to object that an experience e is unreliable because the perceptual judgments $\Gamma_e(v)$ are sometimes false is to misunderstand the nature of experience. The reliability of e consists in this: *if* the view v is correct, *then* the judgments $\Gamma_e(v)$ are true. The falsity of perceptual judgments $\Gamma_e(v)$ does not impugn the reliability of e. The question of the reliability of experience (and, derivatively, of the senses) is often construed as a question about the truth and falsehood of the deliverances of experience (and the senses). But this construal rests on a category mistake. The deliverances of experience are not the kinds of things that can be true or false.[11] Experience is reliable in

10. Of course, the propositional contents expressed by the perceptual judgments may be different in the two cases. Indeed, with dreams, the perceptual judgments may fail to express propositional contents altogether.

11. Kant wrote, "It is therefore correct to say that the senses do not err—not because they always judge rightly but because they do not judge at all" (*Critique of Pure Reason*, A293/B350).

the only sense that matters. It is the best and our most perfect guide to the knowledge of the world. But experience does not guide us by providing us with pristine truths. Its mode of operation is different.

In classical empiricism, the occurrence of an experience ensures the truth of the corresponding sense-datum judgments. A being that undergoes an experience e and proceeds to affirm the sense-datum judgments can rest assured that its judgments are true, irrespective of the character of the surrounding world. Something similar holds under the present proposal. A being that undergoes e can rest assured that the transition "v, therefore $\Gamma_e(v)$" is proper, irrespective of the surrounding world. Classical empiricism gains the assurance by the special meaning it imparts to the sense-datum vocabulary; the present proposal gains it by making the given hypothetical.[12]

This way of meeting the Reliability constraint raises a question, however. In the present account, the rational requirements imposed by experience seem to be very weak; they are merely conditional. How can these conditional requirements be at all substantial? How can they translate into any absolute requirements on a rational being? It is plain that experience can make it irrational for us to believe many things—for example, that the tides are caused by giant turtles. This irrationality is categorical, not conditional. If, however, the given in experience is purely conditional in nature, how can it impose a categorical, unconditional requirement of rationality on us?

The strategy I want to follow in developing a response to this question is the same one that we saw in the theory of interdependent definitions. I want to use the given in experience to generate a revision process, with the hope that this process will enable us to extract categorical requirements from the conditional ones yielded by experience. The revision process for knowledge is quite different in character from that for definitions, and it is also more complex. I shall sketch an idealized account of it in §4B. In chapter 7 I discuss how the removal of idealization affects the proposed theory.

---

12. Note that the present proposal does not *require* any of the four constraints. The proposal can be accepted even though the constraints are rejected.

4B. Transition to the Categorical

A rational being, let us imagine, holds initially a view v_0 and undergoes a succession of experiences $\mathscr{E} = \langle e_0, e_1, e_2, \ldots, e_n, \ldots \rangle$. The being will successively revise its view in light of these experiences. At the initial stage—stage 0—the rational being has the view v_0 and has the experience e_0. Consequently, it revises v_0 in light of the perceptual judgments $\Gamma_{e_0}(v_0)$ entailed by e_0. Set

$R(v, e) =$ the result of revising v in light of the judgments $\Gamma_e(v)$
   entailed by e.

So $R(v_0, e_0)$ is the view to which the rational being is moved after it undergoes e_0. This is the view that the being takes away from stage 0 of revision. Let me highlight some terminology that will prove useful. At any stage of revision, there will be the *input* view, the view that the rational being *brings to* the stage of revision. And then there will be the *output* or *resulting* view, the view that the being *takes away from* the stage of revision. In the present example, at stage 0, the input view is v_0 and the output view is $R(v_0, e_0)$. Set

$v_1 = R(v_0, e_0).$

Now the view that the rational being takes away from stage 0 is the view it brings to stage 1. So the input view at stage 1 is v_1. At this stage, the rational being undergoes experience e_1 and will therefore need to revise v_1. Set

$v_2 = R(v_1, e_1).$

Then v_2 is the view that the rational being takes away from stage 1 and that it brings to stage 2, the stage at which it undergoes experience e_2. This experience will move the being to yet another view, v_3. Similar revisions are forced by successive experiences at higher stages of revision. In general, at stage n, the being brings with it view v_n and takes away view v_{n+1}, where

$v_{n+1} = R(v_n, e_n).$

Let us call the sequence of views $\mathcal{V}\ (= \langle v_0, v_1, v_2, \ldots, v_n, \ldots \rangle)$ that the rational being goes through when it begins with view v_0 and undergoes the sequence of experiences $\mathscr{E}$ *the revision sequence generated by $\mathscr{E}$ and v_0*. Let us designate the nth member of $\mathcal{V}$ by

V_n,[13] and let us say that V *is generated by* $\mathscr{E}$ iff V is generated by $\mathscr{E}$ and V_0. Finally, let us call a sequence of views V an *epistemic revision sequence* iff there is a sequence $\mathscr{E}$ of experiences that generates V. The notion of an epistemic revision sequence is fundamental to what follows. Let me make a few observations about it.

First, the notion obviously involves a high degree of idealization. In practice, the result of revising a view v in light of an experience e is not always a particular view. Sometimes the result is a family of views, perhaps together with some plausibility ordering on the family. I think this fact can fairly be neglected at the present stage of our inquiry; incorporating it greatly complicates matters but promises little benefit. There is another dimension of idealization in the notion of revision sequence. I am treating experience as coming in discrete steps, when actually it is mostly continuous. I think, however, that this idealization is harmless in the present context. We can approximate the continuous with the discrete in a familiar way. We can slice up continuous experience as finely as phenomenology allows, and we can view the slices as discrete steps. There is a final, and most consequential, dimension of idealization: we have not considered action. Action shapes experience, but this fact is neglected in our account. I consider the bearing of action on experience and knowledge in chapter 7. But in the interim I shall persist with the fiction that our rational knower is a passive being.

Second, epistemic revision sequences differ in important respects from definitional revision sequences of §3B. The latter are generated purely by revision rules yielded by definitions. These sequences are abstract, and their stages are not, properly speaking, in time at all. Epistemic revision sequences, on the other hand, are products of successions $\mathscr{E}$ of experiences. These sequences can well be actualized, and their stages could well be stages in time. A rational being may actually go through a succession of views V generated by $\mathscr{E}$, holding the view V_0 at one moment of time, the view V_1 at the next moment, V_2 at the next, and so on.

Third, an epistemic revision sequence does not necessarily consist of views that are successively richer; it is not always cumulative. A later view in a revision sequence may abandon some of the judgments in an earlier view. It is a commonplace that experience can make it rational for us to abandon some of our

13. Similarly, $\mathscr{E}_n$ is the nth member of $\mathscr{E}$.

earlier beliefs about the world and about ourselves. I may believe (with good reason) that it will be a fine day tomorrow. But, after listening to the latest weather report, I may have ample reason to change my mind. For another example, I may believe that my daughter, Donna, is playing in her room. But a glance through her open door may give me sufficient reason to conclude the very opposite. These examples illustrate shifts in views about the world. Ordinary examples that illustrate shifts in views about ourselves are most readily found in our experiences with other people. I meet a gentle and sensitive friend on the street and experience him to be unaccountably overbearing. Given my mind set, my experience entails the judgment "the friend is being overbearing." But the rational response may not be to accept this judgment. Instead, it may be to shift my view of myself: "my friend is not overbearing; the problem is with me—*I* am grumpy from a sleepless night." Our experiences with other people often require us to adjust our view not only of those others but also of our own selves.

Fourth, and this is the most important observation for our purposes: views in the later stages of an epistemic revision sequence may be radically different from views in the earlier stages. A course of experience can precipitate radical changes in view. In ordinary life, such changes are rare. Outside of the classroom, they occur, if at all, mostly in our views of people close to us. A series of experiences may lead one to conclude "my parents are not founts of goodness; they are selfish and mean." And one's conception of one's whole childhood changes.[14] The most spectacular examples of radical change are to be found in the sciences, where the cumulative force of the experience of generations of humans is brought into play. Here is a simplified example: One can imagine an ancient civilization systematically measuring distances between cities. It discovers that the straight distance between a city X and a city Y, directly north of X, is 3,000 stadia and that between X and a city Z, directly east of X, is 4,000 stadia. But it discovers that the straight distance between Y and Z is significantly less than the expected 5,000 stadia. We can imagine that the civilization discovers similar anomalies for other cities, and the combined weight of empirical evidence results in a fundamental revision of its view: Earth is not flat but spherical. (Pythagoras, it is believed,

---

14. I personally have not suffered such a series of experiences.

was the first to have proclaimed the sphericity of Earth, but his reasons are not known.[15] I am purposely making the example fictional.)

CONSIDER WHAT AN IDEAL EPISTEMIC REVISION SEQUENCE might look like. Recall, to begin with, the ideal revision sequence for definitions. Here, we begin with a hypothesis—one that could be quite off the mark as an interpretation of the definiendum—and we revise it repeatedly using the revision rule. We find that eventually we arrive at a stage after which the same hypothesis occurs again and again in the sequence. (We arrive, i.e., at a fixed point of the revision rule.) Now, with epistemic revision we might find the following: We begin with a view. This view may be quite erroneous. It may attribute to us unusual perceptual abilities. It may put us in perceptual contact not only with the properties of ordinary objects but also with those of the gods. It may have us occupying a flat Earth. It may grant us visions of the future. And so on. Anyhow, we begin with this view, however erroneous, and we revise it in light of a succession of experiences. Now, it would be too much to expect, even in the ideal case, that in the course of revision we reach a stage after which our view does not change at all, that the same view v is repeated again and again as we suffer new experiences. Even in the ideal case, one expects that experience can result in trivial additions to a view—for example, new facts about the weather in one's vicinity. Experience can even result in small alterations of the earlier view—for example, a shift in Pythagoras's birth year from 572 B.C.E. to, say, 571 B.C.E. Such changes can be multiplied and still they need not detract at all from the ideal. Let us say that views v and v' are *equivalent in fundamental respects* or, more briefly, *fundamentally equivalent* (notation: $v \equiv v'$) if, and only if, v and v' offer the same basic account of the self and the world. Views that are fundamentally equivalent may be vastly different in some respects. For example, one view may include within it a long historical record encompassing thousands of years, while the other may include only a very short record. For another example, the views may conflict with each other over a sea of details. Still, as long as these conflicts do not point to a divergence in the basic account of the self and the world, the views remain fundamentally equivalent.

15. See Thomas L. Heath, *Greek Astronomy.*

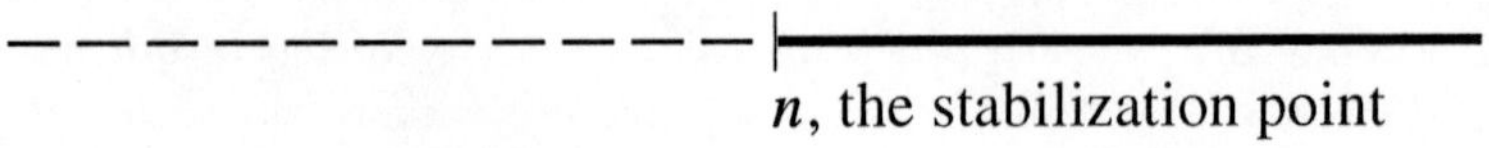

$$n, \text{ the stabilization point}$$

Figure 4.1. A stable revision sequence and its stabilization point.

We would have an ideal epistemic revision sequence, I suggest, if we reached a stage after which the successive views, though distinct, were fundamentally equivalent to one another. Let us call such a sequence 'stable'. More formally:

> A sequence of views V is *stable* iff there is stage n such that, for all stages $m \geq n$, V_m is fundamentally equivalent to V_n—that is, $V_m \equiv V_n$. Otherwise, V will be said to be *unstable*.[16]

The least number n that satisfies the condition in the above definiens will be called the *stabilization point of* V. Once the stabilization point is reached, all subsequent views in the sequence are fundamentally equivalent. From this point on, there are no Kuhnian paradigm shifts. We may picture a stable revision sequence as shown in figure 4.1. (The dashed line before the stabilization point n represents, here and in the figures below, the part of the sequence where substantial changes occur in the view; the solid line after n represents the part in which all views are fundamentally equivalent.)

It is easy to construct examples of stable revision sequences. Given a coherent view v, there is always a succession $\mathscr{E}$ of experiences that only confirm and never undermine any fundamental tenet of the view. The sequence of views V generated by $\mathscr{E}$ and v will be stable. (Indeed, the stabilization point of V will be 0.) Here is a concrete example. Suppose that a being begins its existence with the following view v: there is a God that is the creator of all things, and this God has imprinted on my mind such-and-such fundamental laws and facts about the self and the world. Suppose, further, that the view is indeed correct. Finally, imagine a succession of experiences $\mathscr{E}$ that repeatedly confirm the laws and facts that the rational being takes to be imprinted on its mind. It is even possible to imagine that $\mathscr{E}$ confirms the idea that the fundamental laws and facts are innate to the rational being, and even the idea

---

16. Note that the notion of fundamental equivalence is vague, and different ways of making it precise will yield different notions of stability.

that they are God-given. The sequence of views generated by $\mathscr{E}$ and v will be stable.

WE HAVE SEEN SO FAR HOW AN INITIAL VIEW v EVOLVES into a succession of views $\mathcal{V}$ as it is adjusted in light of experiences $\mathscr{E}$. Let us now vary the initial view v while holding $\mathscr{E}$ fixed. If we begin with a different initial view v', then, obviously, we shall end up with a distinct succession of views $\mathcal{V}'$. Now, despite the distinctness of $\mathcal{V}$ and $\mathcal{V}'$, it is possible that $\mathcal{V}$ and $\mathcal{V}'$ *converge*—that is, after some distinct early stages, the stages of $\mathcal{V}$ and $\mathcal{V}'$ are *virtually identical*. Consider again the example of my turning the street corner and finding myself before a large, light green wall. As noted above, I can bring to bear the following two distinct views on my experience: first, the ordinary view in which I take everything to be normal—call this view v; and second, the ordinary view in which I take my eye lenses to be tinged yellow by disease and in which I believe that things that look green to me are actually blue—call this view v'. Imagine that after experiencing the wall, I undergo a series of experiences with color charts in an optometrist's office. It is easy to imagine that, as a result of these experiences, there is convergence in the sequences of views generated by v and v'. The experiences can easily force me to revise v' and to conclude that my eyes are normal after all, that they were not diseased, and that the wall I faced was in fact light green. Two ideally rational beings that suffer the experiences I suffered and that begin respectively with the views v and v' will, after a time, have virtually identical views. Their views will differ slightly because of their different histories. One will believe, correctly, that it had taken the wall to be blue, while the other will have no such belief. But, setting aside such minor differences caused by the differences in their initial views, their later views will be identical. They will believe the same things about the wall and about the functioning of their eyes. Let us mark this sort of relation between views by calling them *virtually identical* (notation: $v \approx v'$). And let us define convergence as follows:

$\mathcal{V}$ and $\mathcal{V}'$ *converge* iff there is a stage n such that, for all stages $m \geq n$, $\mathcal{V}_m$ is virtually identical to $\mathcal{V}'_m$—that is, $\mathcal{V}_m \approx \mathcal{V}'_m$; the least such n will be called *the convergence point* of $\mathcal{V}$ and $\mathcal{V}'$.

We can picture the convergence of $\mathcal{V}$ and $\mathcal{V}'$ as shown in figure 4.2.

The virtual identity of the stages of $\mathcal{V}$ and $\mathcal{V}'$ is represented, here and below, by the identity of the corresponding points. Note that

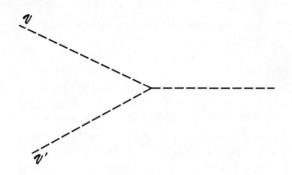

Figure 4.2.   Convergence of two sequences.

the picture represents V and V' as unstable, but this is not forced by the notion of convergence. Stable sequences can also converge.

We now have two distinct relations on views, "fundamental equivalence" and "virtual identity." Let us observe some of their properties and interrelationships. First, "fundamental equivalence" and "virtual identity" are both equivalence relations.[17] Second, "virtual identity" is a stricter relation than "fundamental equivalence":

(5) If $v \approx v'$, then $v \equiv v'$.

The converse does not hold, however; views that are fundamentally equivalent may fail to be virtually identical. Third, views that are virtually identical yield the same perceptual judgments when they are brought to bear on the same experiences. Hence, the revisions of these views in light of an experience e are also virtually identical. That is,

if $v \approx v'$, then $R(v,\ e) \approx R(v',\ e)$.

This claim does not hold for "fundamental equivalence," however. Views that are fundamentally equivalent may fail to be so when revised in light of an experience. Of two fundamentally equivalent views v and v', one may be much richer in detail than another. Hence, it is possible that an experience precipitates an incoherence in one without doing so in the other. In such cases, the results of revision may well fail to be fundamentally equivalent. Fourth, and

17. I.e., they are reflexive, symmetric, and transitive. A less idealized account would treat "fundamental equivalence" and "virtual identity" as vague relations. It would deem them to be only "approximately transitive," not fully transitive.

this is just a consequence of the previous point, if two epistemic revision sequences $\mathcal{V}$ and $\mathcal{V}'$ generated by $\mathcal{E}$ are virtually identical at a stage, then they are virtually identical at all later stages:

If $\mathcal{V}_n \approx \mathcal{V}'_n$, then, for all $m \geq n$, $\mathcal{V}_m \approx \mathcal{V}'_m$.

The parallel claim fails, of course, for "fundamental equivalence."

Let us observe that two sequences $\mathcal{V}$ and $\mathcal{V}'$ generated by $\mathcal{E}$ can converge, even though they begin with views v and v' that are fundamentally nonequivalent. We have seen in the wall example above a situation in which two variants of our ordinary view converge under the guidance of experience. The point now is that convergence can occur even if we begin with views that are fundamentally different. Consider an extraordinary view that takes dream experiences and waking experiences to be on par. Both types of experiences, according to this view, yield perceptual judgments of equal authority. Both reveal features of one and the same reality. Such a view might be sustained by a course of experience. But, equally, a course of experience is easily imagined that will make the extraordinary view converge to the ordinary one.

CONSIDER A *RAIMEX*—THAT IS, AN IDEAL *RATIONAL*, *im*aginative, and *ex*periencing being—that suffers a succession of experiences $\mathcal{E}$. This being can determine the evolution $\mathcal{V}$ of a view v under the pressure of $\mathcal{E}$. Now $\mathcal{V}$ reveals *conditional* rational obligations on our raimex. It tells us what views our raimex should hold in succession *if* it begins with the view v. But it does not reveal any *absolute* obligations, since as matters stand there is no rational obligation on the raimex to begin with v as its initial view. So the question arises: can experiences $\mathcal{E}$ impose any absolute rational obligations on the raimex?

Our raimex, being an imaginative being, can consider the effects of $\mathcal{E}$ on *any* view. Now, some of these views will be unacceptable as starting points of revision, and the raimex will be able to rule them out on general grounds. For example, it will be able to rule out views that are internally incoherent. A view that is like the ordinary commonsense view except that it takes the visual experience of a purple octagon to yield the perceptual judgment that there is an omniscient god—logically consistent though this view may be— makes little sense and is legitimately excluded from the starting points of revision. For another example, a view that yields only one of two judgments "red" and "not-red," no matter how rich the experience, is also quite reasonably rejected as a starting point of revision. It is proper to require that an initial view v yield rich perceptual judgments, that it be *receptive* in the following sense:

> For all experiences e and e' that are subjectively distinct, $\Gamma_e(v) \neq \Gamma_{e'}(v)$.[18]

I shall return later to more substantial requirements on initial views (§5E). For now, I wish to stress the following points. (i) It is a fundamental difference between definitional and epistemic revision processes that, whereas the former contain no restrictions on starting points of revision, the latter do contain such restrictions. These restrictions, we shall see, are both legitimate and essential. (ii) The restrictions concern only the *inputs*, the views that may serve as starting points of revision. No restrictions are placed on the *outputs*. Views that are barred as starting points may end up occurring later in the course of revision. (iii) The restrictions are a priori. They are independent of the actual course of experience.

Let us call views that may serve as starting points of revision *acceptable initial views* or, more briefly, *admissible views*. Let us have our raimex consider the effects of $\mathscr{E}$ on every admissible view. The result is the *(epistemic) revision process generated by* $\mathscr{E}$—in symbols, $\Pi_{\mathscr{E}}$—which we can define as follows. $\Pi_{\mathscr{E}}$ is the function that takes admissible views as arguments and yields epistemic revision sequences as values and, furthermore, satisfies the following condition: if v is an admissible view, then

$$\Pi_{\mathscr{E}}(v) = \text{the revision sequence generated by } \mathscr{E} \text{ and } v.$$

It will be convenient to adopt the following terminology. If v is an admissible view, then

$$\Pi_{\mathscr{E}}(v, n) = \text{the } n\text{th value of } \Pi_{\mathscr{E}}(v).$$

Finally, let us say that a sequence $\mathcal{V}$ *is in* $\Pi_{\mathscr{E}}$ iff, for some admissible view v,

$$\mathcal{V} = \Pi_{\mathscr{E}}(v).$$

---

18. A stronger version of receptivity requires that, for all numbers n, the revisions effected by finite sequences of experiences E and E' of length n are distinct if E and E' are not subjectively identical—i.e., if, for some $m < n$, E_m and E'_m are subjectively distinct.

So, $\mathcal{V}$ is in $\Pi_\mathcal{E}$ iff $\mathcal{V}$ is generated by $\mathcal{E}$ and some admissible view v.

We are now in a position to extend the notions of stability and convergence to epistemic revision processes. The concept of stability extends in a straightforward way:

> The revision process $\Pi_\mathcal{E}$ is *stable* iff all sequences in $\Pi_\mathcal{E}$ are stable; *the stabilization point* of $\Pi_\mathcal{E}$ is the least of the stabilization points of the sequences in $\Pi_\mathcal{E}$.[19]

There are, however, two distinct concepts of convergence. We can define the first concept as follows.

> $\Pi_\mathcal{E}$ is *strongly convergent* iff there is a stage m such that, for all admissible v and v', $\Pi_\mathcal{E}(v, m) \approx \Pi_\mathcal{E}(v', m)$; the least such m will be called the *convergence point of* $\Pi_\mathcal{E}$.

In a strongly convergent process, there is a stage—the convergence point—by which all acceptable initial views are revised to views that are virtually identical. Figure 4.3 is a picture of such a process.

The second concept of convergence is defined as follows.

> $\Pi_\mathcal{E}$ is *convergent* iff all pairs of sequences $\mathcal{V}$ and $\mathcal{V}'$ in $\Pi_\mathcal{E}$ converge.

A merely convergent process $\Pi_\mathcal{E}$ differs from a strongly convergent one in that it provides no assurance that the points of convergence of pairs of sequences in $\Pi_\mathcal{E}$ have an upper bound.[20]

The differences between the two concepts of convergence can be illuminated through the notion of "surviving view." Let us define the concept *the views surviving at a stage n in the revision process generated by $\mathcal{E}$*—in symbols, $\sigma_\mathcal{E}(n)$—as follows: $\sigma_\mathcal{E}(n)$ is the class of views such that

$$v \in \sigma_\mathcal{E}(n) \text{ iff for some admissible view } v', v = \Pi_\mathcal{E}(v', n).$$

In other words, v belongs to $\sigma_\mathcal{E}(n)$ iff v is the nth member of one of the revision sequences in $\Pi_\mathcal{E}$. Think of our raimex as proceeding in this way: It considers all the acceptable initial views at stage 0—that is, it considers all the views in $\sigma_\mathcal{E}(0)$. It then revises each of these views in light of the experience $\mathcal{E}_0$. The result is a class of views, namely, $\sigma_\mathcal{E}(1)$.

---

19. The notion of stabilization point is well defined only for stable processes.

20. The concepts "convergent" and "strongly convergent" are equivalent for processes that contain only finitely many revision sequences. Hence, if there are only finitely many acceptable initial views, then all convergent processes are strongly convergent.

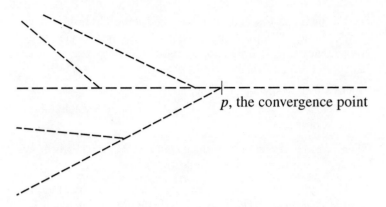

Figure 4.3. A strongly convergent process and its convergence point.

Next, it revises each of the views in this new class in light of $\mathcal{E}_1$, obtaining thereby the class $\sigma_{\mathcal{E}}(2)$. And so on. Now the crucial difference between strong convergence and plain convergence is this: in a strongly convergent process, there is a stage n at which all surviving views are virtually identical, but in a process that is merely convergent and not strongly convergent, no such stage exists. In fact, in such a process, there may be, at all stages, surviving views that are fundamentally nonequivalent.

These observations have an important consequence. *Strongly convergent processes generate absolute rational obligations.* Suppose experiences $\mathcal{E}$ generate a revision process that has n as its point of convergence. Let m be any stage higher than n. Then, at stage m, all surviving views are virtually identical. They contain the same basic account of the self and the world, and furthermore, they agree on numerous details as well. At stage m, our raimex has no obligation to accept elements on which the surviving views differ, but it does have an absolute obligation to accept the massive core on which the views agree.

More generally, at any stage n, the raimex has an absolute rational obligation to accept all that is common to the views in $\sigma_{\mathcal{E}}(n)$, the views that survive at stage n. This obligation may be narrow if, for example, $\sigma_{\mathcal{E}}(n)$ contains many fundamentally nonequivalent views. Or it may be wide if, as in the higher stages of a strongly convergent process, $\sigma_{\mathcal{E}}(n)$ contains only views that are virtually identical. Let us say that $\mathcal{E}$ *entails a judgment P at stage n* iff P belongs to the common part of the views in $\sigma_{\mathscr{E}}(n)$. And let us say that $\mathscr{E}$ *entails P simpliciter* iff there is a stage n such that $\mathscr{E}$ entails P at all stages higher than n.

Two further useful characteristics of revision processes can be obtained by combining the property of stability with those of convergence. The first characteristic is this:

$\Pi_{\mathscr{E}}$ is *good* iff $\Pi_{\mathscr{E}}$ is both stable and convergent.

The second is a stronger version of the first.

$\Pi_{\mathscr{E}}$ is *perfect* iff $\Pi_{\mathscr{E}}$ is both stable and strongly convergent. If $\Pi_{\mathscr{E}}$ is perfect, then its *perfection point* is the greater of its stabilization and convergence points.[21]

Figure 4.4 is a picture of a perfect revision process, in which the perfection point is identical to the convergence point and occurs later than the stabilization point n. There are other kinds of perfect processes also: in some, all three points are identical; in the others, the perfection point is identical to the stabilization point and occurs later than the convergence point.

From now on, I shall apply the predicates of revision processes to the corresponding sequences of experiences. I shall say that $\mathscr{E}$ is *perfect (good, convergent, . . .)* iff the revision process, $\Pi_{\mathscr{E}}$, generated by $\mathscr{E}$ is perfect (good, convergent, . . .). Suppose that a sequence of experiences $\mathscr{E}$ is perfect and that its perfection point is p. Then, at p and each stage after p, $\mathscr{E}$ dictates that our raimex accept a specific view. Of course, the views that $\mathscr{E}$ dictates at higher stages may differ significantly in details from the view $\mathscr{E}$ dictates at p. Nevertheless, since $\Pi_{\mathscr{E}}$ is stable, all these views must be fundamentally equivalent; they must all agree on the basic account of the self and the world. Let a *conception of the self and the world* be that which all fundamentally equivalent views have in common. A conception is, so to speak, the skeleton that remains when a view is stripped of all its details. Then, the present point can be expressed thus: if

---

21. Observe that if a (strongly) convergent process has one stable sequence, then the process is bound to be good (perfect), for if one sequence in a convergent process is stable, then all sequences in it are bound to be stable. Suppose $\mathcal{V}$ and $\mathcal{V}'$ are arbitrary sequences in a convergent process $\Pi_{\mathscr{E}}$, and suppose that $\mathcal{V}$ is stable. Then there is a stage n such that, for all $m \geq n$,

$$\mathcal{V}_m \approx \mathcal{V}'_m.$$

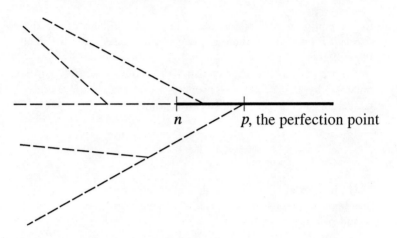

Figure 4.4. A perfect revision process and its perfection point.

$\mathcal{E}$ is perfect, then it entails a particular conception of the self and the world. A raimex that suffers $\mathcal{E}$ comes eventually under a rational obligation to accept, and to continue to accept, this conception.

Sequences of experiences that are good also yield—though they may fail to entail—a unique conception of the self and the world. Consider a sequence $\mathcal{E}$ that is good, and consider the views that occur in the revision sequences in $\Pi_{\mathcal{E}}$ after their respective stabilization points. These views must all be fundamentally equivalent, because $\Pi_{\mathcal{E}}$ is convergent. Hence, these views must share a conception of the self and the world. Let us call this *the limit conception* of $\mathcal{E}$. A raimex who suffers $\mathcal{E}$ may be under no rational

---

Let p be the greater of the two numbers, n and the stabilization point of $\mathcal{V}$. Let q be an arbitrary number $\geq p$. To establish that $\mathcal{V}'$ is stable, it suffices to show that
  (i) $\mathcal{V}'_p \equiv \mathcal{V}'_q$.
Convergence of $\mathcal{V}$ and $\mathcal{V}'$ tells us that
  $\mathcal{V}_p \approx \mathcal{V}'_p$ and $\mathcal{V}_q \approx \mathcal{V}'_q$.
Since "virtual identity" is a stricter relation than "fundamental equivalence"—see (5)—we have
  (ii) $\mathcal{V}_p \equiv \mathcal{V}'_p$ and $\mathcal{V}_q \equiv \mathcal{V}'_q$.
Further, since $\mathcal{V}$ is stable and p, $q \geq$ the stabilization point of $\mathcal{V}$,
  (iii) $\mathcal{V}_p \equiv \mathcal{V}_q$.
But "fundamental equivalence" is transitive. Hence, (ii) and (iii) imply (i).

obligation to accept the limit conception at any stage of its epistemic progress. For at each stage n, the surviving views $\sigma_{\mathscr{E}}(n)$ may include some that are fundamentally nonequivalent. Still, this conception is the limit point of the raimex's epistemic development. This is the ideal toward which its experience is inexorably guiding it—an ideal, though, that it may fail to reach at any stage of revision.

There is no a priori guarantee that a sequence of experiences will be stable or convergent, much less that it will be perfect. Experiences can generate revision processes that exhibit all sorts of pathologies, including those we noticed in chapter 3 with interdependent definitions. Elements of a view may exhibit "paradoxicality" in the course of revision. Empirical evidence may first point to 572 B.C.E. as the year of Pythagoras's birth, and then to 571 B.C.E., and then back again to the original date of 572 B.C.E., and so on ad infinitum. It can even be that this kind of oscillation occurs with large-scale structural features of a view. Similarly, elements of a view, large and small, may exhibit other types of pathology. For example, some elements may exhibit "truth-teller" type pathology.[22] A course of experience may be such that if a rational being begins with, say, the wave view of light, then everything in experience speaks in its favor. But the same may hold for the contrary corpuscular view as well. None of this should be surprising or worrisome. Pathology in epistemic revision processes threatens neither our self-conception nor any of our logical presuppositions. It is only the pressure of philosophical difficulties that has led some empiricists to declare that a course of experience must be good (i.e., stable and convergent), and indeed to define truth in terms of limit conceptions. The empiricism I shall defend will not need to resort to this maneuver.

WE HAVE CONSIDERED SO FAR ONLY DENUMERABLE SEQUENCES OF experiences. Let us now turn briefly to finite ones. The following simple observation allows us to extend the basic concepts introduced above to finite sequences. Let $\mathscr{E}$ and $\mathscr{E}'$ be denumerable sequences of experiences that are identical up to the stage n—that is, $\mathscr{E}_m = \mathscr{E}'_m$, for all $m \leq n$. Then, the revision processes generated by

---

22. This is the pathology exhibited by the sentence "this very sentence is true." It is also found in the behavior of o in definition (6) of chapter 3.

$\mathscr{E}$ and $\mathscr{E}'$ are identical up to the stage $n+1$. That is, for all $m \leq n+1$ and all admissible views v,

$$\Pi_{\mathscr{E}}(v, m) = \Pi_{\mathscr{E}'}(v, m).$$

Let E be a finite sequence of experiences of length $n+1$, and let $\mathscr{E}$ be a denumerable sequence that extends E—that is, $E_m = \mathscr{E}_m$, for all $m < n+1$. We can set the revision process, Π_E, for E to be the segment of the revision process for $\Pi_{\mathscr{E}}$ up to the stage $n+1$. So, for all $m \leq n+1$ and all admissible views v,

$$\Pi_E(v, m) = \Pi_{\mathscr{E}}(v, m).$$

Hence, for all $m \leq n+1$, the set of surviving views at stage m for the revision process for E, $\sigma_E(m)$, is simply $\sigma_{\mathscr{E}}(m)$. Now, we can say that E *entails a judgment* (*view, conception, . . .*) iff the judgment (view, conception, . . .) belongs to the common part of $\sigma_E(n+1)$. And E and the revision process Π_E that it generates are *convergent* iff all views in $\sigma_E(n+1)$ are virtually identical.[23] It is easily seen that if E is convergent, then any denumerable sequence $\mathscr{E}$ of experiences that extends E is bound to be strongly convergent, and its convergence point will be less than or equal to $n+1$. The notions of stability and the other notions that rely on them have little meaning with finite experiences. Still, some notions in their vicinity are worth noting. Let us say that E is *possibly stable* (*possibly perfect, . . .*) iff there is a denumerable sequence $\mathscr{E}$ of experiences that extends E that is stable (perfect, . . .). I am inclined to think that every finite sequence of experiences is possibly stable and possibly perfect, and that it is also possibly nonstable and possibly nonperfect. No finite segment fixes the epistemological character of later experiences. The conclusions mandated by a finite segment may be completely overturned by the boundless experiences that lie ahead.[24]

---

23. For finite sequences of experiences, the notions of convergence and strong convergence collapse into one.

24. Observe that our model allows finite sequences of experiences to be treated as a single experience. The epistemological force of an experience is captured in the present model by the revisions that the experience induces in all views. The same sort of force is associated, of course, with finite sequences of experiences. Let E be such a sequence and let $\mathscr{E}$ be a denumerable sequence that extends E. Then E forces a view v to be revised to $\mathcal{V}_n$, where n is the length of E and $\mathcal{V}$ is the revision sequence generated by $\mathscr{E}$ and v. Whether E is treated as a single experience or as

THE BROAD OUTLINES OF THE MODEL OF EXPERIENCE AND knowledge I wish to defend are now visible. The contribution of experience to knowledge is hypothetical in character. It has the form: given such-and-such a view, so-and-so perceptual judgments follow. An experience taken in isolation is mute; it does not say anything about the world. However, once we bring a view to bear on it, experience speaks. It yields perceptual judgments and thus adds new details to our view. The perceptual judgments are not guaranteed to be pristine truths. They may be false; they may even be fundamentally confused. Nevertheless, the very fact that experience speaks means that a force is in play that can improve our view both materially and conceptually.

A single experience entails small, almost insignificant, changes in a view. But just as a succession of rain drops can crack the hardest rock, similarly, a succession of experiences can entirely transform an initial view. A succession of experiences can have a further property, that of *strong convergence*: it can transform *all* acceptable initial views to essentially one view (i.e., to views that are virtually identical). This property is important because a strongly convergent succession yields substantial rational obligations. It can mandate a specific conception of the self and the world.

I wish to argue that this account of the structure of experience and knowledge can illuminate our epistemic situation. In particular, I wish to defend the idea that the succession of our past experiences can render reasonable our ordinary conception of ourselves and the world. There is a further idea here with which I shall not be much concerned: that the succession renders reasonable our scientific conceptions also. The philosophical problems posed by our empirical knowledge concern the very core of our ordinary conception—a core that humans acquired before they began inscribing marks on clay tablets and that most children

---

a sequence of experiences, the overall epistemic effect remains the same. My seeing an orange oval and then hearing a loud noise can, from the epistemological point of view, be treated either as one experience or as a sequence of two experiences; it does not matter. The same applies to highly complex and extended experiences— e.g., those obtained in the course of determining the conductance of a power line.

There is, nonetheless, this difference between individual experiences and finite sequences. The epistemological force of individual experiences can be captured by a class of perceptual judgments, but not necessarily that of finite sequences.

acquire before reaching the age of three. Once the core is secured, the further idea that experience renders reasonable the refinements of the sciences presents few fundamental difficulties. The bearing of experience on the sciences (and other disciplines) can be understood in the standard way: experience issues perceptual judgments and can thus serve as a tribunal for them.

The present model succeeds in combining the virtues of coherentism and foundationalism. Coherentism is motivated by the insight that our empirical knowledge does not rest on a foundation of special propositions, propositions whose truth is certified by experience. But it has difficulty making sense of the rational bearing of experience on knowledge. Indeed, coherentism is often strongly antiempiricist: it denies experience any rational contribution whatsoever. Foundationalism is motivated by the sound intuition that experience does have at least *some* rational bearing on empirical knowledge. But it finds itself forced into positing special propositional foundations. Our account enables a synthesis of the two theories. It allows us to see that the root intuitions of foundationalism and coherentism are perfectly correct. There *is* a given in experience; hence, foundationalism is right to insist that experience makes a rational contribution. The given is not propositional; hence, coherentism is right to deny propositional foundations.[25]

Finally, let me say that I do not claim any great novelty for the model of experience and knowledge sketched here. Any novelty that there might be can lie only in the motivation and defense of the model. The proposed model rests on the interdependence of views and perceptual judgments—an interdependence that has not escaped the notice of philosophers.[26] The principal elements of the model are dictated by this interdependence. Wherever there

25. For exposition and defense of coherence theories, see Laurence BonJour, *The Structure of Empirical Knowledge*; Keith Lehrer, "The Coherence Theory of Knowledge"; and Nicholas Rescher, *The Coherence Theory of Truth*.

For foundationalist theories, see Robert Audi, "Contemporary Foundationalism"; Richard A. Fumerton, *Metaphysical and Epistemological Problems of Perception*; Paul K. Moser, *Knowledge and Evidence*; and Timothy McGrew, "A Defense of Classical Foundationalism." For a critical assessment of the two theories, see Ernest Sosa, "The Raft and the Pyrimid."

26. The interdependence was recognized by Norwood Russell Hanson, Paul Feyerabend, and Thomas Kuhn, all of whom stressed that observation statements can be theory-laden. The interdependence was recognized also by Wilfrid Sellars; see, for instance, *Empiricism and the Philosophy of Mind*, §36.

is interdependence, one finds the same elements: revision rules, revision processes, and convergence. One finds these elements in the theory of interdependent definitions—which was my own starting point in developing the present model—as well as in, for example, the theory of numerical approximations. Charles Sanders Peirce recognized long ago the importance of convergence. He wrote in §IV of his essay "How to Make Our Ideas Clear":

> Different minds may set out with the most antagonistic views, but the progress of investigation carries them by a force outside of themselves to one and the same conclusion.... No modification of the point of view taken, no selection of other facts for study, no natural bent of mind even, can enable a man to escape the predestinate opinion. This great law is embodied in the conception of truth and reality. (pp. 138-39)

Finally, one finds all the elements—revision rules, revision processes, and convergence—in subjectivist Bayesianism.[27] Indeed, remarkable convergence theorems have been proven about the Bayes rule for deriving posterior degrees of belief from prior ones. The present model is more general, however, and does not require an acceptance of Bayesianism or even of its fundamental notion "subjective degree of belief."[28]

4C. Some Objections

The model of experience and knowledge sketched above needs considerable development. But even in its sketchy state, it is liable to provoke objections. "The model cannot be right," an objector may say, "because of its sharp separation of view and experience. Experience is not independent of concepts, conceptions, and beliefs—in short, of what you call 'view'. Our view shapes our experience. Even detailed elements of a view can affect experience.

27. See John Earman's *Bayes or Bust?* for an account of Bayesianism and of challenges facing it.

28. The Bayesian convergence theorems are of little use to us in defending the idea that our experience entails the commonsense view. These theorems are too weak: they do not assure us of convergence when initial views fail to agree on what is certain. The theorems are also too strong: the convergence they establish holds irrespective of the course of experience.

Your visual experience of the foliage will change when you are brought to recognize a bird within it. More generally, Kant's point that experience is the product of both sensibility and understanding is surely sound. But you seem to neglect it altogether. If our experience is constituted, in part, by our view, little sense can be made of your hypothetical given. A view is woven into the very fabric of experience. It makes little sense to ask what perceptual judgments an experience issues with respect to a different view."

In response, let me observe that the separation between view and experience that the model requires is only epistemological. It requires neither a causal nor a metaphysical separation. No doubt views causally influence and even shape experience. But this does not undermine the epistemological autonomy of experience. A theoretical belief may lead us to perform certain experiments, and these experiments may produce some special experiences in us. It may even be that we would not suffer the experiences were it not for the experiments, and furthermore, we would not perform the experiments were it not for the theoretical belief. The belief is thus an essential part of the causal ground of our experiences. Nevertheless, the experiences can retain their epistemological autonomy. They can undermine the belief that is their causal ground. Epistemological independence is therefore compatible with causal dependence. It is compatible also with metaphysical dependence. Perhaps, as the objection suggests, views are somehow a part of the constitution of experiences. More specifically, perhaps experiences are individuated by their contents, and concepts and conceptions literally constitute these contents. (I myself am highly doubtful of this idea, but I allow it for the sake of the argument.[29]) Even so, the epistemological autonomy of experience is not undermined, for there remains the possibility of an aspect of experience, distinct from its content, that is epistemologically significant. Indeed, there had better be such an aspect, for the epistemological significance of an experience cannot be located in its content. If views constitute contents, we need a prior acceptance of the constituting view before we are in a position

---

29. Let me note, *en passant*, that there have been two principal motivations for making concepts, conceptions, etc., constitutive of experiences. First, this move makes available the synthetic a priori; second, it ensures that experience can stand in rational relation to beliefs. The first motivation is no longer in play; there is no pressing need to sustain the synthetic a priori. The second *is* in play, but, as I have argued, it does not direct us to conceptual contents. See also §5B.

to accept the content of an experience. Hence, the rational force that experience exerts on us to accept a view cannot come from the content. It must come from some other aspect. Indeed, there is little doubt that this aspect is nothing other than the phenomenology of experience, how experience is from the subjective viewpoint. In experience, we are not presented with contents. We are presented, if anything, with elements that yield different perceptual judgments as different views are brought to bear on them. The phenomenology need not change as I learn that the light I took to be a distant lamp is in fact an image, or that it is an illusion, or even that it is a hallucination. The same phenomenology leads me to different judgments as I consider different hypotheses about the light. A person suddenly coming to a solipsist view may exclaim "*this* is all there is!" but there may be no accompanying shift in the phenomenology of his experience—visual, auditory, tactile, or other.

The objector may respond: "Your invocation of phenomenology does not help your case. You are not true to the phenomenology, and you do not respect its epistemological significance. It is beyond question that the 'phenomenological feel' of, for example, typical visual and tactile experiences is that one has in them a direct awareness of objects and their properties and relations. As you look at that coaster near you, you have a direct awareness of an orange something. A simple examination of your experience reveals to you the presence of an orange object in your consciousness. The relationship of this object to the coaster itself may be debated—some will say that the relationship is that of identity, others that it is that of representation. But there is no denying that you are directly aware of an object and of a particular property (the color orange). Before we can so much as entertain a view of the world, our thoughts must have content; they must be *about* the world. This is impossible, however, without experience. Our language and thought gain their connections to the world through our acquaintance with objects, properties, and relations. This fundamental fact is utterly neglected in your model. You talk about the contribution of experience to knowledge. But you neglect the prior issue: the contribution of experience to content. Without direct awareness, there is no content, there is no thought. Direct awareness must be prior to views, not mediated by them or somehow internal to them.

"Furthermore," the objector may continue, "if direct awareness exists—as it undoubtedly does—then there must be a propositional given. Indeed, in light of your acceptance of much of the framework of classical empiricism, you must acknowledge that the given includes sense-datum judgments. The meaning assigned to the sense-datum vocabulary assures us that these judgments are rendered true by the very occurrence of experience. The judgments meet all the constraints on the given. Hence, you have no grounds for denying that they belong in the given.

"This points to a further difficulty," the objector may add, "one that is internal to your proposal. Even if you can somehow reject the sense-datum theory as untrue, you must admit that the theory is at least coherent. But now there is a major problem facing you since convergence is bound to fail. Suppose you begin the revision process with the following view, which may be called the *epistemological solipsism of the present moment*:

> I am a mind that has direct awareness of my present sense-data. My current experience entitles me to affirm the existence of an oval orange sense-datum, a soft whirring auditory sense-datum, a faint memory sense-datum of an odor, etc. Everything else I believe must be justifiable on the basis of my sense-datum judgments.

You would then affirm the existence of different sense-data from moment to moment, but you would never move beyond sense-data. Your sense-datum judgments will not entitle you to affirm the existence of anything external to yourself. For all you know, you and your current sense-data are the only things in the universe. Note, incidentally, that the same is bound to occur with the other variants of epistemological solipsism—for example, one in which a mind has direct awareness of its experiential states.

"You are back in the old epistemological predicament. With a solipsist view in play, there is at best convergence only on subjective judgments. Hence, you fail to establish that experience validates our commonsense conception of the world, and we are back in the hole in which traditional epistemology finds itself. Or perhaps in a deeper one. Before, we could at least understand how our thoughts might have content, and now we have lost even that little grip on reality."

These objections require an extended response, and I attempt to provide one in chapter 5. Let me note for now one significant difference between the present proposal and traditional epistemological theories. In traditional epistemology, solipsist views appear as a part of the *solution* to the problem of the external

world; they provide the ideal foundations for empirical knowledge.[30] It is true that traditional epistemology allows itself to work
with broader materials, for example, sense-data of other minds,
and even possible sense-data. But it does so only because solipsist
foundations create for it problems that are insuperably difficult. To
stay true to its own fundamental thought, traditional epistemology must build solely on solipsist foundations. In contrast, in the
picture I have painted, solipsist views are in no way a part of the
solution to the problem of the external world. They are rather
irritants that must somehow be removed. They are debris that
threaten to clog up the engine of knowledge, not—as in traditional epistemology—ideal fuel for running the engine. Solipsist
views pose a problem, I admit, for the account of experience and
knowledge that I wish to defend—a problem that must be solved
if the account is to remain viable. Nevertheless, it speaks in favor
of the account that solipsist views pose the particular problem that
they do for it. Solipsist views belong in the problem box of
empirical knowledge, not in the solutions box. An adequate account of empirical knowledge must somehow rule solipsist views
to be unacceptable, not embrace them as foundational.

30. Russell writes in *Problems of Philosophy*, "We must therefore, if possible, find,
in our own purely private experiences, characteristics which show, or tend to show,
that there are in the world things other than ourselves and our private experiences"
(p. 22). See also Carnap, *The Logical Structure of the World*, §64.

❀

FIVE

DIRECT AWARENESS,

SEMANTICS, AND SOLIPSISM

❀ The problems facing our model of experience and knowledge can be solved only through a study of the semantical significance of "direct awareness." Let us begin this study with a review of the semantical picture found in classical empiricism; here "direct awareness" is assigned a straightforward, foundational role (§5A). A critical examination of the picture will provide us with some resources to address the problems before us (§§5B–5E).

5A. The Semantics of Classical Empiricism

A simple and familiar picture of truth and falsity is this. Our sentences and thoughts have logical structure: they are built using logical resources (e.g., predication and negation) from names, predicates, function symbols, and so on. The sentence 'Socrates is wise', for example, is built from the name 'Socrates' and the predicate 'is wise' using the logical resource of predication. The name 'Socrates' picks out a particular individual, and the predicate 'is wise' picks out a particular property, wisdom. When we affirm 'Socrates is wise', we commit ourselves to the judgment that the man Socrates exemplifies the property of wisdom. The sentence 'Socrates is wise' is thus true (or expresses a truth) if Socrates exemplifies wisdom; it is false, otherwise. More generally, according to this picture, the simplest elements of our language and thought are connected to the world by certain representational relations. These relations fix the truth and falsity of sentences in the manner dictated by logical form. For instance, the logical form of 'Socrates is not wise' dictates that this sentence is rendered false by the fact that Socrates exemplifies wisdom.

Classical empiricism adopts this simple and familiar picture and enriches it. According to classical empiricism, there is a part of our language and thought that has a privileged connection with the world. This is the part that concerns the self and its sense-data. The self has direct awareness or apprehension of itself and its sense-data, and of (some of) their properties and relations.[1] It can set up names for the directly apprehended entities and can then proceed to think and talk about them.[2] The connection of the names to the apprehended entities is immediate, transparent, and tidy.

In semantics, as in the theory of knowledge, classical empiricism takes over a natural, commonsense idea and transforms it. It is a natural idea that we can name objects and properties that are presented to us. A child is presented with a doll; she names it 'Martha', and then she goes on to talk about it. I am presented with a new color; I name it 'metallic blue', and then I go on to make claims about it. The whole thing is easy and trouble-free. Similarly, in classical empiricism, the self, presented with certain objects and their properties, can name them and can then go on to think and talk about them. Classical empiricism keeps the structure of the

---

1. As I indicated in §2A, the notion of direct awareness goes under various names in the philosophical literature, including 'direct perception', 'immediate experience', and 'sensing'. I shall use 'direct apprehension' and 'direct perception' as variants of 'direct awareness'.

As also noted in §2A, followers of classical empiricism have not been in perfect agreement on the objects of direct awareness. Some theorists have, for instance, denied—while others have affirmed—that the self has direct awareness of itself. There have also been disagreements on the nature, and even the existence, of sense-data. I am concerned here to bring out the general character of the classical empiricist account of content. For ease of exposition, I work with a particular conception of the objects of direct awareness. Theorists who subscribe to different conceptions of the objects of direct awareness would give accounts of content that differ in detail from the account sketched below but that are similar to it in structure.

2. Locke writes in his *Essay* that "*Words in their primary or immediate Signification, stand for nothing, but the* Ideas *in the Mind of him that uses them*" (III.ii.2; emphasis original).

commonsense idea but substitutes special entities for the ordinary objects of the commonsense scheme.

The semantical picture offered by classical empiricism fits neatly with its account of the given in experience. According to this account, the logical form of the given is that of proposition—indeed some of the propositions in the given are *atomic* (of the form, e.g., *x* is *F* and *xRy*). This implies that some individuals, properties, and relations are also given in experience, that they are directly apprehended. So, the account lends plausibility to the semantical picture: in naming, one is simply labeling a thing; one is simply setting up a connection between a symbol and an object (or a property or a relation) that one has apprehended. The semantical picture, in turn, lends plausibility to the classical account of the given. The linkage between thoughts about current sense-data and the sense-data themselves is so close and intimate that it precludes any mismatch between the two. The propositional conception of the given thus goes hand in hand with the simple model of language and thought.

The semantical picture offered by classical empiricism, like its epistemological picture, is foundationalist in character. In the epistemological picture, there is a realm of judgments—basic judgments—that is simply given in experience. And the rest of our empirical knowledge receives its justification through these basic judgments. Similarly, in the semantical picture, there is a part of our language and thought (that concerning the self and its present sense-data) whose connections to the world are privileged and direct. And the rest of our language and thought gains content through its connection to this privileged part.[3]

---

3. I understand the notion "*X* is *privileged*" to include the ideas (a) that *X* has a *tidy* semantical link to the world—i.e., *X* picks out an actual object if *X* is a name, an actual universal if *X* is a predicate, etc.; and (b) experience is the immediate ground of the linkage (and so the linkage is not mediated by semantical linkages of other terms). The notion is thus parallel to that of "basic empirical proposition," which applies to propositions that are (a′) true and (b′) whose truth is immediately grounded in experience. Experience provides the subject with suitable access in both cases: in the case of terms, to their referents; and in the case of propositions, to their truth.

I shall not take other related ideas—e.g., that privileged vocabulary constitutes the semantical foundation for the rest of language—to be part of the concept of privileged term, but as substantive theses about it.

The foundationalist picture in semantics receives support from a reflection on ordinary meaning. Intuitively, the contents of such terms as 'red' and 'Donna', as I understand them, are, it appears, easily explained.[4] The content of 'red' is the property that I encounter in experience; the content of 'Donna' is similarly a person I often encounter, namely, my daughter. But what about the meaning of a non-basic term such as 'Bismarck'—to use Russell's example—whose referent I do not, and cannot, encounter in experience? A natural response is that what I mean by 'Bismarck' is captured by a description such as 'the most astute diplomat of nineteenth century Germany'. This description, it is true, contains expressions—for example, 'diplomat' and 'nineteenth century'— whose meanings are not the objects of my experience; they are not entities with which I am, in Russellian terminology, *acquainted*. But, again, it is a natural thought that their contents can also be spelled out in terms of further descriptions. Now, just as a natural regress argument leads to a foundationalism about epistemic justification, a parallel regress argument leads naturally to a foundationalism about content. The regress about meaning ends in basic, privileged terms—that is, terms that acquire meaning through their links to entities I encounter in experience. (Of course, for classical empiricism, the basic terms denote such things as sense-data, not physical objects and persons. For according to classical empiricism, underlying our conceptualization of physical objects and persons, there is a conceptual subbasement of the self and its sense-data.[5]) Thus emerges the idea that reflection on the meanings of my terms will reveal the deep logical grammar of my language. It will lay bare how the various parts of my language connect to the world. All these connections flow through the basic acts of meaning, acts that connect names to entities I directly apprehend in experience.

In the semantical picture of classical empiricism, as in the epistemological picture, there are various grades of connection between terms that are foundational and terms that belong in the superstructure. The simplest grade is *direct reduction*: a term *t* is said to be *directly reducible* when there is an equivalent expression of the same logical type as *t* that is built solely from foundational (i.e.,

---

4. In the present exposition, I use the terms 'meaning' and 'content' interchangeably.

5. Quine's metaphor; see *Word and Object*, p. 3.

privileged) terms. The reduction of 'is an apple' to 'is round, and tart, and...' would count as direct if the '...' in it could be filled in in a satisfactory way.[6] However, few empiricists in the twentieth century committed themselves to such direct reductions for physical-object terms. They opted instead for a looser kind of reduction, which may be called *contextualist reduction*. Here, terms are not reduced to equivalent ones, but every legitimate context—more specifically, every legitimate sentence—containing the terms is claimed to be equivalent to one that is free of them. This sort of reduction is inspired by Russell's theory of definite descriptions. Russell showed how a sentence containing a definite description could be analyzed into one that is free of the description. It turns out that the Russellian analysans contains no constituent that corresponds to the original definite description.[7] Russellian reduction is thus a genuine liberalization; its effect cannot be duplicated by a direct reduction. So, even though a physical object term such as 'apple' may not have a direct reduction, it may still be possible to reduce each legitimate sentence containing 'apple' to a complex of sentences containing only privileged terms. If so, then the term 'apple' would be, in Russellian terminology, an *incomplete symbol*. It would not have any independent meaning in isolation, but it would contribute systematically to the meanings of sentences in which it occurs. Russell's reflections on meaning led him to espouse (in 1912) a reduction of this form:

> The fundamental principle in the analysis of propositions containing descriptions is this: *Every proposition which we can understand must be composed wholly of constituents with which we are acquainted.*[8]

---

6. Perhaps Berkeley's dictum that things are ideas committed him to a direct reduction of some physical-object terms. But this is not the only type of reduction that can be recovered from his writings.

7. Russell analyzed the sentence 'the King of France is bald' as 'there is a King of France, and no one else is a King of France, and he is bald', i.e., in logical terminology,

$\exists x(x$ is a King of France $\& \forall y(y$ is a King of France $\rightarrow x = y) \& x$ is bald$)$.

Observe that the analysans contains no constituent corresponding to 'the King of France'. I should note that some sentences containing psychological verbs such as 'look' and 'worship' prove to be resistant to the Russellian treatment. Nevertheless, the scope of the Russellian theory is impressive.

8. Russell's *Problems of Philosophy*, p. 58; emphasis original.

Russell's idea was greatly influential on the empiricism of the early twentieth century and led to the development of various versions of phenomenalism.

The picture of meaning that now emerges is this. Each legitimate sentence has a deep logical structure. This structure is generally quite unlike grammatical structure, and it is revealed by analysis—deep analysis!—of meaning. The ultimate nonlogical constituents of the analysans of a sentence are terms of the privileged vocabulary. The meanings of these terms we grasp in acts of direct awareness. It is thus that experience connects our language and thought to the world. Experience is the foundation not only of knowledge but also of meaning.[9]

A virtue of classical empiricism is that it grants us substantial conceptual freedom. It does not treat the commonsense conceptions of, for example, space, time, and physical objects as sacrosanct. It makes room for the possibility that, in our attempts to understand the world, we may find it necessary to radically revise these conceptions. It is true that classical empiricism makes this possibility available only at a price: it denies us all conceptual freedom in one realm, namely, that of the self and sense-data.[10] Classical empiricism, though it approximates the ideal of complete conceptual freedom, does not achieve it.

One problem with the semantical picture offered by classical empiricism is that the promised reductions prove difficult to construct. No matter how deep the reflection on meaning, it is hard to spell out the content of even simple claims (e.g., "that is a

---

9. Observe that the picture is not committed to idealism. The possibility remains open that some of the properties that we apprehend directly, e.g., "square" and "red," are true of external, objective particulars. It may even be that "red square" is true precisely of one particular, and that this particular is objective and external. If so, we can refer to and talk about such a particular. In Russellian terminology, we may be able to know this particular by "description" even though we cannot be acquainted with it.

10. Further, while classical empiricism allows us to revise *sentences* we accept about space, time, and physical objects, it does not permit a radical shift in *view*. Classical empiricism rigidly adheres to one view, that of the self and sense-data. Radical changes in theories—e.g., from a Newtonian to a relativisitic mechanics— are, as classical empiricism conceives them, simply shifts in the way sense-data are "bundled" in various physical-object sentences.

.

door knob") in terms of privileged vocabulary.[11] But perhaps this problem can be overcome by liberalizing the notion of reduction beyond the Russellian limits to what may be called *indirect contextualist reduction*. We now allow the possibility that some of the legitimate sentences containing a nonprivileged term fail to possess an independent meaning. These sentences, we can maintain, are like incomplete symbols in that they contribute to the meanings of wholes—more specifically, theories—but they cannot be assigned any independent parcel of meaning. The theories themselves have, of course, independent meaning: they are reducible to theories built using only privileged terms. But no such reduction is available for the sentences themselves. Plane geometry supplemented with the talk of "points at infinity" and "the line at infinity" provides an illustration of this sort of reduction. The supplemented geometry is equivalent to ordinary geometry (on theorems formulated using ordinary geometrical vocabulary), but there is no sentence-by-sentence reduction of the former into the latter. Ramsey's account of theories can also be seen as an instance of this broader sort of reduction.[12] Quine's empiricism is another instance. One of the main sources of Quine's distinctive doctrines—for example, holism about meaning, the indeterminacy of translation, and his pragmatism—is the idea that (empirical) meaning can be attributed only to theories as a whole, not to the individual sentences that constitute them.

The fundamental problem with the semantical picture of classical empiricism lies, of course, in its core idea: that the semantical links of our language and thought are effected through entities

---

11. Especially influential criticisms of empiricist reductions were given by Chisholm ("The Problem of Empiricism") and Quine ("Two Dogmas of Empiricism").

12. Ramsey proposed that the content of a theory $\Theta(O_1, \ldots, O_m; T_1, \ldots, T_n)$, containing privileged terms $O_1, \ldots, O_m$ and nonprivileged terms $T_1, \ldots, T_n$, is given by the sentence (nowadays called the *Ramsey sentence for* Θ)

$$(\exists X_1, \ldots, X_n) \, \Theta(O_1, \ldots, O_m; X_1, \ldots, X_n),$$

where $X_1, \ldots, X_n$ are variables of types corresponding respectively to $T_1, \ldots, T_n$. Ramsey pointed out that Θ and its Ramsey sentence are equivalent in the sense that if one logically implies a sentence containing only privileged vocabulary, then so does the other. For a fuller account of Ramsey's proposal and for some of the difficulties with it (and with related approaches), see William Demopoulos, "On the Rational Reconstruction of Our Theoretical Knowledge."

directly apprehended in experience. We need to find our way to seeing clearly that this seductive idea is mistaken, and also *how* it is mistaken. Wilfrid Sellars's *Empiricism and the Philosophy of Mind* contains one of the most explicit and extended criticisms of the idea.[13] Let us consider this criticism briefly, for even if—as I think—it does not provide a compelling rationale for rejecting the classical picture, it does help to dissipate some of the picture's enchantment.

5B. The Sellarsian Criticism

Sellars argues that there is no direct awareness or apprehension of the type required by classical empiricism. He rejects the "Myth of the Given," which holds (in part) that "the awareness of certain *sorts*... is a primordial, non-problematic feature of 'immediate experience'."[14] The Myth of the Given takes several forms, and Sellars marshals a variety of considerations against these forms. His principal arguments rest, I think, on some "Priority Theses" and the claim that

(1) All awareness is conceptual.

Chief among the Priority Theses are the following:

(2a) *The Priority of the Linguistic to the Conceptual*: All concepts presuppose the use of language.
(2b) *The Priority of Physical-Object Concepts to Mentalistic Concepts*: Mentalistic concepts, including those used to describe experience, presuppose physical-object concepts.[15]

---

13. Sellars's criticism evidently builds on the work of Wittgenstein and Gilbert Ryle.

14. *Empiricism and the Philosophy of Mind* (henceforth, *EPM*), §26. Unless otherwise indicated, all parenthetical references in the present section are to this book. Also, all italics in the extracts from Sellars's writings are from the original.

15. Sellars explicitly commits himself to a strict priority of physical-object concepts to mentalistic concepts. But whether he is committed to a strict priority of the linguistic over the conceptual is debatable. On Robert Brandom's interpretation, for instance, Sellars is not committed to the idea that language use is possible without the possession of concepts (see Brandom's "Study Guide"). I do not need to decide the proper interpretation of Sellars on this point. Let us agree to read thesis (2a) in a weak way: it does not rule out the possibility that the possession of language implies the possession of concepts.

Now, the defenders of the classical picture can easily concede (1), for it requires them to give up only a naive abstractionist account of sensory concepts—an account that is implausible in any case. Thus, it is the Priority Theses that are crucial to Sellars's arguments. The thesis of the Priority of the Linguistic implies, in conjunction with (1), that all awareness presupposes the use of language. This conclusion is closely related to Sellars's "Psychological Nominalism," which he formulates as follows:

> *All* awareness of *sorts, resemblances, facts*, etc., in short, all awareness of abstract entities—indeed, all awareness even of particulars— is a linguistic affair. According to it, not even the awareness of such, resemblances, and facts as pertain to so-called imme- diate experience is presupposed by the process of acquiring the use of a language. (§29)

In "Some Reflections on Language Games," Sellars says emphat- ically, "There is no more such a thing as a non-symbolic noticing that something is red, than there is a non-symbolic saying that something is red."[16]

Sellars's famous Myth of Jones aims to render plausible the Priority Theses and, with them, Psychological Nominalism. In outline, the Myth of Jones is as follows. Sellars imagines a com- munity of people—the *Ryleans*—whose language has no psycho- logical vocabulary. The Ryleans talk of public objects, and they offer behavioristic descriptions of each other. And, most impor- tant, the Ryleans are theoretically sophisticated: they use sub- junctive conditionals, they possess semantical concepts, and they understand the theoretical introduction of new entities and states. But the Ryleans lack all vocabulary for talking about thoughts, impressions, and experiences. Sellars shows how a genius in this community, Jones, can guide the Ryleans to the acceptance of new theoretical entities, *thoughts*, which are modeled on sentences and whose intentionality is explained in analogy with the semantical properties of sentences. Sellars goes on to show how members of the community can learn *reporting* uses of the new theoretical terms. Thus, members of the community can learn to make such reports as "I am thinking that it will snow" directly, without going through any inferences. In this way, Sellars tries to show how the

---

16. Sellars, *Science, Perception and Reality*, p. 336.

intersubjectivity of the concept of thought can be reconciled with one's privileged access to one's thoughts. (Sellars thinks that this privileged access is limited, not of the full-blooded Cartesian sort.) In the final stage of the myth, Jones introduces *impressions* as theoretical posits. These are modeled on "inner replicas" (e.g., a red and triangular wafer) and are "the end results of the impingement of physical objects and processes on various parts of the body" (§60). Here, too, the community can learn a reporting use of the new theoretical terms. And, again, Sellars uses this to explain how the intersubjectivity of our talk of impressions can be reconciled with our privileged access to them.

It should be stressed that Sellars does not take the Myth of Jones to be a *mere* myth. In the last section of *EPM*, he writes, "I have used a myth to kill a myth—the Myth of the Given. But is my myth really a myth? Or does the reader not recognize Jones as Man himself in the middle of his journey from the grunts and groans of the cave to the subtle and polydimensional discourse of the drawing room, the laboratory, and the study" (§63).

According to Sellars, an experience has a propositional content and a descriptive content. The two stages in the Myth of Jones, sketched above, aim to put these two contents on the Sellarsian gold standard,[17] the standard of Methodological Behaviorism.[18] The statement "Jones sees that there is a green tree," Sellars holds, ascribes the propositional content "there is a green tree" to Jones's experience and, indeed, endorses the content. (Note that the ascribed content does not exhaust all the content belonging to an experience. As Sellars understands it, the latter is generally more complex and determinate; see *EPM*, §22.) The first stage of the myth aims to put the notion of propositional content on the gold standard. This content is modeled on sentence meaning, which Sellars understands as inferential role broadly construed.[19] There is,

17. Sellars invokes the metaphor of the gold standard in the first of the two sections numbered 16 in *EPM*.

18. Note the way Sellars understands Methodological Behaviorism: "The behavioristic requirement that all [mentalistic] concepts should be *introduced* in terms of a basic vocabulary pertaining to overt behavior is compatible with the idea that some behavioristic concepts are to be introduced as *theoretical* concepts" (§54).

19. Sellars draws attention to three sorts of roles that may constitute the meaning of a sentence. First, there are the language-entry roles; these link the use of a sentence to certain worldly conditions. E.g., it may be part of the meaning of 'that's

of course, something more to an experience than its having a particular propositional content. This something more, "what philosophers have in mind when they speak of 'visual impressions' or 'immediate visual experiences'" (the second §16), is the descriptive content of the experience. Sellars puts this content on the gold standard in the second stage of his Myth of Jones.

Sellars insists that the two notions of content—propositional and descriptive—are radically different. Propositional content requires concepts and presupposes language. As Sellars sees it, it is only because experience has propositional content that it belongs in the logical and conceptual realm. Descriptive content, on the other hand, requires no learning or concept formation, and it is devoid of epistemic significance. Descriptive content can be instantiated in brutes without any language, brutes without any sense of giving and asking for reasons. To say that "red" belongs to the descriptive content of an experience is to say that the corresponding impression is *of* red, and this claim concerns only the typical causes of the impression. Thus, experience, according to Sellars, has two radically different sorts of "aboutness." The first sort of aboutness is that of *thoughts*, and the second is that of *impressions*. The first is a reflection of the fact that experience belongs in the realm of reasons; the second, of the fact that it belongs in the realm of causes. Sellars thinks that one of the central errors of the sense-datum theory is the confusion of the aboutness of impressions with that of thoughts. This confusion enables the theory to read epistemic significance into epistemically inert impressions (§§7 and 24–25).[20]

Sellars's criticism of classical empiricism may now be summed up as follows. Classical empiricism claims that there is in experience a direct awareness of certain objects and properties (e.g., red sense-data

---

red' that it is appropriate to assert the sentence in the presence, under normal conditions, of certain apples. Second, there are language-language roles; these relate the use of one sentence to that of others. E.g., it may be part of the meaning of 'that's red' that its correct affirmation entitles one to affirm 'that's colored'. Finally, there are language-departure roles; these connect uses of a sentence to actions. E.g., it may be part of the meaning of 'I will move my arm' that, on affirming this sentence, it is appropriate to move one's arm. See Sellars, "Some Reflections on Language Games."

20. For a critical discussion of Sellars's account of impressions, see Romane Clark, "The Sensuous Content of Perception."

and triangularity) or states (e.g., "looking to me as if there is a red triangle"). It claims further that this awareness can justify knowledge claims; in particular, it can justify claims lying at the foundations of empirical knowledge. But the Sellarsian analysis of experience reveals nothing that can play the required role. Plainly, direct awareness cannot be identified with an experience's possession of propositional content, for this content is typically about physical objects. It is tempting to identify direct awareness with impressions. That is, it is tempting to think that one has direct awareness of, for example, red when one has an impression of red. But this temptation rests on confusing two sorts of aboutness that Sellars has sharply separated: the aboutness of impressions with that of thoughts. Epistemically inert impressions cannot constitute direct awareness of anything. They are of the wrong logical type to justify any propositions. There is thus in experience no primordial awareness of reality. There are primordial interactions with reality, but these generate only epistemically inert impressions. There are seeings, for example, *that there is a green tree*, but these are not primordial; they presuppose concepts and language.

A proponent of the classical picture may try to abandon talk of "direct awareness" and retreat to the idea that concepts such as "red," when restricted to sense-data and appearance talk, are independent of physical-object concepts. But this comes into conflict with the Sellarsian thesis of the Priority of Physical-Object Concepts. Sellars holds that the "fundamental grammar of the attribute *red* is *physical object x is red at place p and at time t*" (§23). Therefore, uses of "red" as applied to sense-data—and even its uses in "looks" and "appears" talk—are derivative; they rest on applications of "red" to physical objects. Sellars says,

> The concept of *looking* [*red*], the ability to recognize that something *looks* [*red*], presupposes the concept of *being* [*red*], and . . . the latter concept involves the ability to tell what colors objects have by looking at them—which, in turn, involves knowing in what circumstances to place an object if one wishes to ascertain its color by looking at it. (§18)[21]

Sellars is thus led to a holism about physical-object concepts: "One can have the concept of [red] only by having a whole battery of

---

21. Sellars offers also a reductive analysis of "looks" talk (see §22). The reduction is open to several objections, however. (In this and the next extract, Sellars's actual example is "green," not "red.")

concepts of which it is one element" (§19). And possession of this battery of concepts requires knowledge of general truths.[22] Sellars concludes that the use of "red" in sense-datum or appearance talk does not have the logical autonomy that classical empiricism accords to it. Indeed, according to Sellars, *no* empirical proposition has this logical autonomy. Our empirical knowledge does not rest on a body of logically autonomous propositions.

Sellars turns the classical picture inside out. The classical picture takes the deliverances of immediate experience to be fundamental both semantically and epistemologically. And it views our talk and thought of physical objects to be problematic—something that has to be understood in experiential terms. Sellars reverses the order: he takes our talk of experience—and, more generally, the mental—to be problematic and aims to rehabilitate it within a broadly behaviorist perspective. The classical picture is foundationalist in both epistemology and semantics. Sellars rejects foundationalism in both domains. According to him, our empirical knowledge does not rest on a foundation of basic propositions. And the semantical links between our language (and thought) and the world are not mediated by acts of "direct awareness." As Sellars writes,

> Once sensations and images have been purged of epistemic aboutness, the primary reason for supposing that the fundamental associative tie between language and the world must be between words and 'immediate experiences' has disappeared, and the way is clear to recognizing that basic word-world associations hold, for example, between "red" and red *physical objects*, rather than between "red" and a supposed class of private red particulars. (§29)

The word-world associations are thus effected not through acts of direct awareness or through immediate experience but through the *use* of words in a public language. For example, the language-world relationship of 'red' is fixed not by an inner direct awareness of the property "red" but by the role of 'red' in our linguistic system: by the language-entry, language-language, and

---

22. Sellars says in "The Structure of Knowledge" that there isn't "a level of perceptual knowledge of singular truths which presupposes no knowledge of general truths about material things and our perception of them" (lecture I, §6).

language-departure roles of such sentences as 'this is red' and 'pick up that red apple'.[23]

SELLARS'S CRITICISMS OF THE CLASSICAL PICTURE ARE RICH and instructive. But I must confess that they do not enable at least *this* fly to see his way out of the fly bottle. Sellars's criticisms rest, we have seen, on the Priority Theses: the Priority of the Linguistic and the Priority of Physical-Object Concepts. Proponents of the classical picture can pose a reasonable challenge here. They can ask about the sort of priority that is claimed by Sellars. Sellars's arguments place stress on the priority of *acquisition*: physical-object concepts are acquired first, and 'looks' talk later; language and its semantic concepts are acquired first, and the talk about thoughts and experiences only later.[24] But if 'priority' is understood in this way, the proponents of the classical picture can happily accept Sellars's claims and still retain their account.[25] They can argue that the order in which concepts are acquired does not always reflect the logical order. Some concepts (e.g., "area") are acquired fairly quickly, but the elements in their proper definition require considerable conceptual sophistication and are typically acquired

---

23. See Sellars, "Some Reflections on Language Games." See fn. 19 for a brief description of these roles.

24. There is a problem with Sellars's argument here. The Myth of Jones assumes that the Ryleans have semantical vocabulary even before the appearance of Jones. Thus, it assumes that semantical concepts can be introduced in the absence of the concepts of thinking and of experience. But it is not at all obvious that this assumption is correct. Intuitively, it appears that to make sense of a concept such as reference, one needs to appeal to thoughts and experiences. The referent, e.g., of a particular utterance of 'Mary' by John may depend on John's intentions on the occasion of his utterance and on features of his experience. Unless we are shown that this intuition is erroneous, we must regard the Myth of Jones as a *mere* myth, for we have little reason to regard the Rylean community as anything more than a merely fictional steppingstone from "the grunts and groans of the cave" to the "polydimensional discourse of the drawing room."

25. The proponents can also argue that the concepts "red" and "looks red," for instance, are interdependent and must be acquired simultaneously. They can in this way reject some of Sellars's priority claims. But I do not pursue this avenue in the text because it creates no fundamental problem for the Sellarsian critique of classical empiricism. If the two concepts are interdependent, Sellars can point out, "looks" talk cannot be the logical and semantical foundation for our talk about physical objects. (Sellars himself notes the possibility of interdependence in a footnote added to the reprinting of *EPM* in *Science, Perception and Reality*.)

later. Similarly, it may be that the concepts necessary to articulate the semantical and epistemological grounds of our talk of physical objects are acquired at a late stage of our conceptual development.

The sense of 'priority' that brings the Sellarsian claims into conflict with the classical picture is not "priority in the order of acquisition" but "priority in the logical order" and, at several points in his argument, this is the sense that Sellars has in mind.[26] But here, it appears, the proponents of the classical picture can hold their ground. Claims such as "that looks green to me," they can point out, do not presuppose any substantive claims about "green." Even if the concept "green" is erroneous and confused, the concept "looks green" can be in perfect order. (Compare: the truth of the statement "those events look to be simultaneous" is not impugned by the defects in the concept of simultaneity.) "Looks green," the proponents can say, has a logical autonomy that makes it suitable for a foundational role. In the only sense that matters, they can insist, "looks green" *is* logically prior to "green."

A further, and more important, set of difficulties centers on Sellars's account of experience. In the first place, Sellars's account obscures the rational contribution of experience to knowledge. In the Sellarsian account, this contribution can come only from the propositional content that is attributed to experience since impressions, we are told, are epistemically inert. But for the following two reasons, the propositional content cannot be the rational contribution. (i) It would violate the Reliability constraint (see §2B); the propositional content Sellars associates with an experience is sometimes false.[27] (ii) The propositional content of an experience, as Sellars conceives it, carries various presuppositions. And entitlement to these presuppositions cannot issue from any particular experience. Hence, an experience by itself does not entitle one to accept

---

26. E.g., in §12, Sellars writes, "*being red* is logically prior, is a logically simpler notion, than *looking red*"; in 38, he says that there is a "logical dimension" in which observation reports rest on empirical propositions (including empirical generalizations); and, in §59, Sellars claims that the fact that overt behavior is evidence for inner states, e.g., thoughts, "*is built into the very logic of*" the concept of thought.

27. Whether the Equivalence constraint would be violated is less clear, for Sellars does not tell us in sufficient detail the propositions that belong to the content of an experience.

the propositional content associated with it.[28] Let us observe that
Sellars himself does not take an experience to yield entitlement to
the propositional content: before the content—or a part of it—can
rationally be endorsed, one needs to have, according to Sellars,
knowledge of certain reliability facts (see *EPM*, §§35–37).

Now, if the propositional content is not the rational contribution of an experience, what might the rational contribution
be? The difficulty of finding an adequate answer to this question
within the Sellarsian framework suggests that Sellars is committed
to rejecting empiricism: experience understood in the Sellarsian
way makes no rational contribution to knowledge.[29] Indeed,

---

28. This argument holds even if experience is conceived as *affirming* its propositional content. Sellars's view of the mode under which experience has its propositional content is not perfectly clear. In the first §16 of *EPM*, Sellars says that
experience makes "an assertion or claim," but he also prefixes this with a 'so to
speak'. Further, the idea that experience affirms its propositional content does not sit
well with Sellars's analysis of "looks" (§22). It follows from Sellars's analysis that a
proposition, e.g., "*x* is red," can be a part of the content of an experience even when
the particular experience provides grounds for thinking that conditions are not
normal and that the object in question is not red.

If experience has its propositional content under a mode other than that of
affirmation, then there is little reason to take the content to be the rational contribution of experience. Plainly, the mere fact that a conceptual item (e.g., a supposition) has a particular propositional content tells us little about its rational
contribution. For all we know, the item may make no rational contribution at all (it
may just be a passing thought), or its contribution might be something quite distinct
from the content.

29. Note that Sellars's account is not fundamentally different from that of Davidson, who assigns only a causal role to experience. Recall Davidson's claim from
"A Coherence Theory of Truth and Knowledge" cited in chapter 1: "No doubt
meaning and knowledge depend on experience, and experience ultimately on
sensation. But this is the 'depend' of causality, not of evidence or justification"
(p. 146). Compare this with what Sellars writes in "Phenomenalism": "The direct
perception of physical objects is mediated by the occurrence of sense impressions
which latter are, in themselves, thoroughly non-cognitive. . . . this mediation is
causal rather than epistemic" (pp. 90–91).

Recall also the following famous remark of Sellars: "For empirical knowledge,
like its sophisticated extension, science, is rational, not because it has a *foundation* but
because it is a self-correcting enterprise which can put *any* claim in jeopardy,
though not *all* at once" (§38). It is remarkable that Sellars explains the rationality of
empirical knowledge without any mention of the contribution of experience.
(I myself think that the mere fact that an enterprise is "self-correcting" does not
make it rational, for the starting point of the enterprise, as well as the methods of
correction, may be irrational.)

Brandom has claimed that "one of the major tasks of the whole essay [*EPM*] is to dismantle empiricism."[30]

In the second place, Sellars's account does not fit with the phenomenology of experience. Take an ordinary experience—say, the visual experience one has when one looks at a pile of red apples in a grocery store—and consider what its propositional content might be. We find ourselves confronted with a host of questions. Does the propositional content contain the individual apples as its constituents—which ones?—or only individual concepts of the apples, or perhaps only some general concepts? Does the content contain the concept of apple and, if so, which concept? The scientific one, or the perceiver's concept, or some other? What if these concepts are all erroneous and embody some fundamental misconceptions? Suppose the experiencing subject is a demented skeptic, one who is convinced of the sense-datum theory and is skeptical of the external world. What is the propositional content of his experience of the apples? Is it different from the experience of one who is a full believer in the commonsense view? More fundamentally, how do we tell what belongs to the propositional content of an experience considered in itself, isolated from all views? I must confess I am at a loss to answer these questions. I have enjoyed the experience of looking at piles of red apples on visits to grocery stores. On some occasions, I have contemplated what the propositional content of my experience might be. The experience itself was vivid, but the propositional content was hard to discern. It was dim, if not entirely absent.

I believe it is not the phenomenology of experience that leads philosophers to the idea of propositional content, but their desire to place experience in the conceptual realm. This desire in turn has its source in the legitimate idea that experience has a rational role to play in our cognitive lives. But, as I have already argued, one can acknowledge this rational role without placing experience in the conceptual realm—that is, without assigning any propositional content to it. Indeed, the idea of propositional content gets in the

30. "Study Guide," p. 168. There is disagreement among scholars about Sellars's intentions regarding empiricism. Brandom, Rorty, and Sosa read Sellars as rejecting empiricism. McDowell and Bruce Aune, on the other hand, read Sellars as aiming to reform empiricism. See Rorty, *Truth and Progress*, chapter 6; Sosa, "The Mythology of the Given"; McDowell, "Transcendental Empiricism"; and Aune, "Sellars, Wilfrid Stalker."

way of a proper understanding of the rational role of experience. There is in present-day philosophy a vigorous debate whether experience has any "nonconceptual" content. I wish there were an equally vigorous debate whether it has any conceptual content.[31]

Let us now turn to Sellarsian impressions. Where are these to be found in, or around, experience? Consider again the phenomenology of visual experience. (The points I am concerned to make hold also for other types of experience.) Visual experience supports what may be called "an identification question about a visual object." Typically, in a visual experience, one seems to apprehend some objects, and one can ask the question "what is that?" of any of these objects. For example, on a clear summer night, I can have a visual experience of a distant small reddish light, and I can wonder "what is that?" I may on reflection come to the conclusion that it is Antares, or that it is a light belonging to an airplane, or even that it is an illusion or a hallucination. The question "what is that?" when asked in this way in connection with a visual experience, I shall call a "visual-identification question" or, more briefly, an "identification question." The point to note is that experience can ground a "what is that?" question—it can render the question meaningful—even though the demonstrative in it fails to pick out any material or objective particular.[32] Moreover, an identification question can make perfect sense even though not everyone is in a position to grasp its sense. A sharp-sighted ranger may ask "what is that?" and the question may be lost on those of us with eyes that are untutored or myopic. In an extreme case, an identification question may make sense only to the one having the experience; others may have an insufficient fix on what is being asked.[33]

31. Let me stress that, as far as my principal claim is concerned—that the rational contribution of experience is not propositional in form—I can remain neutral on the issue of propositional or conceptual content. Even if an experience has a propositional content, the point I insist on is that this content is not its rational contribution.

32. I am not saying that in such a case the demonstrative picks out a nonmaterial or subjective particular—this path leads to philosophical error. I am only drawing attention to the fact that the identification question is meaningful. I am not attempting to explain the fact.

33. From the subjective viewpoint, the identification question is just as substantial and meaningful when it is directed to a rainbow or to a snake hallucinated in the river below as when directed to the waterfall above.

Now, in a typical visual experience, the self and the experience itself are not *within* the experience in the following sense: it is incorrect to answer a visual-identification question with "that is the experiencing self" or "that is the experience itself."[34] People, cats, and illusions are found within ordinary experiences; viruses, electrons, and hallucinations, within specialized experiences; and experienc*ings* within rare, if any, experiences. Sellarsian impressions, too, are not to be found within ordinary experiences: it is incorrect to answer identification questions for ordinary experiences with "that's a Sellarsian impression." Sellarsian impressions are located, if anywhere, in the complex processes leading up to, and perhaps constituting, the state of experienc*ing*. Note the contrast with sense-data: sense-data are not to be found in these processes; they are to be found (if anywhere) within experience itself. The sense-datum theorists arrive, through their logical and phenomenological reflections, at the conclusion that the strictly proper answer to an identification question is invariably "that's a sense-datum." Sense-data are intimately connected to the phenomenology of experience, to what it is like to have an experience; not so for Sellarsian impressions.[35]

The sense-datum theory—and, more generally, classical empiricism—is motivated by two genuine features of ordinary experience: its phenomenology and its rational power. Phenomenologically, in experience, one seems to be confronted with objects, and the rational power of experience seems to lie in the epistemic access it provides to these objects. The sense-datum theory tries to refine these commonsense ideas using the correct observation that there is no unmediated access to the external world. Thus, it arrives at the notion that objects one is confronted with in experience are special and subjective. Sellars's account of experience fails to do justice to both vital elements of experience, its phenomenology and its rational power. Hence, it cannot be an

34. Are there any visual experiences when such answers would be strictly correct? I look at a mirror and ask "what is that?" Is the answer "that's me" strictly correct only insofar as it is an abbreviation of "that's my image"?

35. It is hard not only to recover propositional contents and Sellarsian impressions from the phenomenology of experience but also to recover the phenomenology from the contents and impressions. How, e.g., can we explain the meaningfulness of identification questions if we have only propositional contents and Sellarsian impressions to work with?

objection to the sense-datum theory that the Sellarsian account of experience precludes it, for the account precludes much about ordinary experience that is genuine and legitimate.[36]

My principal complaint about Sellars's critique, however, does not concern his account of experience. It concerns the resources that the critique deploys. The critique rests on hefty philosophical ideas— ideas such as Methodological Behaviorism, the Priority of the Linguistic, and Psychological Nominalism. These ideas are powerful—a little too powerful. They can be used to call into question not only classical empiricism but the entire commonsense conception of the mind. (Indeed, Quine argued for a radically skeptical conclusion about mind and language starting from a position virtually identical to Sellars's Methodological Behaviorism.) Classical empiricism makes specific epistemological and semantical claims. Why not criticize it directly on epistemological and semantical grounds? Why invoke hefty assumptions about the nature of thought and experience, and about their relationship to language? Critics of classical empiricism sometimes aim to establish not only that it is false but also that the entire conception of the self it contains is absurd: that it is logically incoherent, or that it rests on a conceptual confusion or on a mis-understanding of the logic of our psychological vocabulary. Perhaps this explains why hefty philosophical guns are brought to bear on the classical account. But these guns are best put away; it is not necessary to destroy the account so completely. We can allow that the classical-empiricist conception of the self is logically coherent. All we need show is that the classical account is simply false: As a matter of fact, and as experience shows, our interactions with the world are mediated by our bodies; we have no mental pliers that enable a direct grasp of objects and universals. As a matter of semantical fact, the connections between our words (and thoughts) and the world are not effected solely by experience. And, as a matter of epistemological fact, the rational contribution of experience is not propositional in form. I have already argued a little for the epistemological claim. Let me turn now to the semantical one. In arguing for it, I shall stress yet again the critical importance of interdependence.

36. I do not find convincing Sellars's diagnosis of the error in classical empiri-cism, namely, that it confuses the aboutness of impressions with the aboutness of thoughts. One can be quite clear about *this* distinction and still find the classical picture compelling on the phenomenological and rational grounds just sketched.

5C. Remarks on Reference and Truth

When classical empiricists assert such things as "that orange sense-datum is oval" and "I am sensing a red sense-datum," what are they talking about? What objects are they referring to by singular terms such as 'that orange sense-datum'? What state are they denoting when they speak of "sensing a red sense-datum"? And what are the grounds of their assurance that their claims are true? In order to address these questions, it is necessary to first make some simple observations about the concepts of reference and truth.

To begin with, let us observe that we have great conceptual freedom as we go about exploring the world. We can think about surfaces, about points and lines, and about numbers. We have the freedom to introduce the line at infinity and points that lie on it. We conceptualize parts of the world as containing committees, organizations, and nations. We find it useful to count passengers and customers. Finally, in our philosophical moments, we find ourselves reflecting on "time-slices of persons," "the nonexistent fountain of youth," and "the arbitrary man." It is generally recognized that we have wide freedom in defining predicates. We can introduce vocabulary for, for example, "being green before 1 January 2100 and blue afterward," "being Michael Jackson and being bald," and "being either a prime number or the nose of a U.S. president." The predicates introduced may be philosophically revealing, they may be merely amusing, or they may be downright useless. Nonetheless, they are all *logically* legitimate. The freedom that we have with predicates extends to common nouns and singular terms. We exploit this freedom when we talk of points at infinity, of the U.S. government, of passengers, and of the arbitrary fat man in the doorway. There is nothing logically illegitimate in this talk. Any assessment of it must center on the functions that the talk is meant to serve. In the same way, there is nothing logically illegitimate in the empiricist talk of "that orange sense-datum" and of "sensing a red sense-datum." Nothing in their doctrines dictates that empiricists be especially constrained when exercising their conceptual freedom.

It must be stressed that our conceptual freedom is not merely *nominal* in character. This freedom is not merely the linguistic one to make up new names and predicates—or, more generally, to clothe our thought in a variety of different surface linguistic forms. It is not as if genuine conceptual constraints were to be found at the level of deep logical form, as if the legitimacy of our surface forms had to be earned by showing the legitimacy of their deep logical analyses—analyses that need to be recovered by some peculiar sort of logical excavation. There is no level of "the deep logical form." We can analyze our sentences in different ways, and there is no unique answer to the question of which of the analyses captures *the* deep logical form—at least, none that is independent of the functions that the analyses are meant to serve. Our interest may be to work up a simple set of rules that will generate a large swath of grammatical sentences of English. We may then find that a particular parsing of sentences is forced upon us. Our interest may instead be in rigorous and precise rules of logical inference in a fragment of special interest (e.g., mathematical language). We may find this interest best served by a different parsing of sentences. One of Gottlob Frege's great logical discoveries is precisely that inference rules for mathematical languages are most crisply stated using the devices of quantifiers and variables. The subject-predicate analysis of sentences, which looms large in traditional grammar, disappears entirely in Frege's logic.[37] For another example, certain purposes may be served best by treating "knowledge" and "necessity" as predicates, while some others might dictate that they be treated as sentence operators.[38] We do have linguistic freedom— we can introduce, for example, new names and predicates by definitions—but our conceptual freedom extends beyond it. Our talk of surfaces, points, nations, and passengers—and also of sense-data—is legitimate even if it is not eliminable via definitions (including contextual ones).

37. Traditional grammar treats the sentences 'Socrates is mortal' and 'every man is mortal' as having the same form. In particular, it takes 'Socrates' and 'every man' to belong to the same grammatical category. The Fregean analysis, in contrast, assigns to the two sentences radically different logical forms. It does not recognize 'every man' to be a genuine logical unit at all. The Fregean account is not the last word, however. Even when our interests are logical, it is possible to retain the traditional analysis, and some purposes may best be served by doing so. Richard Montague discovered an ingenious way of preserving the subject-predicate analysis of 'every man is mortal'. See his "Proper Treatment of Quantification in Ordinary English." For a more accessible account, see Richmond Thomason's "Introduction" in *Formal Philosophy*.

38. For a discussion of this example, see Belnap's and my *Revision Theory of Truth*, §6E. I have found Belnap's "Grammatical Propaedeutic" to be especially useful as an antidote to absolutism about logical form.

Nothing is more perplexing to a beginner in philosophy than a peculiar schizophrenia that philosophy seems to exhibit in matters of ontology. On the one hand, the beginner encounters a finicky puritanism: colors, odors, and sounds are deemed unreal; theoretical entities are viewed with suspicion; and doubts are expressed even about the reality of ordinary, familiar objects such as cups and saucers. The beginner naturally wonders what qualifications must be met before philosophy would allow something into the sacred realm of Being. On the other hand, the beginner encounters an unrestrained license: the present Queen of Britain is countenanced, of course, but so also are her time-slices; no suspicions are raised about the present King of France—he, too, is given a place in the realm of Being; and doubts about arbitrary numbers and arbitrary men are quashed. The beginner now naturally wonders whether any shady character is excluded from this slum of Being. Why this strange mixture of puritanism and licentiousness in questions of ontology?

The answer, I think, is that disparate concerns lead to these opposite tendencies. The second tendency issues from the concern to rebuff, as far as possible, a priori constraints on our conceptual freedom. Here we learn that a broad notion of object is, from the logical point of view, perfectly coherent. We can treat such terms as 'the King of France' and 'Vishnu', and even pronouns and variables, as genuine singular terms. Even in their deep logical grammar—if one believes in deep logical grammar—these expressions can be treated as denoting objects. Let us call objects in this broad sense *Meinongian* objects.[39] Let us allow that a term such as 'the King of France' has a denotation, and let us call this denotation the *Meinongian referent* of the term. The common-noun phrase 'time-slice of the Queen of Britain' may or may not be true of objects of the familiar sort, but it is true of some Meinongian objects; let us call these objects *Meinongian referents* of the phrase. The expressions 'that orange sense-datum' and 'state of sensing a

39. So named, of course, after Alexius Meinong (1853–1920), who argued for the broader notion of objects. The work of Kit Fine, Terence Parsons, Edward Zalta, and others has greatly clarified and extended the conception inaugurated by Meinong. See Fine's *Reasoning with Arbitrary Objects* and Parsons's *Nonexistent Objects*, and Zalta's *Intensional Logic*.

Note that ordinary objects count as Meinongian. So, e.g., Queen Elizabeth II is a Meinongian object also.

red sense-datum' are thus assured to have Meinongian referents. But let us not pause to figure out what precisely these might be.

We have noted our great conceptual freedom. We should now take notice of a correlative constraint: we have no freedom to make up the world. The world is what it is quite independently of us (at least for the most part; our influence on the world at large is, fortunately, minuscule). We need to discover through judicious interactions with the world the objects that inhabit it, the properties that they have, and the relations that they bear to each other. It is this concern and the difficulties of addressing it adequately that result in the first tendency mentioned above: the finicky puritanism in ontology. Even die-hard Meinongians will recognize the necessity of a little constraint here, a little puritanism, for even the Meinongians will recognize that there is an important distinction between two categories of objects: those that constitute our actual contingent world and those that do not. Finicky puritanism is fundamentally concerned with gaining an inventory of the *actual* objects (and their properties and relations). As a step toward this goal, it is concerned with discovering how far objects can be denied actuality while conforming to the phenomena. Thus, the seemingly opposite tendencies in ontology: the puritans trying to eliminate even familiar objects from the realm of Actuality and the Meinongians trying to give even the shadiest of them a place in the realm of Being.[40] The constraints that result in the puritanical tendency and the freedom expressed in the Meinongian are both genuine. Both must be recognized by any account of our knowledge of the world. There would be no genuine object of knowledge without the constraint, and without the freedom, we would lack sufficient means of gaining it.

The mere logical coherence of a term assures us that there is a Meinongian referent for it. But logical coherence is insufficient to establish that the term has an actual referent. Reference construed as a relation between terms and Meinongian objects may be simple,

---

40. Let me make explicit my terminology. I am using 'actual' to mark out the objects, properties, and relations that constitute the world. Whether an object is actual depends, in general, on the nature of the world, not on our thoughts and decisions.

My use of 'Being' does not coincide with that of Meinong, who applied it only to existent and, to what he called, "subsistent" things—things such as numbers, universals, and propositions.

tidy, and even purely logical. But when it is construed as a relation between terms and actual objects, reference is complex, untidy, and substantive.[41] Consider, for example, our talk of passengers. Let us suppose that Fred takes a one-hour flight on United Airlines from Pittsburgh to Chicago on 1 January and takes a return flight a few days later on 4 January 2003. United counts him as two passengers: Passenger 568, say, on the first flight and Passenger 682 on the second. What are the referents of the terms 'Passenger 568' and 'Passenger 682'? Suppose we say that both terms refer to the man Fred. This implies that the statement

(1) Passenger 568 $\neq$ Passenger 682

is false and leads us to conclude that United Airlines is confused in its method of counting of passengers. Shall we say instead that the referents of the two terms are hour-long time-slices of Fred, one occurring on January 1, 2003, and the other a few days later? If we do this, we can judge (1) to be true and are thus not forced to attribute to United an absurd error. But we are slipping into a confused Meinongianism. We wish to understand the relationship of the two terms to *actual* objects; the invocation of Meinongian objects is therefore improper. When we think about logic and semantics, we seem to get confused about the simplest of things even when the relevant facts are in plain view.

In the present example, plainly, the truth and falsity of statements containing 'Passenger 568' and 'Passenger 682' are grounded in facts about Fred, not in facts about some manlike thing without an adolescence or a childhood. 'Passenger 568 checked in two bags' is true precisely because Fred checked in two bags on his first flight. 'Passenger 682 drank coffee on the plane' is true because Fred had coffee on his second flight. The terms 'Passenger 568' and

---

41. There is a significant movement in the philosophy of language, namely, *deflationism*, that denies that reference and truth are substantive notions. It regards these notions to be purely logical, fit to serve only specific logical functions (e.g., to express certain sorts of generality). For expositions of this point of view, see Dorothy Grover's *A Prosentential Theory of Truth*, Paul Horwich's *Truth*, Brandom's *Making it Explicit*, Scott Soames's *Understanding Truth*, Hartry Field's *Truth and the Absence of Fact*, and Hill's *Thought and World*. I do not wish to enter into a discussion of deflationism here. For my reservations about it, see my essay "A Critique of Deflationism." I discuss Hill's view, which I find to be in many ways attractive, in "Remarks on Christopher Hill's *Thought and World*."

'Passenger 682' plainly bear an important semantical relationship to Fred. But the relationship is not simple, and it differs from the relationship 'Fred' bears to Fred. The crucial difference is, of course, that the terms 'Passenger 568' and 'Passenger 682' carry a different principle of identity than that carried by 'Fred'. The difference can be captured, I think, by taking the key language-world relation between names and things to be a *relativized* notion of reference R. 'Passenger 568' bears R to Fred only during the course of his one-hour flight on New Year's Day, 'Passenger 682' bears R to Fred only during his flight a few days later, and 'Fred' bears R to Fred throughout Fred's existence.[42] It is now easy to see why the truth of, for example, 'Passenger 682 drank coffee on the plane' depends on Fred's behavior during his second flight. It is also easy to see how (1) can be assessed to be true: 'Passenger 568' and 'Passenger 682' never bear R to the same object.[43]

We should admit that the terms 'Passenger 568' and 'Passenger 682' can legitimately be viewed as referring to numerically distinct objects (and not to Fred) and, for certain semantical purposes, this viewpoint is fruitful. The shadowy character of the referents should not stand in the way of this recognition. Why allow the mathematician the entire transfinite hierarchy of sets—much of it entirely useless (and, it must be added, stunningly beautiful)—yet balk at a liberal Meinongian notion of object that is useful to the semanticist? Why should the semanticist's exercise of conceptual freedom raise our dander when the mathematician's exercise of the same freedom arouses only our admiration and wonder? We should be fair. We should recognize the Meinongian notion of object as coherent, legitimate, and useful. We should allow that the Meinongian referents of 'Passenger 568' and 'Passenger 682' are numerically distinct. The only point to insist on is that Meinongian reference is not the only semantical relation of interest. Our two terms bear an important semantical relation to an actual entity, Fred,

42. Note that, in the present proposal, reference is relativized to time along two dimensions. One dimension is governed by the principle of application of a term; thus, the singular term 'the passenger that Martha is serving' can pick out the different passengers whom Martha serves at different times. The second dimension, which is our present concern, is governed by the principle of identity.

43. I tried to implement a semantics based on the idea just sketched in my *Logic of Common Nouns*. I should note that I was concerned in that book primarily with modal contexts and with representing "transworld" principles of identity.

and it is this relation that is of particular interest to us at present. This semantical relation is not as simple and tidy as Meinongian reference. It does not relate to truth in a simple, straightforward way—as we have seen with example (1)—but it is real and actual.

Language-world relationships—I mean, here and below, the semantical relationships between expressions and *actual* objects, properties, and states of affairs—cannot be read off from logical form, no matter how "deep." The fact that an expression is a singular term does not imply that it refers to an actual object. Even if we add that the expression is useful and that it yields truths, still it does not follow that the expression refers to an actual object. We utter 'the U.S. government reduced taxes in 2003' and we speak the truth. There are various goings-on in the world—the actions of the president, the members of congress, and others—in virtue of which our statement is true. The structure of the fact that makes the statement true cannot be recovered through any meditation on the meaning of the statement, no matter how deep or prolonged the meditation. The fact that makes 'the U.S. government reduced taxes in 2003' true may not contain any constituent corresponding to 'the U.S. government'. And this is entirely consistent with the idea that 'the U.S. government' is a genuine singular term. Even if we assume that there is a well-defined totality of inferences that must be accounted for in a semantic analysis of language, and even if we assume that the semantic analysis will result in an assignment of unique logical forms to expressions ("deep forms")—I myself am skeptical about both antecedents—still, we should not assume that language-world relationships can be read off from the resulting logical forms.

My aim in this example, I should stress, is not to lend support to individualism in the philosophy of social sciences.[44] For all I care, perhaps those philosophers are correct who take social wholes—nations, governments, and the like—to be fundamentally real and treat individuals as secondary constructs or fictions. The point I am concerned to make is that this issue cannot be settled by a semantic analysis of our talk about nations, governments, and the like. The semantic analysis of language (including one that appeals to a general notion of object) is a legitimate enterprise. So also is the

---

44. Nor, in the previous example, is it to urge "personism" in the philosophy of transportation!

enumeration of the constituents of the actual world (henceforth, I shall reserve the name 'ontology' for this latter enterprise). But the two are distinct. Ontology bears no closer relationship to semantics than it does to, say, economics. The pronouncements of semantics do not reveal the world more perspicuously than do those of the other sciences.

The close linking of ontology to semantics is detrimental to both disciplines. It is detrimental to ontology because the linkage burdens it with a proliferation of entities. This encourages false pictures (e.g., "the mind grasping universals") and bad questions (e.g., "what is the relationship between the causal powers of passengers and persons?").[45] The linkage is detrimental to semantics because it burdens the subject with alien concerns. Semantics is a specialized discipline with its particular goals (e.g., to account for logical consequence). It is no more concerned with a "synoptic view of the world" or with the metaphysical distinction between appearance and reality than is any other specialized science.[46] Any specialized science that is burdened with metaphysical concerns would be hamstrung, and semantics is no exception.

To summarize, the principal conclusions so far are these: (i) We have considerable conceptual freedom. We can talk about sets, passengers, and nations. And this talk is legitimate even if it is irreducible. (ii) We have no freedom to make up the world. The products of our conceptual activity are not necessarily actual.

45. Wittgenstein says in *The Blue and Brown Books* that "one of the great sources of philosophical bewilderment" is that "a substantive makes us look for a thing that corresponds to it" (p. 1).

46. Just as there is the metaphysical doctrine of physicalism, which makes physics the primary science and accords it authority in matters of ontology, there is a parallel metaphysical doctrine that makes semantics the primary science. If a broad Meinongianism yields the best semantics, then, according to this metaphysical doctrine, Meinongian objects are actual. I think that this metaphysical doctrine is not very attractive, and that the little attractiveness it has stems from a false syntactic conception of our rational activity. On this conception, our rational exploration of the world results in the acceptance of a set of *sentences*, and we read off the ontology by a semantic analysis of this set. (See the discussion of Quine in §2E.) If this way of thinking were correct, then semantics would indeed be the first science. But it is not correct. It makes little sense to ask whether our acceptance of some sentences is rational when those sentences are uninterpreted. Our acceptance of propositions, accounts, and views can be assessed for rationality, but not our acceptance of sentences that are stripped of meaning and interpretation.

Our terms for sets, passengers, and nations may be assured of having Meinongian referents, but they are not assured of having actual referents. (iii) The relationships that obtain between language and world cannot be read off from logical form. These relationships can be complex and obscure while the logical forms are simple and clear. Applied to the classical-empiricist talk of sense-data, these conclusions suggest that the empiricist talk may be legitimate. It may even be that an assertion such as "that orange sense-datum is oval" is both true and contains a genuine occurrence of the expression "that orange sense-datum." Still, this does not establish that the semantical links of the sense-datum vocabulary to the world are tidy, much less that they are privileged.

BUT ARE THE SENSE-DATUM PERCEPTUAL JUDGMENTS true? When experience prompts sense-datum theorists to make an assertion such as "that orange sense-datum is oval," what is the content of their assertion? In particular, how much of the broader sense-datum conception is in play in this content? Let me make the question a little clearer through some examples.

Consider, first, Joseph Camp's example of Fred and the ant colony.[47] Here, a man, Fred, is under the misconception that his ant colony has only one big ant, which he calls 'Charley'. In fact, the colony has two big ants—Ant A and Ant B—that look very similar. The two ants avoid each other and are rarely found together on the surface of the colony, so Fred's misconception is sustained. Suppose Fred says, as he and a visitor are looking down at the colony, "Charley is nibbling on a leaf." Suppose also that, as a matter of fact, it is Ant A that lies in Fred's and his visitor's field of vision. Now, what is the content of Fred's claim? Is it a part of the content that there is just one big ant in the colony? Or is the content simply that Ant A is nibbling on a leaf? Or is the content something different?

Imagine that an ancient astronomer inscribes in his diary "The Sun is in the constellation Capricorn today." Is the astronomer's inscription false because of his misconceptions about the constellations? Or is it a true record of the Sun's position relative to the Earth?

---

47. The example occurs in chapter 3 of Camp's wonderful book *Confusion.*

Imagine a girl who has inherited a primitive conception of person from her linguistic community. Say that she takes persons, including herself, to be spirits, and that she takes spirits to be parcels of a subtle and ethereal fluid that permeates bodies. What is the content of her assertion "I am in pain," made after a visit to the local medicine man? Is she speaking erroneously because of her misconceptions about the pain and the self? Or is she truly expressing how things are with her?

I think it best not to give straight answers to these questions. It is better to recognize that there are (at least) two different kinds of contents that can be associated with the assertions in the above examples. One kind of content—let's call it *absolute* content—includes within it the relevant elements of the subject's conceptions; it captures the inferences that are licensed by the subject's assertion. The ancient astronomer, for example, would infer from his report—and be entitled to infer—that if the Sun was not in Capricorn the previous week, then the Sun must have moved. We capture the validity of this inference by making the ancient conception of the constellations a part of the absolute content of the astronomer's assertion. For a similar reason, Fred's assertion has as a part of its absolute content that Charley is the unique big ant in the colony. The girl's assertion has as a part of its absolute content that she is a parcel of spirit and that pain is a particular kind of agitation of the spirit.

There is another kind of content—let's call it *effective* content—that is not as rich as absolute content and that captures the content in play in a speech situation. Suppose that the sole point of interest, practical or theoretical, in Fred's conversation with his visitor was the behavior of the big ant before them; the existence or nonexistence of the other big ant was of no importance. Under these circumstances, we may associate "Ant A is nibbling on a leaf" as the effective content of Fred's assertion. While the absolute content of Fred's assertion is false, its effective content is true. If we consider Fred's assertion not from an absolute, all-encompassing viewpoint, but from the narrow viewpoint of his conversation with his visitor and of what is at stake in this conversation, we should find Fred's assertion to be proper and right. Similarly, the ancient astronomer, despite his misconception, is right (in a sense) about the position of the Sun, and this rightness explains why, for example, he has sound advice to give the farmer about the best time to plant seeds. The girl has a misconception about the self and about pain. She is not a spirit, let alone a spirit agitated in a certain specific way. Nonetheless, the girl's assertion is a true expression. Her report communicates useful information and may enable her to gain relief.

Absolute content, as its name suggests, is not relative to speech situation—at least this is so when indexical elements are absent from the assertion. In contrast, effective content expressed by an assertion—even one without indexical elements—may vary from speech situation to speech situation. Fred's use of the sentence 'Charley is nibbling on a leaf' may have, in a different conversation, the effective content that Ant B is nibbling on a leaf. It can even happen that an assertion has absolute content but fails to have any effective content at all. The engine of language can run idle, failing to engage productively with the world.

The distinction between absolute and effective contents allows us to capture the double character of Fred's, the astronomer's, and the girl's assertions. There is something erroneous in all three assertions, and this is captured by the absolute contents. There is also something right in the assertions, and this is captured by the effective contents. A person—or a community—may be under a great misconception about the layout of reality, about the self, and about its situation in the world. Our forefathers were under such misconceptions; we as children were under such misconceptions; and it is not inconceivable that, though we have libraries full of science and philosophy, we are still under such misconceptions. The assertions made under a spell of misconception are in a sense erroneous—their absolute contents are false. Nonetheless, these assertions can succeed in doing significant cognitive and practical work—their effective contents may well be true. Perceptual judgments are particularly liable to display this sort of double character. Perception for us finite mortals is, typically, a taking in of reality through a veil of misconception.[48]

---

48. See my "Meaning and Misconceptions" for a little more on the distinction between absolute and effective content. For a different perspective on language use under misconception, see Camp's *Confusion*. Essays 6 and 7 in Field's *Truth and the Absence of Fact* contain an important early treatment of the phenomenon. See also lecture 4 in Bas C. van Fraassen's *Empirical Stance*. My own thinking has been greatly influenced by discussions with Mark Wilson. Wilson's book *Wandering Significance* is a rich source of example and theoretical reflection. See also his "Predicate Meets Property" and "Inference and Correlational Truth."

Returning to the original example, "that orange sense-datum is oval," we can grant that its effective content is indeed likely true. A person making this assertion is genuinely expressing a fact, perhaps about himself, or about the world outside, or both. We can also grant that some Meinongian object is picked out by the expression 'that orange sense-datum' and that this object is oval. Still, to grant all this is not to grant that the absolute content of the assertion is true. The absolute content may be false. The sense-datum conception that gives life to the assertion may be all wrong. But is it all wrong? Don't we have in experience a direct awareness of certain actual objects, properties, and relations? And isn't this awareness fundamental to semantics? I now address these questions.

5D. The Significance of Direct Awareness

Philosophers, even those as sensitive to skeptical argumentation as Berkeley and Russell, find the phenomenon of direct awareness so evident that they feel little need to argue for it. Russell explains "direct awareness" briefly in the course of introducing his notion of acquaintance: "We shall say that we have *acquaintance* with anything of which we are directly aware, without the intermediary of any process of inference or any knowledge of truths."[49] And he hurries on to the task of enumerating the objects of acquaintance. Russell's manner of proceeding here is reminiscent of Berkeley's, whose Hylas readily accepts that "in truth the senses perceive nothing which they do not perceive immediately: for they make no inferences," and then debates with Philonous what objects are "immediately perceived."[50] These astute philosophers are not talking about nothing when they speak of "direct awareness" or "immediate perception." The phenomenon of direct awareness is definitely real, and it is of the utmost psychological importance. But it does not have, I want to argue, the epistemological or semantical significance that has been assigned to it. It is not a source of unmediated justification or of privileged semantical links.

Let me begin with the positive: the existence and importance of the *ordinary* phenomenon of direct awareness. (A few paragraphs

---

49. Russell, *Problems of Philosophy*, p. 46.
50. See the first dialogue in Berkeley's *Three Dialogues*. The citation is from pp. 174–75 in the Luce and Jessop edition (p. 62 in the Dancy edition).

further below, I shall turn to the classical-empiricist conception of direct awareness.) Consider the experience of driving a car in a city. The following sort of experience is not untypical for me: I am driving along, I see the traffic light ahead change to red, I want to stop the car, I push on the brake, and the car comes to a stop. In this experience, there seems to be—and there is—a direct awareness of the traffic light and of its change of color. I go through no conscious inferences—or, I suspect, any unconscious ones—to achieve this awareness. The traffic light is transparently and immediately present before me. It feels as if I have a direct connection with it: no intermediaries seem to intrude in my perceptual interaction with the light, even though the interaction is, of course, causally mediated by a complex of factors. The situation with action is parallel. My act of pushing down on the brake is direct also. I want to push the brake down, and right off, I do it: I am focused on the road and have no time to dwell on the muscles in my leg or on the movement of my foot. I do not push down on the brake by performing a different act—as, for example, I might turn the wipers on by looking for and then turning the right knob. Quite the contrary: the pushing on the brake is—and feels to be—as direct as the act of moving my thumb. The brake, and even the car itself, can seem to become an extension of one's body—even of oneself. "I should slow down," I can think, and I slow down: there is no thought of the brake or of the car. Perception and action involve highly complex processes, but it is of their phenomenological essence to telescope the complexity.

Direct awareness, as well as direct action, is affected by training and learning. An adult sees at a glance that the thrown die shows a five, but the young child has to count to gain the same awareness. The action of pushing down on the brake is simple and direct for a mature driver. But a beginner may well need to remind himself of the position of the brake, or there is risk he will push the accelerator instead. Even highly complex activities can be telescoped into direct perceptions and actions. A doctor may be able to tell at a glance that the patient is likely suffering from jaundice. The drive to work may, for a long-time commuter, become a simple and direct action. She may attend more to the news on the radio than to the road ahead, yet her driving may be flawless. It is as if, having delegated some routine task to a subpersonal assistant within, one can remain oblivious to the humdrum details of executing it.

There is a certain flexibility to direct perception and action. I may be directly aware of the coaster at one instant and then can decide to focus on its surface. I can even enter into a Cartesian meditation and reflect to myself, "Well, the surface is right there, but perhaps the object is not a coaster but a papier mâché copy, or perhaps the entire thing is a hallucination." At one moment, the act of typing my thoughts can feel—and be—direct, but at another, I can start attending to the movements of my fingers and can type the words deliberately (and laboriously) letter by l-e-t-t-e-r. Before, my mind was centered on my subject matter and on typing out my thoughts. Later, it was focused on the movement of the fingers, and it became harder to keep the subject in view.[51]

Direct awareness can move outward—to distant buildings, stars, and beyond—and it can shrink inward—to one's body, one's sensations and feelings, and to how-things-seem-to-one-right-now. This flexibility is not merely curious and accidental. It is vital to our lives. Conscious awareness is a highly valuable resource, and our well-being requires that it be allocated wisely. There is a subtle interplay between things that can be left, in a particular context, to subpersonal routines and those that need to be before our consciousness. Much, though not all, of this interplay occurs without our conscious intervention.

Direct awareness is not without semantical and epistemological significance. We can and do name things (and universals) that are directly apprehended. And acts of perceptual judgment are as much guided by direct awareness as, for example, acts of threading needles. Further, we can appeal to direct awareness to justify our claims. I tell a friend that the Penguins won, and I am called to provide justification for my incredible claim. I can answer, "I was there, I saw them win."

The phenomenology of direct awareness is striking. One seems to take in a bit of reality-as-it-is. One opens one's eyes and reality seems to flood in. The objects and facts appear to be right there before us to behold, to name, and (on occasion) to manipulate. The self seems to be transparent in direct awareness: reality seems to enter one's consciousness unobstructed and unsullied.

---

51. Direct action presupposes direct perception. There could not be a direct act of pushing the brake unless there were a direct perception of the brake. The flexibility of direct action requires, therefore, the flexibility of direct perception. And the practical importance of the former translates into that of the latter.

Sometimes—for instance, in the course of an intense practical activity—the transparency is so great that one loses all sense of the self ("one seems to become one with reality"). This phenomenological character of direct awareness—transparent self and vividly present reality—is undoubtedly of the greatest practical value. But in philosophy, it is a powerful source of illusion and error. It tempts us to overly simple semantical and epistemological pictures. It tempts us to think that the act of direct awareness *by itself* brings us into a cognitive relationship with the world. However, just as there is nothing *causally* simple about direct awareness, though it seems to be so; similarly, there is nothing semantically or epistemologically simple about it, though there is a natural temptation to take it to be so. The immediacy and transparency of direct awareness are a *mere* seeming, one of great practical value but of no semantical or epistemological significance whatsoever.

Consider the car example again: I saw the traffic light change to red, I pushed on the brake, and the car came to a stop. My pushing on the brake was immediate and direct; it was not mediated by any other consciously performed acts. However, though my act was direct, there was no direct connection between my decision to push the brake and the movement of the brake. My decision did not bring about the movement by magic. Far from it: my direct act was possible only because a highly complex structure was in place. In the context of this structure, my decision to push the brake translated into the direct action of pushing the brake. If there is any magic here, it is to be found in the subtlety with which the resources of consciousness are allocated, in how irrelevant complexity is kept out of view.

The semantical and epistemological situations are parallel. In my experience, the traffic light was vividly before me. It was easy for me to give it a name if I wished to do so, and I was entitled to make various perceptual judgments about it (e.g., "it is red"). But the simplicity with which the naming ceremony is performed, and the entitlement gained, is not indicative of the nature of the underlying mechanisms. (Compare: It is easy for me to stop the car even on an icy road. Yet the underlying mechanism that makes this easy is complex—and *has* to be complex.) Experience does not have the capacity to establish, as if by some mental magic, a connection between a name and an object. The connection is made possible by certain facts (e.g., that there indeed was a traffic light before me) and by the complex linguistic and conceptual structure that is already in place (e.g., that I use names in a particular way and that I have the concept of traffic light). The semantical connection established in an ordinary naming ceremony depends, in part, on the semantical linkages of some preexisting terms—for example, that of 'traffic light'. And these latter depend in turn on the linkages of yet other expressions. Hence, ordinary terms do not receive an unmediated semantic foundation in experience.

The situation with justification is similar. My perceptual judgment "the light is red" was justified but only because a rich epistemological structure was in place. In particular, I had a justified view about traffic lights, about the normal functioning of my eyes, and other such things. In the context of such a view, the experience entitled me to the judgment that the traffic light was red. Outside of such a context, there is no entitlement.[52]

Skeptical arguments prove conclusively that the phenomenological transparency of experience has no epistemic or semantical force: it yields no unmediated entitlement to ordinary judgments of perception, and it establishes no privileged semantic links for ordinary terms. Phenomenologically, I can be in exactly the same situation as I was when I saw the red traffic light. Yet the judgment "the light is red" may not be justified, and the naming ceremony may be impossible. This would be so if, for instance, I had knowledge that I was suffering from a certain sort of illusion. Hence, neither the semantical linkage nor the justification issues solely from the experience. Some other factors must also be in play. (Compare: there cannot be a direct link between the decision to push the brake and the movement of the brake, for the former may occur without the latter, e.g., when the leg is paralyzed.)

THE CLASSICAL EMPIRICISTS ARE WELL AWARE, OF COURSE, that the justification of *ordinary* perceptual judgments is not

---

52. Wittgenstein stressed the importance of background factors in his discussion of the mental. In §6 of part I of *Philosophical Investigations*, where he remarks on the ostensive teaching of words, Wittgenstein offers the following comparison:

"I set the brake up by connecting up rod and lever."—Yes, given the whole of the rest of the mechanism. Only in conjunction with that is it a brake-lever, and separated from its support it is not even a lever; it may be anything, or nothing.

In philosophy, a neglect of "the rest of the mechanism" tempts us to imbue the mental with magical powers.

unmediated and that the semantical links of our *ordinary* terms are not privileged. The very point of their invocation of sense-data (and the like) rests on this recognition. What is foundational in epistemology and semantics, according to the classical empiricists, is not the direct awareness of physical objects but the direct awareness of sense-data. It is here that they claim to gain unmediated justification and privileged semantical links. Let us now turn to this claim—the core claim of classical empiricism.

To begin with, we should allow that sense-data are logically legitimate (§5C). Classical empiricists are within their "logical rights" when they introduce the sense-datum vocabulary. Furthermore, their explanations are clear enough for us to report our experiences using this vocabulary (notwithstanding some residual worries about how precisely to report the experience of the speckled hen). It may even be that the vocabulary is especially useful for some purposes. (It seems to be fairly effective for saying in a compact and noncommittal way how things seem to one.) We should allow, furthermore, that the sense-datum conception is coherent: it is not impossible that we are minds that have a primitive direct apprehension of private sense-data. A world such as this is weird, I think, but it is not conceptually impossible.

So much for the concessions. Consider now the core claim in the context of an example. I have a red ball near me, I look at it, and I have a familiar sort of experience—say, *E*. The classical empiricist tells me: "The red and round object so vividly before you in your experience is really a fleeting sense-datum. (Strictly speaking, you commit an error—though an excusable one—in taking the object to be a ball.) Your experience is fully transparent with respect to the sense-datum and its apprehended properties: you can establish privileged semantical links here, and you gain unmediated justification." I understand the empiricist well enough, and I perform an "inner ostension" and name the sense-datum 'Sandy'. Further, I declare (internally) my intention to use 'red' and 'round' for the two properties that are so vividly before me. My terms 'Sandy', 'red', and 'round' have, according to the classical empiricist, privileged semantical links, and my judgment that Sandy is red and round has immediate epistemic justification.

Is it true, though, that the semantical relationship of 'Sandy' to the world is privileged, that it is assured of having a denotation

simply in virtue of my experience?[53] The Meinongian referent of
'Sandy' (see §5C), we can allow, is fixed by my experience and by
my inner acts of pointing and naming. But that is not what our
question is about. We are asking about the semantical relationship
of 'Sandy' to *existent* objects, not nonexistent Meinongian objects.
Can this relationship be read off the character of my experience
(and my "inner" naming ceremony)? Does my experience guarantee that 'Sandy' denotes an actual object in the world?

If things are as the classical empiricist paints them to be, then the
semantical relationship of 'Sandy' to the world is tidy: it denotes
an actual object, and that object is a sense-datum. But there are
other possibilities. I might be so constituted that I have a primitive
direct-awareness of color expanses in public space. That red and
round thing so vividly before me in my experience E could, as far
as the phenomenological character of E is concerned, be a color
expanse in public space. The phenomenological character of my
experience is as compatible with this idea as it is with the one
favored by the classical empiricist. I cannot read off from my experience that the object before me is fleeting, or mind dependent,
or private. For all that I can tell, it may be long enduring, mind
independent, and graspable by many.

If the scenario just imagined obtains—call it the "color-
expanse" scenario—then the semantical relationship of 'Sandy' to the
world is not simple and tidy. The color expanse I apprehend—say,
O—is not the denotation of 'Sandy' in the way that, for example,
Fred is the denotation of 'Fred'. We must either rule that 'Sandy' is
a vacuous name and does not denote anything actual, or more
charitably, we may recognize that there is an important semantical
relationship between 'Sandy' and O. This relationship would be
somewhat like the one we saw in the Passenger example above:
'Sandy' picks out O in the way that 'Passenger 568' picks out a
particular person and, like the latter, 'Sandy' carries a deviant
principle of identity. This option has the virtue that it does not let
an erroneous conception drain all truth from simple perceptual
judgments containing the concept "Sandy." (If 'Sandy' is regarded
as a vacuous name, then these judgments have to be ruled false or

---

53. Since classical empiricists will grant that the semantical links of spoken and
written words are mediated, let us take 'Sandy' to be a thought-token in my mind.
And let us imagine further that the token occurs during the course of my experience.

without truth-value.) In any case, whatever option we follow, 'Sandy' fails to have a privileged semantical link to the world.

The color-expanse scenario is not the only possibility compatible with my experience *E*. Here are some others. (i) I have a primitive direct-awareness of certain physical objects: I am so constituted that I have a capacity to take in directly, without distortion and causal intermediaries, the color and shape of certain physical objects. So in my experience *E*, I am directly apprehending a ball and its color and shape. (ii) I acquire a primitive direct-awareness of some properties of physical objects, but only under certain particular conditions (under other conditions, I am susceptible to error and illusion). These conditions do, as a matter of fact, obtain for *E*, and I am directly apprehending a ball in *E*. Note that under this and the previous scenarios (i), a charitable interpretation of 'Sandy' would require an even more complex relationship of perceptual judgments to the world than that under the color-expanse scenario. (iii) I have a direct awareness of color expanses and their shapes but not of their positions. My present experience is actually of two different semicircular color expanses that I misperceive to be touching each other along their bases. Again, phenomenologically, the experience would be no different. Under the charitable interpretation, the semantical relationship of 'Sandy' to the world is perhaps like that of a term such as 'Passenger 123' to two different persons whom the airline mistakenly regards as one passenger. . . . There are other possibilities; let these suffice for now.[54]

The situation is the same with general terms such as 'red' and 'round'. The sense-datum theory sketches one metaphysical possibility: perhaps these terms denote attributes of sense-data. But the character of my experience is compatible with other possibilities. Perhaps these are attributes of color expanses, perhaps of physical objects, perhaps shape is an attribute of physical objects but not color, and so on.[55] It may even be that I am not directly aware of any universals in my experience, that the objects of my direct

<hr />

54. I have deliberately confined myself to the restricted range of possibilities in which 'direct awareness' picks out a simple and primitive relation in the world. More interesting and more realistic possibilities exist in which this is not so.

55. More realistically, perhaps these are confused concepts that pick out more than one property. See Camp's *Confusion* and Wilson's *Wandering Significance*.

awareness are all particulars. When I introduce the terms 'red' and 'round' through inner ostensions, the denotations of the terms are fixed by something extrinsic to the objects of my direct awareness—for example, by objective similarities in nature or by what I *regard* as the instantiations of the same universal.

It may be suggested that privileged semantical links are established not between terms and the *objects* of direct awareness (and their properties and relations) but between terms and *states* of direct awareness (and their properties and relations). When I had the visual experience of the red ball, the suggestion goes, I am in a position to establish privileged semantical links between terms and my state of experiencing and its characteristics (e.g., "being a state of experiencing red"). However: (i) The suggestion is phenomenologically implausible. In visual experiences, for instance, we are not presented with our states of experiencing or with their intrinsic characteristics. (ii) The phenomenology of experience leaves the nature of these states as wide open as it does the objects of experience. The experiencing may be a primitive relation that obtains between a Cartesian mind and a fleeting sense-datum; or it may be a relation between a self and a color-expanse; or, perhaps, it might even be a brain state. We certainly are in a privileged position with respect to our mental states. But this privilege does not amount to transparent knowledge. The nature of our mental states is as much open to empirical discovery as is the nature of the external world.

The general point is that no experience, taken in isolation, reveals to us our nature and our capacities. Even if we allow ourselves an occult power of "direct apprehension," the character of experience fails to fix the entities and states that can be directly apprehended. The same experience remains "factorizable" into different world-self combinations (§1B). The idea of a transparent self directly apprehending objects, properties, and facts gets around the relativity of perception, but it does not get around the multiple-factorizability of experience. Sense-data, for instance, are so conceived that they are immune to relativity: they are what they appear to be, and the appearance-reality distinction collapses for them. Striking though this feature is, it does not establish the sense-datum conception to be the unique factorization of experience (even granting a transparent self). This is the principal reason why sense-data are of no help in gaining privileged semantical links. The status of the sense-datum vocabulary is no different from that of ordinary vocabulary. The semantical linkages of sense-datum terms are also dependent on contingent features of the world and on antecedent semantical linkages of other terms.

IT IS A THEORETICAL CONCEPTION, NOT THE PHENOMENOLOGY of experience, that leads one to the idea of privileged semantical links. One begins to think, under the influence of a foundationalist picture, that if our language is to have content, experience *must* enable us to set up privileged semantical links. But the picture is dispensable and indeed erroneous. Just as we can understand how our beliefs can be reasonable even though experience provides no unmediated justification, similarly, we can understand how our language can have content even though experience provides no privileged semantical links. Why does 'Tomato A' refer, in Fred's idiolect, to *that* particular tomato? The answer can be straightforward: because Fred was looking at that tomato when he introduced the name, and he wanted to call the tomato before him 'Tomato A'. The linkage of the name to object depends not just on Fred's experience but also on parts of Fred's view (e.g., his belief that there was a tomato before him) and on contingent features of the world (e.g., that Fred was not hallucinating a tomato). We can understand the connection of name to object without needing to invoke the idea of privileged semantical link. Experience makes a critical contribution to content, as it does to rationality. But this contribution does not take the form of making available semantical links that are privileged.

It is the idea of privileged vocabulary that motivates the philosophical fiction of deep logical form. It suggests that philosophical reflection on meaning allows us to peer through a thicket of linguistic convention and stipulation to discern the truth-conditions for our sentences. I am arguing that there is no privileged vocabulary—not even 'I' is privileged—and thus there is no deep logical form. The connections of our words to the world depend on experience, on view and, of course, on contingent features of the world. A particular vocabulary may have a tidy semantics under one set of worldly circumstances but may fail to do so under a different set. No vocabulary is guaranteed to have a tidy semantics by experience. No vocabulary has a privileged status.

Classical empiricists, remaining unswayed, may offer the following argument to buttress their viewpoint: "The meaning stipulations governing sense-datum vocabulary guarantee that the sense-datum perceptual judgments are bound to be true. These stipulations tie the truth of a judgment such as 'there is a red and round sense-datum' solely to the subjective character of an experience. Hence, if experience is of the right subjective sort, then the judgment must be true, and one must indeed be aware of a red and round sense-datum. The subjective character of experience thus guarantees the existence of sense-data and one's awareness of them."

This argument confuses things that we have already distinguished. We can certainly introduce sense-datum vocabulary in the manner suggested by the classical empiricists; we have the requisite linguistic and conceptual freedom. We can stipulate—better, implement—the rule that 'that is a red sense-datum' is assertible in the context of a certain set of experiences (and certain internal intentions concerning 'that'), that 'that is a green sense-datum' is assertible in the context of a different set of experiences, and so on. Once all this is done, I am entitled to assert 'there is a red and round sense-datum' when, for example, I am having the experience E mentioned above. Furthermore, there are senses in which the assertion is true. But these are senses in which the phrase 'there is' has no ontological force: the truth of the assertion does not establish the actuality of sense-data. For example: (i) The assertion may be true in the sense that it has a true effective content. The assertion may be practically efficacious in certain contexts. However, no ontological conclusions about sense-data are warranted by truth in this sense. (ii) It may be true in a correspondence sense. There may indeed be a Meinongian object that is a sense-datum and that is also red and round. But this sort of correspondence is cheap; it does no ontological work. (iii) The assertion may be true in the sense of being right, of being warranted by experience and meaning. But now the truth of 'there is a red and round sense-datum' is tied only to the subjective character of experience, and this character does not force a particular factorization of experience. For example, as we have seen, it does not exclude the possibility that the object of my direct awareness is in actuality a color expanse in public space. Hence, truth in this sense also fails to yield the ontological conclusion desired by the classical empiricists.

We have freedom in stipulating meanings. We have freedom in stipulating conditions of correct assertion. But we have no right to draw ontological conclusions from the logical forms of these assertions. We have no right to insist that language-world relations must be tidy. In fact, our linguistic and conceptual freedom is possible only because our language and thought bear a flexible relationship to the world. The structure of fact bears only a contingent relationship to—and may be quite different from—the structure of sentence or thought. To insist on rigid language-world relationships in the context of conceptual freedom is to insist that we are free to make up the world. This is absurd, though I suppose not so absurd as to preclude some philosophers from embracing it as their own cherished view.

The truth of the sense-datum conception, then, cannot be read off experience. Further, it cannot be derived from the meaning stipulations governing the sense-datum vocabulary. The sense-datum conception has, in short, no special claim to truth. It is one among many possible conceptions of the self and the world. Hence, sense-datum perceptual judgments have no special authority, and sense-datum vocabulary no special semantical privilege. It follows that sense-datum judgments no more belong to the given in experience than do ordinary judgments of perception.[56]

A STRIKING FEATURE OF THE *ORDINARY* PHENOMENON OF direct awareness is its flexibility. At one moment, I can be directly aware of the stick in my hand. At another moment, I can focus on the feelings in my hand. And at yet another, I can be directly aware only of the unseen ball behind the dresser that I am trying to roll up with the stick. I seem to touch the ball directly, and the stick seems to become an unperceived part of me. The flexibility of direct awareness is essential to our ability to efficiently manipulate things in the world and is of critical importance to our survival. But its nature is highly puzzling. How can the self be in such a seemingly transparent relationship with a shifting range of elements in the world? Indeed, what is this self that exhibits direct awareness, the self that is seemingly both diaphanous and protean? These are questions that only a subtle psychology can help us answer. Whatever the answers may be, it is plain that ordinary direct awareness, though fundamental in many ways, provides us neither with unmediated justification nor with privileged semantic links.

The principal motivation for the sense-datum conception is theoretical: to secure unmediated justification and privileged

---

56. Since the sense-datum conception has no special authority, absolute contents of sense-datum judgments have no special claim to truth. Notice that this fact creates no difficulty for our account of the given. *If* the sense-datum conception is correct, *then* the sense-datum judgments are (absolutely) true.

semantical links. It is for this sake that it transforms the ordinary
phenomenon of direct awareness into something metaphysical and
bizarre. The vital link between direct awareness and direct action is
broken. The objects of direct awareness are frozen and banished
to a private space, one that the self can peer into but not occupy
(somewhat like a transcendent god peering into an immanent reality). The protean self is congealed and shrunk into an extensionless
something. Even allowing this transformation, the sense-datum
conception fails to gain, I have argued, unmediated justification and
privileged semantical links. And the failure is not to be lamented.
We can understand the contribution of experience to knowledge,
and the semantical links between language and the world, while
dispensing entirely with the notions of "unmediated justification"
and "privileged semantical links."

Let me stress that the above argument against classical empiricism
is neutral on the nature of direct awareness (and, more generally, of
the mental). It makes no assumptions, for example, about the relative priority of thought and language or about the status of Methodological Behaviorism.

5E. The Problem of Solipsism

I can now address the problem solipsist views pose for convergence
(see §4C). I wish to grant the premiss on which the problem rests,
namely, that the pressure of ordinary experience will not transform
solipsism into our commonsense view of the world. But I wish
to insist that this fact does not threaten the convergence of the
revision process, and thus that it does not undermine empiricism. *Solipsism is not an admissible view*; it is not an acceptable
starting point of revision. Solipsism has this peculiar *rigidity*: irrespective of the series of experiences that impact it, the solipsist
view never shifts.[57] It does not evolve into an essentially different

---

57. More precisely, the notion of rigidity is defined thus:
A view v is *rigid* iff, for all sequences of possible experiences $\mathscr{E}$ and all
sequences of views $\mathcal{V}$ and all numbers n, if $\mathcal{V}$ is the revision sequence
generated by $\mathscr{E}$ with v as the initial view, then v is fundamentally equivalent
to $\mathcal{V}_n$.
See §4B for explanations of the notions "generation of a revision sequence" and
"fundamental equivalence."

view.[58] The world can be structured in all sorts of different ways. Things in the world, including the self, can have a variety of different natures and can bear a variety of different relationships to each other. But solipsism is blind to all these possibilities. It is unable to pick up clues from experience to adjust itself, to bring itself more into alignment with the way the world is. No matter what the structure of the world, no matter what the experience, solipsism remains the same rigid view. Solipsism is an unacceptable starting point of revision because it is insensitive. No rigid view is an admissible view.

Solipsism holds out the promise of a great dialectical advantage. A solipsist can rest assured that he cannot be refuted, that no appeal to logic or experience can budge him from his adopted stance. A solipsist, it seems, can be rational in his stubbornness. But it is important to distinguish here two kinds of rationality, one narrow and the other broad. Individuals are rational in the narrow sense iff they respect the constraints of logic and experience. That is, they ensure that their views conform to the principles of logic and evolve in the manner dictated by experience. Individuals are rational in the broad sense iff they respect the constraints not only of logic and experience but also of imagination. That is, they take full account of the available *possibilities* in forming their views. A lunatic can be rational in the narrow sense: he starts from a crazy and insensitive view, he pays attention to logic and experience to the last nitpicky detail, but he is never budged from his view. (Philosophy—alas!—is fertile ground for such lunatics.) We can try desperately to refute the lunatic, but we shall fail. A solipsist is a rational lunatic. The fact that we cannot bring him around to our view using only logic and experience casts no doubt on the rationality of our view. To talk a solipsist out of his view, we need to appeal to his imagination, to his sense—if he has it—of the different possible views and of different possible arrangements of things in the world. A solipsist can keep his dialectical advantage only as long as he feigns a dull imagination. Or else the solipsist must insist that, given his

---

58. Of course, the solipsist view does change in the sense that new sense-datum judgments are added to it. The present point is that the solipsist conception of the self and sense-data remains fixed, irrespective of experience.

experience, the world *has* to be the way he conceives it to be. However, as we have seen, this is not so. The phenomenology of his experience would be no different if the solipsist were a being that could directly sense orange ovals in public space. It would be no different, I venture to say, if he were a materially embodied being that stood in certain physical relations to certain kinds of physical objects. Perhaps the most compelling source of the solipsist illusion is the thought that experience could not serve as the ground of meaning and knowledge unless there were epistemically privileged direct awareness of something like sense-data. This thought, we have seen, is natural but erroneous.

Solipsism holds out the promise of absolute certainty. A Cartesian meditation on perceptual judgments gravitates toward a solipsist formulation of them (e.g., "I am sensing an oval sense-datum"). But the gain in certainty here is worthless, for it is obtained at the expense of content. If the solipsist perceptual judgments are understood absolutely (i.e., as implicating the solipsist conception), then, as we have seen, they are not certain at all; they are as susceptible to error as ordinary perceptual judgments. The solipsist judgments are certain only if they are read as having a thin content—content such as "I am now being so affected that my view entitles me to such-and-such sense-datum judgments." And again, we must so understand this content that it does not implicate any specific conception of the self and sense-data. In effect, under the weak reading, the very disposition to make a perceptual judgment can render the judgment correct.

The solipsist view is pathological. It puts the solipsist in a position somewhat like that of a paranoid who interprets everything he hears and sees in a way that confirms his paranoid fantasy. The solipsist, like the paranoid, is in an epistemological rut, one that makes it impossible for him to make ordinary rational transitions to different sorts of views. The existence of this kind of pathology is not surprising in light of the main thesis of this essay: the interdependence of views and perceptual judgments. If views affect perceptual judgments, it is understandable that there are views that tilt perceptual judgments in their favor or that render perceptual judgments so weak and ineffective that they make themselves immune to empirical refutation. We find similar phenomena in other cases of interdependence, for instance, with truth and circular definitions.[59] The existence of solipsism is not a problem for our theory; it is instead a powerful confirmation of it.

A solipsist enjoys a special sort of immunity, an immunity that philosophers often covet: an immunity from refutation. Traditional epistemology regards this immunity to be a virtue—indeed, a virtue of such import that solipsist perceptual judgments are seen as lying at the very foundations of knowledge. Thus arises the traditional project of showing how our knowledge of the external world could be built on these slender foundations. The present approach, in contrast, regards the immunity as a grave defect—a defect so great that solipsism deserves to be ruled out as a starting point of revision. This, as I have indicated, is an advantage. Solipsism does not deserve a place of honor at the foundations of knowledge; it deserves instead to be excluded and ignored.

In order to reject solipsism, we do not need to entertain such strong theses as that it is meaningless or that it violates some rule of language. We can reject solipsism on the basis of its dynamical behavior: the way solipsism evolves under the pressure of experience. The rejection of solipsism consists of two stages. First, the dynamical behavior entitles us to rule solipsism (and similar views)

---

59. The behavior of solipsism is somewhat reminiscent of the behavior of the Truth-Teller ("this very sentence is true"). The Truth-Teller, if it is assumed to be true, confirms itself; a person who insists that the Truth-Teller is true cannot be internally refuted. But the parallel here is not perfect, for the denial of the Truth-Teller is as arbitrary as its affirmation; not so for solipsism. A stronger parallel obtains with (*):

    (*) (*) is true and snow is black.

The denial of (*) is not arbitrary, yet its affirmation can be at best only pathological. Similarly, the denial of solipsism is not arbitrary, while its affirmation is pathological.

There are, of course, important differences between the behaviors of solipsism and (*). For instance, solipsism can—but (*) cannot—be both true and pathological. These differences issue from the fact that the interdependence responsible for the pathology of (*) is *definitional*, while that responsible for the pathology of solipsism is *epistemic*. The principles governing the concept of truth make the truth of (*) pathological under certain conditions (namely, those in which snow is black). In contrast, the truth and falsity of solipsism are not pathological. What is pathological is its epistemic behavior. These differences notwithstanding, important structural similarities remain between the behaviors of solipsism and (*).

as inadmissible. Second, the actual course of our experience entitles us to deny solipsism altogether, for all views that survive the revision process are contrary to solipsism.

IT DESERVES EMPHASIS THAT BY RULING SOLIPSISM TO BE inadmissible, we are not violating the empiricist maxim that reason has no a priori insight into the nature of reality; we are not declaring a priori that solipsism is false. We are placing restrictions only on the *starting points* of revision. These restrictions do not exclude solipsism from the revision process. They do not even exclude the possibility that the revision process converges to a solipsist view, for it may be that some extraordinary series of experiences renders it rational to accept a solipsist view—just as an extraordinary series of events might render it legitimate to overthrow a democratic constitution in favor of a despotism. The dangers in the two cases are parallel: in the one case, we are falling into an epistemological rut; in the other, into a political one. Nevertheless, the present point is that a restriction on starting points does not by itself eliminate these dangers. The possibility remains that a solipsist view occurs in some revision processes.

The present approach to the given in experience provides empiricists with a new resource. In their quest to show that the rationality of our view of the world is grounded in experience, the empiricists can appeal not only to the static logical relationships between perceptual judgments and views. They can appeal also to the dynamical properties of views. This additional resource, it seems to me, helps to make the debate between rationalism and empiricism less one-sided. In the traditional, propositional conception, with its thin given, rationalism wins the debate hands down. The propositional conception burdens the poor empiricist with the impossible task of building the external world from a thinned out given. The rationalist's task is easy: to show that a substantial contribution of reason is essential if we are to justify our knowledge of the world. It is no wonder that, in the modern period, rationalism is seen as the only viable alternative to skepticism; to be a coherent empiricist is to be a skeptic. The propositional given masks the virtues of empiricism and makes it a thoroughly unattractive idea.

In contrast, under the present approach, empiricism gains a fighting chance. The issue between empiricism and rationalism is now this. Rationalism insists—and empiricism denies—that convergence must fail unless the revision process is constrained by some substantial a priori truths.[60] In this debate, the burden on rationalism is to produce such truths. The burden on empiricism is to articulate a rich conception of admissible views—a conception that is a priori and yet is powerful enough to ensure convergence. This debate reflects the traditional disagreement between rationalism and empiricism: rationalism insists—and empiricism denies—that reason has the capacity to provide us with a substantial insight into the nature of the world and, furthermore, that this insight is essential if we are to justify our knowledge. But unlike the traditional debate, rationalism is not now assured of an easy victory. Empiricism, under the present account, has available not only a richer conception of experience; it has available a richer conception of reason. Empiricism can insist, as usual, that there is no a priori insight into the nature or structure of the world. But this insistence does not entail a commitment to the traditional empiricist idea that the contribution of reason is merely formal and logical. Reason has, in the present account, a substantial role to play: that of ruling on the admissibility of views. The admissibility of a view depends on the dynamical behavior of the view under possible streams of experience, and this is something that can in principle be determined a priori; it is the proper domain of reason. So, even though reason yields no substantial *truths*, it can make a substantial contribution to our knowledge.

Indeed, under the present approach, empiricism has an advantage over rationalism. Rationalism needs to introduce a spooky element to explain why the world accords with the substantive deliverances of reason: some *anamnesis*, or some imprinting of the mind by God, or some form of transcendental idealism. Empiricism, on the other hand, can assign a substantial role to reason and at the same time supply a relatively straightforward rationale for this role. The substantive role of reason is to institute admissibility requirements on views, and these requirements derive their motivation from the goals of inquiry. For instance, it is relatively easy to motivate the restriction that admissible views must be nonrigid: Our aim in inquiry is truth; we want our inquiry to yield a view

---

60. In the present framework, as in the traditional one, rationalism and empiricism agree on the nature of the given. Their debate is over the relationship between the given and the commonsense (or scientific) conception of the world.

that fits the world. Hence, we want the results of our inquiry to be sensitive to the way the world is and, in particular, to our inter-actions with the world. A rigid view is completely insensitive. It is like a watch that has stopped working. The watch may accidentally display the right time, but we would accept its reading only if we were led to it by the guidance of better watches. Similarly, a rigid view may be true, but we would accept it only if we were guided to it by better views.

Under the present approach, the burden on the empiricists, though lighter, remains considerable. The empiricists need (i) to formulate and justify specific requirements of admissibility on views and (ii) to maintain that views that meet these requirements converge under the force of experience. There is an interplay in the demands generated by the two parts of the empiricists' task. Weak requirements of admissibility make part (i) of the task easier and part (ii) correspondingly harder; stronger requirements have the opposite effect. Compare, for instance, the requirement that admissible views be nonrigid with the stronger requirement that they be *protean*, where a view is protean iff it is transformable into any other view under the pressure of experience.[61] The latter requirement makes part (ii) of the empiricist task much easier, but only at the expense of making part (i) harder. It is relatively easy to provide an a priori justification of the requirement that admissible views be nonrigid; it is not so easy to do so for the stronger requirement that they be protean. *If* protean views can be shown to exist, then there certainly are plausible reasons to require admissible views to be protean. The difficulty lies in establishing existence.

In conclusion, the present approach makes possible a nontrivial empiricism. We shall see in chapter 6 that the resulting empiricism is also attractive and defensible.

---

61. More precisely:
v is *protean* iff for every view v' there is a sequence of possible experiences $\mathscr{E}$ and a sequence of views $\mathcal{V}$ such that $\mathcal{V}$ is the revision sequence generated by $\mathscr{E}$ with v as the initial view and, for some number n, v' is fundamentally equivalent to $\mathscr{E}_n$.
A weaker, and more plausible, requirement can be obtained by restricting the range of the variable v' in the above definition (e.g., to views that are nonrigid).

SIX

A REFORMED EMPIRICISM

We have seen that classical empiricism, with its tendency toward skepticism and idealism, is an inevitable consequence of the idea that the rational contribution of experience is propositional in form (chapter 2). I have argued that we should abandon this idea in favor of the hypothetical given, the idea that the rational contribution of experience is hypothetical in character (chapter 4). I shall now argue that this change yields a distinctive and reformed empiricism, one that coheres with realism.

6A. Epistemic Justification and Skepticism

Empiricists have long insisted that our view of the world is, and should be, shaped by our experience. We need to probe and explore the world if we are to gain an accurate conception of it and of our place in it. Our experience yields a mass of particular perceptual judgments, yet these judgments can, with the aid of a genius or two, guide us to a substantial revision of our conception of ourselves and of the world. The changes in our view have been profound: we have, under the guidance of experience, radically changed our view of the shape of Earth, the structure of space and time, the nature of physical objects, and even of life itself. The empiricist injunction to probe and explore rests plainly on a realism about the external world; if the external world is taken to be merely a fiction of our minds, the injunction makes little sense. The world is there independently of us, and in the normal course of life, we encounter a small fragment of it. Only by increasing our exposure and by probing judiciously can we hope to form a just conception of it.

This simple picture of empiricism is familiar and worth preserving, but it faces a logical difficulty. The picture assumes that our ordinary judgments of perception (e.g., "this paper is blue" and "that star is red") are rational and thus authoritative. But what is the source of their rationality? If we say that the source is simply experience by itself, then we are committing ourselves to Naive Epistemological Realism: we are taking experience to provide us with an (epistemically) unmediated access to a bit of external reality. On the other hand, if we acknowledge that experience does not by itself make our judgments of perception rational, then we have to recognize the dependence of our perceptual judgments on our view. The resulting logical situation is troublesome: the rationality of our view depends upon the rationality of our perceptual judgments, but the rationality of our perceptual judgments in turn depends upon the rationality of our view. The fundamental problem for any empiricist theory of knowledge is to explain the rationality of our ordinary judgments of perception in the face of this interdependence.

Naive Epistemological Realism seems to receive support from the phenomenology of ordinary experience: it seems as if in experience we are sometimes directly presented with a bit of external reality (e.g., tables and traffic lights). But skeptical arguments, ancient and modern, show that this appearance is illusory. Classical empiricism is born from a recognition of the force of the skeptical arguments. It maintains that we have a direct awareness of a subjective realm (e.g., ideas, impressions, and sense-data), and it attempts to found the rationality of our ordinary perceptual judgments on this subjective awareness. But, unfortunately, it encounters formidable problems. Classical empiricists face a standing temptation to acquiesce in the idea that ordinary perceptual judgments are not rational (skepticism) or to attempt to reduce them to the subjective contents of experience (idealism).

A different response to the problem is that the rationality of the view is epistemologically prior—that is, the view, or a suitable fragment of it, can be established a priori. But to follow this approach—whether in a direct form or in a Kantian transcendental form—is to abandon empiricism.[1] In any case, the burden that the approach imposes is not one that our poor reason is fit to bear. A variant, neo-Kantian response follows Kant's footsteps only part of the way. It endows experience with a rich content but does not attempt an a priori justification of the underlying view.[2] This idea succeeds in establishing strong logical links between experience and perceptual judgments. But without a satisfactory account of why it is rational to accept the content of an experience, the idea fails to explain the rationality of perceptual judgments.

The only remaining option is to take seriously the interdependence between view and perceptual judgment. We do not first gain perceptual judgments, as a naive empiricism supposes, and then work up an adequate view of the world. Nor do we first gain an adequate view, as a naive rationalism urges, and then fill it in with the aid of perceptual judgments. Neither the view nor the perceptual judgment is prior. Nevertheless, it is possible to understand how both can be rational. The key lies in the proper appreciation of the logical power of experience.

Experience yields judgments not only when we bring to it a view that is rational and true. It yields judgments also when we approach it with a view that is false, confused, and even downright crazy. I have argued that we should think of the rational contribution of experience—the *given* in experience—to be hypothetical in character. Experience does not entitle us to perceptual judgments outright. It entitles us to them only conditionally: provided that the view that we bring to bear on experience is rational, the resulting perceptual judgments are rational. The rational contribution of experience consists in the links it creates between views and perceptual judgments. As I suggested above (§4A), the contribution is analogous to that of an argument-form.

---

1. In his essay "Rationalism and Empiricism," Hans Reichenbach writes, "Kant's philosophy ... though advanced with the claim of offering a solution by embracing rationalism and empiricism in the form of a higher synthesis, appears to the critical eye as a rationalism of the purest form without any injection of empiricism" (p. 333).

For a critique of some twentieth-century attempts to revive transcendental arguments, see Barry Stroud's "Transcendental Arguments."

2. See Bill Brewer, *Perception and Reason*.

Experience is rich, but its richness does not consist of a capacity to deliver weighty perceptual judgments. It consists instead of its ability to guide a range of erroneous views toward truth. In one respect, the given, in the account I recommend, is even thinner than that of Cartesian conceptions. Even the lightweight judgments of the Cartesian conceptions (e.g., "I am sensing an orange sense-datum") have, in the present account, at most a conditional entitlement: *if* the Cartesian conception is justified, *then* so are the subjective perceptual judgments. But in another respect, the given is thick: it yields conditional entitlements irrespective of the view that is brought to bear on experience. The power of experience is not like that of a sage who delivers hefty pronouncements in a subtle language. It is like that of a counselor who can empathize with widely different views, who can address different individuals in their own preferred vocabulary, and who can communicate with the sane as well as the insane. The special power of experience lies in the fact that it can, through gentle admonition, bridge the gap between radically different views; it can even guide the insane to sanity. (This is not to say that it can cure the incurable.)

The present account of the given does not require us to deny the obvious phenomenological fact that in experience one seems to be—and is—in direct touch with external objects (and some internal ones as well). The phenomenological fact is of great practical importance; it is also of theoretical importance for an account of the nature and function of our consciousness. But it is not epistemologically significant. Phenomenological directness does not imply epistemic directness. There is no epistemic direct access to the world, external or internal. Experience by itself delivers no propositions as rational; it delivers rational judgments only when it has the aid of a rational view.

Even though the given in experience is hypothetical, a series of experiences can entail, I have argued, a specific view. The hypothetical given generates a revision process—a process that captures how each acceptable view is revised in light of experience. This revision process can have the property of convergence: all acceptable initial views end up being revised to ones that are virtually identical (see §§4B and 5E). The very interdependence of view and perceptual judgment can thus be a basis for understanding how they both can be rational. It is a commonplace that revision of view is a part of our epistemological situation. What has not been recognized is that this revision is dictated by the very character of the given in experience.

THE PRESENT ACCOUNT, LIKE ANY EPISTEMOLOGICAL THEORY (e.g., foundationalism), does not aim to provide a psychological description of how we arrive at our knowledge of the world. It aims instead to provide a model for making sense of the rationality of our perceptual judgments (and other knowledge claims). The adequacy of the account must therefore be judged by how well it captures and explains important features of our epistemic practices. Let us look at some of these practices in light of the proposed model.

In the first place, our ordinary judgments of perception are rich with content, yet they serve as the end points of ordinary demands for justification. I may claim "the water in the kettle is boiling" or "the Blue Devils will win tomorrow," and I can be asked to justify my claim. In response I may make further claims, and I may legitimately be asked to provide justification for these new claims. The process of response and new demands may go through several iterations. But once the resulting regress reaches certain ordinary judgments of perception such as "the kettle is whistling" and "I just heard the coach announce that Lefty will pitch tomorrow," the demand for justification, if insisted on, is extraordinary and perplexing. The point to note is that the judgments of perception that serve as the end points of ordinary justification are not thin in content ("it seems to me as if...") but fully objective.[3] They implicate our view of the world. The judgment "the kettle is whistling" is meant to be about a medium-sized material object in public space; the judgment is erroneous if there is no such object. Compare: An ancient astronomer records in his diary words to the effect, "I am seeing an eclipse of the moon in the constellation Leo." This is a fully legitimate perceptual judgment, but it contains error because of the ancient misconception of the constellations. (In the terminology of §5C, the absolute content of the astronomer's judgment is false.)

It is true that not every part of a view is implicated in an ordinary judgment of perception. My perceptual judgment about the kettle is quite independent of my view about the solar system and about the date of Pythagoras's birth. It is also true that parts of

---

3. The demand for justification may be appropriate for certain judgments of perception in certain contexts. You say, pointing to an animal in the zoo, "that's an African elephant." A child asks, "how can you tell?" And you reply, "she has tusks." Observe that the end point of justification here is again a fully objective judgment.

the view that *are* implicated in a perceptual judgment may be inessential for the practical purposes for which the judgment is intended. My judgment "the kettle is whistling" may have as part of its (absolute) content that the kettle is an artifact. But this content may be idle as far as my immediate practical purposes are concerned (to make tea, etc.). (In the terminology of §5C, the proposition that the kettle is an artifact may fail to be a part of the effective content of my judgment.)

These observations, though important, should not lead us to doubt the dependence of perceptual judgments on views.[4] We should not imagine that we can somehow peel away extraneous content from perceptual judgments to reveal a core that is independent. The peeling may leave us with no content at all, or at best, it may leave us with thin sense-datum contents.[5] Nor should we imagine that we can pare down the view on which perceptual judgments depend to reveal a skeleton with a priori validity.[6] This will put an unbearable burden on our reason. It is true that perceptual judgments do not depend upon all parts of a view. But no perceptual judgment is entirely free of the dependence on a view.

4. One important consequence of these observations is that a perceptual judgment is rational as long as the part of the view on which it depends is rational. Hence, a perceptual judgment may be rational even when the *total* view fails to be rational.

5. We can understand the evolution of a view—e.g., from Ptolemaic to Copernican astronomy—to be rational and proper even though the perceptual judgments guiding the evolution are erroneous. Indeed, this is the only available option if we wish to understand the rationality of the change from an internal viewpoint. For, in radical shifts in view, the relevant error-free perceptual judgments are available only from the perspective of the succeeding view (if they are available at all).

6. It may be suggested that there is a core commonsense view—a view about persons, animals, and material things in a delimited region of space and time—that has legitimately stayed the same through all the upheavals in our picture of the world. This core view—shared by the merchants on the streets of Mohenjodaro with their counterparts in Times Square—suffices for the formulation of enough perceptual judgments, it may be suggested, to explain even the most radical changes in our view.

If this suggestion is correct, then a rational reconstruction of the actual evolution of our view can be simpler than that envisaged in the model above. The reconstruction can in effect neglect the dependence of perceptual judgments on views and can thus be foundationalist in character. In contrast, our model takes this dependence seriously and is therefore more complex.

And no part of a view can safely be excluded from this dependence.[7]

It is a virtue of the present account, then, that it works with a thick notion of perceptual judgment and that, consequently, it recognizes the interdependence of perceptual judgments and views. This enables us to understand how ordinary judgments of perception serve as end points of the demands for justification and, at the same time, how these judgments can be challenged and even refuted. My perceptual claim that the shirt is green, for example, may serve as an end point of a demand for justification. But it can be challenged (and even refuted) by the observation that the lighting is nonstandard. It is important to mark the distinction between a *demand for justification* and a *challenge*; they involve different logical and dialectical processes. A demand for justification can be appropriate even though it is not founded in any contrary belief or evidence. You may demand, for instance, justification for my claim that the Blue Devils will win, even though you have no reason to think otherwise. The demand for justification is answered by an argument, which in favorable cases will have some judgments of perception for its premises. The demand for justification is not always appropriate—it is often inappropriate for judgments of perception. But when it is appropriate, it does not require the issuer to possess a special reason or license. A *challenge*, on the other hand, does require a special reason. It requires some special contrary belief or evidence; it cannot be issued *in vacuo*. My perceptual judgment that the shirt is green can be challenged by one who has reason to think, for example, that the lighting is abnormal or that my visual system is messed up, but not by one

---

However, (i) it is a substantial thesis that there is a core commonsense view of the sort envisaged in the suggestion; it calls for a difficult logical and historical inquiry. (ii) Assuming the core exists, its validity would be grounded in experience, for even such a central idea as that physical objects exhibit spatiotemporal continuity is revisable in light of experience. So, even if the possibility envisioned proves to be actual, the revision account will retain its usefulness. It will help explain the rationality of the core.

In any case, the possibility envisaged in the suggestion seems to me interesting and deserving of exploration. It is a worthy successor of the foundationalist programs of an earlier philosophical era.

7. Even if perceptual judgments have no dependence on certain parts of a view, the proposed model is not affected as long as experience is the ground for those parts of the view on which perceptual judgments depend. See fn. 6.

who lacks any such special reasons. It is a harmful fiction to imagine that an ideal justification consists in the possession of an argument that implicitly contains a response to all challenges. The fiction is founded on a conception of perceptual judgments as thin and firmly secure, a conception that is alien to our epistemic practices.

The difference between a demand for justification and a challenge is highlighted by the following observation. There are familiar—and reasonable—ways of responding to a challenge to a perceptual judgment. You challenge my perceptual judgment that the shirt is green by asserting that the lighting is abnormal. I can respond to your challenge in a number of ways. I can thank you for providing me with useful information and withdraw my perceptual judgment. Or I can enter into a debate with you about the lighting conditions, or about some other factors relevant to the perceptual judgment. All this is familiar and makes sense. But what if you issue a bald demand for justification of my perceptual judgment? How am I to satisfy you? You are not blind and see the shirt as well as I do. I can, of course, say such things as that the lighting is normal and that my vision is in good working order, or that I am a reliable indicator of green shirts. But these responses are lame. In giving them I am pretending that I understand your demand—that I understand what would satisfy you—but I do not. In this imagined exchange, you are milking a he-goat and I am holding a sieve underneath.[8]

The skeptic is fond, of course, of issuing demands for justification of perceptual judgments. But the skeptic is no ordinary sort of fellow. He is out to make mischief and to confound us. And he is willing to exploit our weakness to respond to all demands and questions, no matter how absurd. The skeptic would only laugh if we responded to his demands by telling him things such as that our vision is in good working order or that we are reliable indicators of green shirts. The fact is that the skeptic means to call into question the rationality even of our commonsense view. Hence, it does no good to respond to him with claims that presuppose this view. One can, of course, tell the skeptic to get lost. And if he were merely a mischievous fellow, the response would be appropriate. But the skeptic is a genuine philosopher. He does

---

8. Kant, *Critique of Pure Reason*, A58/B83.

not just issue bald demands. He has a powerful argument for calling into question the rationality of the commonsense view.[9] I shall turn to this after I have reviewed a second dimension of our epistemic practices.

I HAVE DISCUSSED SO FAR OUR EPISTEMIC PRACTICES WITH respect to perceptual judgments. Let us consider now our epistemic practices with respect to views. To begin with, it is a fact that in the course of ordinary life we encounter persons with substantially different views about the world. We encounter Christians, devout Hindus, as well as total atheists. We encounter hard-headed materialists and also mind-body dualists. We encounter optimists who paint a rosy picture of human nature, and also conspiracy theorists who see darkness and evil design even in the most ordinary of human affairs. Occasionally, we find ourselves in frustrating conversations with individuals with extreme and exotic views. Histories of science, religion, and philosophy—as well as works of fiction—further enlarge our appreciation of alternative views. Now, when debating individuals with different views, or when trying to decide for ourselves the conception that deserves our rational assent, we encounter a bifurcation that reflects an important feature of revision processes. We find that sometimes disagreements between rival views can be settled, at least in principle, by experience—such disagreements are generally the most instructive and congenial. Let one individual affirm the benefits of taking a dip in the Ganges and let another deny this. Experience can help the individuals converge to a common view (assuming that the concern for truth dominates love of ideology).[10] The disagreement between views may be so wide that it extends even to the formulation of perceptual judgments. Still, experience can bring about convergence: a rational but ignorant

---

9. Stroud has long argued for the seriousness of the skeptic's challenge and the difficulty in meeting it adequately. See, e.g., the essays collected in his *Understanding Human Knowledge*. A less charitable view of the skeptic is articulated by Michael Williams. Williams thinks that the skeptical arguments rest on dubious presuppositions that are easily abandoned—e.g., the presupposition that our beliefs fall into "natural epistemological kinds" (see his "Epistemological Realism and the Basis of Scepticism"). As I have indicated, my own view is that some skeptical arguments are powerful and rest on highly plausible assumptions.

10. See the quotation from Peirce given near the end of §4B.

flat-earther can be brought around, through a course of experience, to radically alter his view. This aspect of our epistemic practices—convergence of views in light of experience—is quite common when the differences between views are relatively narrow. It occurs, though not so often, when the differences between views are wide. It occurs rarely, it must be acknowledged, when the wide differences are rooted in religion. I will not attempt to explain this fact, but I want to insist that it does not refute empiricism. The failure of actual convergence may lie, in part, in the special nature of religious claims and, in part, in the nature of the attitude (e.g., faith) that one takes toward these claims.

Imagine witnessing a conversation between individuals who hold radically different views. Imagine, for instance, that you kibitz a conversation between me and a solipsist—or, better, between me and an individual who acts for the duration of the conversation as if she accepted the solipsist view. She maintains that the world is constituted, as far as she knows, solely by her and her sense-data. I feel strongly that she is wrong, even wrongheaded. I tell her that I see my hands and that I see her. Hence, I conclude, it is obvious that she is wrong: the world definitely contains at least two persons and some physical objects. The solipsist laughs and says, "I sense various annoying visual and auditory sense-data. None of these can be a physical object, let alone a person worth debating." We can go back and forth like this for a while, neither able to budge the other. I end up frustrated, she amused. Each of us is able to argue convincingly from *within our respective views* that the other is wrong or irrational. The arguments I give—for example, "here are two hands; hence, there are physical objects"—are as solid as empirical arguments get. If these are suspect, then so are all empirical arguments found in the sciences. Equally, the solipsist is able to argue from within her view that my belief in the external world is irrational. It is a characteristic of this sort of *alienated* disagreement that each party can easily construct a refutation of the other but in each case the refutation is ineffective. (This accounts for some of the frustration in such disagreements.) There is an important moral here: *the availability of reasons from the internal perspective for the rejection of competing views is insufficient to establish the rationality of a view.* The solipsist may from her perspective be able to reject competing views as erroneous. But this does not establish that solipsism is rational. The same holds, of course, of the commonsense view.[11] Convergence and alienated disagreements are features of our epistemic practices and are reflected in the present model of experience and knowledge.

OUR VIEW, OUR KNOWLEDGE CLAIMS, AND EVEN OUR perceptual judgments are open to challenges. The ordinary practices of asking for justification and of issuing challenges are intelligible, I have suggested, if we keep in mind the interdependence of perceptual judgments and views. These practices are founded on the correct and justified assumption that our view is, for the most part, reasonable. The ensuing perceptual judgments, too, are reasonable, unless there is a reason to call into question some relevant elements of our view.

The skeptical challenges to our view and judgments are extraordinary and can take several forms. First, the skeptic can issue persistent demands for justification. Even when we reach a simple judgment of perception, the skeptic may baldly demand that we provide justification for it. Such a skeptic is an unworthy successor of Arcesilaus and Aenesidemus and can summarily be dismissed. His bald demand for justification is improper.

Second, the skeptic can raise one of the familiar skeptical scenarios. He may say, "You do not know that you are not a brain in a vat. You know you have hands only if you know you are not a brain in a vat. Hence, you do not know you have hands."[12] A straightforward Moorean response is appropriate, it seems to me, to such a skeptic: "I know that I have hands. If I know that I have hands, then I know that I am not a brain in a vat. Hence, I know that I am not a brain in a vat."[13] To be sure, it is a little odd to assert in an everyday

---

11. The commonsense view does not make available a priori refutations of all competing views—this is one of its many virtues.

12. Peter Unger has used a similar argument to defend a skeptical position; see his *Ignorance*.

13. The Moorean response is defended by Gail Stine in "Skepticism, Relevant Alternatives, and Deductive Closure." There is a large philosophical literature on this skeptical argument and on issues related to it. Stewart Cohen, Keith DeRose, David Lewis, and others have attempted to defuse the argument through contextualist theories of knowledge attributions. Crudely, the idea is that the standards for knowledge attributions can shift from context to context. The skeptical premiss

context that one knows that one is not a brain in a vat. But, as Paul Grice pointed out, there are many truths that are odd to assert in everyday contexts. The proposition that I am not a brain in a vat is an easy and known consequence of something I know for sure, namely, that I have hands. So it must be true that I know that I am not a brain in a vat, however odd it may be for me to go around insisting on it.

The skeptic's principal premiss—that I do not know that I am not a brain in a vat—gains plausibility, I think, from an improper application of generalizations that hold in ordinary cases. In ordinary cases, our knowledge claims exhibit convergence: if I know that a contingent claim P holds, then I can (ideally) cite experiences that would correct the contradictory claim that not-P. I know that there is beer in the refrigerator; moreover, I can cite experiences that would correct the idea that there is no beer there. Contrast this with the skeptical hypothesis: I can cite no experiences that will guide the hypothesis that I am a brain in a vat to the truth that I am not a brain in a vat. This failure is to be expected; like solipsism, the skeptical hypothesis is pathological. No experiences whatsoever will rationally force a revision of the hypothesis to its contrary. My failure to bring about convergence with the skeptical hypothesis does not show that my nonskeptical claim is irrational or that I do not know that I am not a brain in a vat. It cannot be a requirement of rationality (or of knowledge) that convergence obtain for all views, no matter how pathological. Rationality cannot require us to move an immovable object.[14]

---

that one does not know that one is not a brain in a vat is true, but the skeptical argument fails because the standards of knowledge attribution shift in the course of the argument. (A different sort of contextualist response is offered by Ram Neta in his essay "Contextualism and the Problem of the External World.") Fred Dretske and Robert Nozick take a more radical course of denying that knowledge is closed under known implication. There are also semantic-externalist responses, provoked by Hilary Putnam, that attempt to show that we know the skeptical hypothesis to be false since we can entertain the thought that is expressed in the hypothesis. For, if we were brains in a vat, our expression 'brain in a vat' and the mental state it expresses would not have the actual content "brain in a vat." See the papers collected in *Skepticism*, edited by DeRose and Ted Warfield. See also Cohen's "How to Be a Fallibilist."

14. Another consideration, one that has been much discussed in the literature, that lends plausibility to the skeptic's principal premiss is this. Ordinary contingent knowledge *tracks* the world: if I know that P, then I would not have believed that P had P failed to obtain. I look out of the window and I know that it is raining.

The argument "I have hands; hence, I am not a brain in a vat" is ineffective—that is, it is incapable of budging the skeptical hypothesis. Nonetheless, the argument suffices to establish the rationality of my belief that I am not a brain in a vat, *provided* my belief that I have hands is rational or reasonable. The key question is whether this is so and, more generally, whether our commonsense beliefs are in fact rational. Skeptics, ancient and modern, have returned a negative answer to such questions. But the skeptical argument under consideration does not further their cause. If the argument is read as an attempt to cast doubt on the rationality of the commonsense view, it simply begs the question. However revealing it may be about knowledge attributions and about our use of the word 'know', the argument has little in it to scare a dogmatist.

Third, the skeptic may argue, in the manner of the ancients and the moderns, that the materials supplied by our senses and reason are insufficient to ground ordinary knowledge claims. The sixth mode in Sextus Empiricus' *Outlines of Scepticism* contains the following argument.

> So because of the admixtures our senses do not grasp what external existing objects are accurately like. But our intellect does not do so either, especially since its guides, the senses, fail it. . . . According to this mode too, therefore, we see that we cannot say anything about the nature of external existing objects, and are forced to suspend judgement.[15]

Hume's skeptical argument is of the same general character. According to Hume, the senses provide us only with impressions and images—they do not "produce any immediate intercourse between the mind and the object."[16] And reason, he argues, is incapable of

---

Moreover, were it not raining, I would not believe that it is raining. Contrast this with the skeptical scenario: were I a brain in a vat, I would still believe that I am not a brain in a vat. So, my belief that I am not a brain in a vat fails to track the world. I think that tracking is not a requirement for knowledge in pathological cases of the sort cited by the skeptic.

15. Sextus Empiricus, *Outlines of Scepticism*, I.127–128, translated by Julia Annas and Jonathan Barnes.

16. Hume, *Enquiry*, 12.1. Hume writes in the *Treatise*, "Properly speaking, 'tis not our body we perceive, when we regard our limbs and members, but certain impressions, which enter by the senses" (1.4.2).

establishing that our perceptions are caused by external objects. Hume concludes, "The profounder and more philosophical sceptics will always triumph, when they endeavour to introduce an universal doubt into all subjects of human knowledge and enquiry."[17]

This kind of skeptical argument is similar to independence proofs in logic but much more ambitious. In an independence proof, one shows that a particular proposition and also its negation fail to be logical consequences of a body of principles (e.g., Peano arithmetic). The skeptical argument aims in effect to establish the independence of a claim such as "I have hands" from the total contributions of the senses and reason. Imagine an ideal cognitive mechanism, one with perfect recall and one that can execute the operations of reason perfectly. The skeptical argument aims to show that such a mechanism, if fed the total contribution of the senses, would be unable to settle the question of whether it had hands. If the argument is sound, then our commonsense beliefs are in an important sense irrational. (The Pyrrhonist conclusion, drawn by Sextus, that we should suspend judgment, requires a further argument. For it may be that there are practical reasons for sticking with commonsense beliefs, or that our nature makes suspension of judgment impossible. But this further argument is not relevant to our present concerns.)

This kind of skeptical argument is powerful and disturbing. It does not beg the question against the commonsense view. It does not *assume*, for example, that I do not know that I am not a brain in a vat. Instead, it offers a powerful argument for this conclusion. Nor does this kind of skeptical argument work by imposing on us persistent demands to provide justification. It bypasses entirely the dialectic of giving and asking for reasons. The argument sets aside most of our cognitive limitations—our limited memory, our limited capacity to draw inferences, and even our confusion about the nature and structure of justification. It focuses on the broad limitations of our senses and of our reason. It aims to show that, even with the most ample supply of the materials provided by the

17. Hume, *Enquiry*, 12.1. Again, Hume writes in the *Treatise*, "Sceptical doubt, both with respect to reason and the senses, is a malady, which can never be radically cur'd, but must return upon us every moment, however we may chace it away, and sometimes may seem entirely free from it" (1.4.2).

senses and reason, one is unable to rationally sustain the commonsense view.[18]

As I have indicated, I think that this type of argument is irresistible if we conceive the given—that is, the contribution of the senses—to be propositional in form. Under the propositional conception, the very possibility of skeptical scenarios thins out the given (§2C) and makes the skeptical conclusion virtually inevitable. The alternative conception I am proposing helps to block the skeptical argument. In this conception, the skeptical hypotheses, far from thinning out the given, highlight its richness: the given yields conditional entitlements even under the peculiar hypotheses entertained by the skeptic. Further, in this conception, reason plays a more robust role in our knowledge than that under the propositional conception: reason demarcates the range of acceptable views. This role, we have seen (§5E), is compatible with the empiricist maxim that reason has no special insight into the nature of reality. Thus, the present theory increases the burden on the skeptic. The citation of skeptical hypotheses, such as the brain-in-a-vat idea, is insufficient to yield the skeptic's conclusion, for these hypotheses are unacceptable starting points of revision. To reach his desired conclusion, the skeptic needs to produce an acceptable initial hypothesis and show that it does not converge to the commonsense view. This is a harder task.

I wish to reject the skeptical conclusion, but I think that the main skeptical argument of the ancients and the moderns is essentially correct: the argument is a *reductio ad absurdum* of the propositional given.

6B. Features of the Reformed Empiricism

The account of experience I have offered yields a more thoroughgoing and, at the same time, reformed empiricism. The empiricism is more thoroughgoing in that it assigns a wider role to experience: experience shapes not only our view of the world but also our view of ourselves. Experience reveals what our nature is, what our capacities are, and what we are capable of knowing. Our

---

18. A simple and familiar instance of this type of argument is as follows: the senses provide us with truths about sense-data, reason provides us with analytic truths, and the proposition that there are material things is logically independent of the totality of all truths about sense-data and all analytic truths.

conception of ourselves and of the scope of human knowledge is contingent on experience.[19]

The resulting empiricism is reformed in that it avoids the excesses of its classical ancestor. It lends no support to the projects of Locke and Hume to determine, once and for all, the scope of human understanding and to reject on general epistemological grounds certain types of inquiries and claims (e.g., religious claims).[20] Locke and Hume proceed on the Cartesian assumption that our capacity for knowledge lies wide open to inspection, quite independently of experience. I have argued, on the contrary, that our account of ourselves is thoroughly intertwined with our account of the world, that we cannot determine the one independently of the other.[21] Just as experience can impose on us a radical revision of our conception of the world, so it can impose on us a radical revision of our conception

---

19. Even knowledge as basic as that we have limbs and the five senses—and indeed, even bodies—is derived from experience.

20. In section 7, chapter 1, book 1 of the *Essay*, titled "Occasion of this Essay," Locke says,

> I thought that the first Step toward satisfying several Enquiries, the Mind of Man was very apt to run into, was, to take a Survey of our own Understandings, examine our own Powers, and see to what Things they were adapted.

A little later in the same section, Locke indicates the result of this examination: "the Extent of our Knowledge ... discovered, and the Horizon found, which sets the Bounds between the enlightned and dark Parts of Things; between what is, and what is not comprehensible by us." Hume echoes Locke in the first section of the *Enquiry*:

> The only method of freeing learning, at once, from these abstruse questions, is to enquire seriously into the nature of human understanding, and show, from an exact analysis of its powers and capacity, that it is by no means fitted for such remote and abstruse subjects.

The "abstruse" questions Hume refers to include those concerning natural theology and revealed religion. According to the testimony of Locke's friend James Tyrrell, questions concerning religion also motivated Locke to pursue his epistemological work.

21. Locke's and Hume's projects, though magnificent, must, unfortunately, be deemed to be complete failures.

The foundations on which they built their epistemological theories land us either in skepticism or in idealism—as Berkeley made plain in his critique of Locke in the *Principles* and *Three Dialogues*. Berkeley, of course, used this point as a lemma in his argument for idealism: since skepticism is false, idealism must be true. But the fact is that the foundations of Locke and Hume provide no plausible demarcation of the scope of human knowledge. Once these foundations are accepted, the scope of empirical knowledge is limited, at best, to the subjective contents of the mind.

of ourselves. It is ironic that the Cartesian picture of experience—the very picture Locke and Hume use to rule out certain claims—is itself ruled unacceptable by our reformed empiricism.[22]

Similarly, this new empiricism provides no support for the attempts of the Logical Positivists to demarcate, on conceptual grounds, science from pseudoscience (and from metaphysics, which they held in as low an esteem as any pseudoscience). The Positivists' demarcation was based on the verification theory of meaning. The statements of science, the positivists held, were testable against experience and hence had meaning. In contrast, the statements of pseudoscience and metaphysics, they maintained, were without any empirical significance and hence were meaningless. The foundations of the Positivists' demarcation, like the earlier demarcation of Locke and Hume, lay in a Cartesian picture of experience—a picture that we have reason to reject.

Our reformed empiricism sustains the intuitive idea that no magic bullet will destroy all pseudoscience and that no such bullet is really needed. Each nontrivial inquiry must be assessed piecemeal before the tribunal of experience. Let an astrologer claim that the main features of a human life can be discovered from the patterns of heavenly bodies at birth. The astrologer's claim is not conceptually incoherent. The claim is undoubtedly strange and outside common experience, but then so is much of the best physical science. No abstract or philosophical refutation is needed here, nor any inquiry into the scope of human understanding (or meaning). All that is needed is deference to experience. The case against pseudoscience and natural theology is strongest when we let experience—not ill-conceived conceptual ideas—do the work for us.[23]

Of course, the more modest project of using our best current understanding of ourselves to demarcate the scope of human knowledge is feasible. Since our current understanding of ourselves depends upon our current understanding of the world, the demarcation is bound to be tentative. And it can be of little force against, say, natural theology. For, in arriving at this understanding of ourselves, we must settle the prior issue whether natural theology constitutes a part of our best current understanding of the world.

22. More specifically, it is ruled unacceptable as an initial view in the revision process.

23. The point is already illustrated in Hume's celebrated attack on the reliability of testimony about miracles. Hume's empirical considerations against such testimony are much more powerful than his purely conceptual arguments.

ANOTHER FEATURE OF OUR REFORMED EMPIRICISM IS THAT it is not at war with commonsense. It does not denigrate the commonsense view as irrational. Nor does it preserve the husk while discarding the content of the view: it does not mouth the *sentences* commonsense endorses while understanding them in novel, idealistic ways. The commonsense view, understood in the ordinary way, is fully reasonable. We are embodied beings who interact with each other and with things around us, and it is only some deep psychological disturbance or philosophical error that can lead us to seriously doubt this.

Any theory that would wage war against commonsense had better come loaded with some powerful ammunition. Philosophy is incapable of providing such ammunition. Empirical sciences are a better source. But before one taps them, one had better explain how these sciences can be acceptable if the commonsense view is irrational, for the commonsense view is woven into the very practice of the empirical sciences. The proper philosophical attitude toward the commonsense view is one of admiration, not denigration. The view guides us in the conduct of our lives; it is wonderfully rich; it gives experience a full and ample voice; and, above all, it is open to radical revision.

The commonsense view has, despite all its virtues, no intrinsic rationality; its rationality derives from experience. The reasonableness of the detailed contents of the commonsense view—contents such as that apples are good to eat, that we humans are mortal, and that the Earth has existed for more than a few centuries—is plainly founded in experience. Experience is also the ground of the core (and structural) elements of the commonsense view—elements such as that we have bodies that mediate our interactions with the external world, that physical objects exhibit spatiotemporal continuity, and that time has a direction. These elements are so thoroughly entrenched in our thinking that they can seem to be valid independently of all experience. The following two considerations may help, however, to shake off this impression.

First, highly deviant and persistent experiences may make it rational for an individual to abandon core elements of the commonsense view. It is easy to imagine experiences that would rationally force us to abandon such ideas as, for example, that we have bodies and that ordinary physical objects are spatiotemporally continuous. A schizophrenic who believes he can hear an all-powerful God is sick, but he is not necessarily irrational. His experiences may leave him with no choice but to accept the unusual belief.[24]

Second, even ordinary experiences can force an abandonment of core elements of the commonsense view. It proved fruitful when dealing with the scattering of alpha particles by a gold foil to abandon the idea that ordinary objects exhibit spatial continuity—that all parts of the space occupied by, for example, a gold foil are filled with matter. Similarly, in order to account for some confounding observed behavior of subatomic particles, a physicist may entertain the hypothesis that certain particles exhibit temporal discontinuity. We philosophers should not try to block the idea by invoking some imagined conceptual necessities. We are not the police: we do not serve by preventing conceptual trespasses. Quite the opposite: we serve by opening up possibilities, by freeing the imagination of the theoretician struggling with perplexing phenomena.

24. Even a casual perusal of Karl Jaspers's *General Psychopathology* provides a fascinating glimpse into actual deviant experiences. Jaspers records the following account given by a schizophrenic patient, Staudenmaier, of a heautoscopy—"the phenomenon when someone vividly perceives his own body as a double in the outer world" (p. 92):

> During the night while I walked up and down in the garden I imagined as vividly as possible that there were three other people present besides me. Gradually the corresponding visual hallucination took shape. There appeared before me three identically clothed Staudenmaiers who walked along in step with me; they stopped when I did and stretched out their hands when I stretched out mine. (p. 93)

Jaspers also gives the following example of an experience of bodily distortion:

> Serko describes himself during mescalin intoxication (the picture presents us with a vivid analogy to some psychotic processes): '... I suddenly have a sensation that my foot has left my leg; I feel it lying apart from my body below the truncated leg.... Then I have the sensation that my head is being turned right around, 180°, that my abdomen is becoming a soft fluid mass, my face growing to gigantic dimensions, my lips swelling.... Among many other things I have the hallucination that my head has become separated from my body and is floating free in the air half a mile behind me. I really feel it floating and yet still belonging to me...' (p. 91)

Jaspers is well aware that reports of deviant experiences cannot always be trusted. Nonetheless, he observes that there is much similarity in patients' accounts of these experiences, and he takes reports such as those quoted above as data for a theory of the human psyche.

In our attempts to work out a coherent and empirically adequate account of the world, we have complete freedom to abandon any core element of the commonsense view. We need heed only one epistemic master: experience. There are conceptual necessities, of course. But from a methodological viewpoint, a greater danger is posed by the threat that misconceptions about these necessities will limit our theoretical imagination than by the threat that we shall entertain conceptually incoherent ideas. Experience itself is an adequate defense against the latter threat. Entertain a conceptually incoherent hypothesis—for example, that snow is both white and black—and experience will help you to correct it. But confine your theoretical imagination within the limits of a misconceived conceptual necessity—for example, speed is bound to be relative to an observer—and you are like a fly in a fly-bottle, persistently running into anomaly and unable to escape it.

THE FINAL FEATURE TO WHICH I WISH TO DRAW ATTENTION is that our reformed empiricism vindicates realism. The term 'realism' has become highly ambiguous in contemporary philosophy. Let me therefore be explicit about the senses in which realism is vindicated.

(A) *Minimal Realism.* The reformed empiricism recognizes that our current view can be radically mistaken. The actual structure of reality may be quite different from our conception of it, and furthermore, future experiences may lead us to substantially revise our current view. Something stronger holds: even an ideal view can be radically mistaken.[25] Experience and rationality, even when supplemented by a perfect imagination, cannot guarantee absolute truth. A perfectly rational creature may explore all avenues available to it. It may diligently set up the best experiments to test its view. It may draw all the requisite inferences from the phenomena. Yet it may arrive at, and persist with, a substantially erroneous view of the world. The concept of truth is not the same as that of rational belief, or as that of rational belief in the long run, or even as that of ideal rational belief. Nothing guarantees that ideal rational beliefs are true. Indeed, it is quite possible that such beliefs involve fundamental errors.

---

25. This can be strengthened yet further: for every world *w* in which a raimex *P* reaches a view, there is a world *w′* in which *P*'s epistemic position is subjectively indistinguishable from that in *w* but *P*'s view in *w′* is radically mistaken.

A position that thus separates the concept of truth from that of ideal rational belief has sometimes been called "metaphysical realism."[26] But this is to give an innocent position an awful and frightening name. I myself prefer to call it "minimal realism." The position simply reflects the commonsense idea that the scope of knowledge depends not only on the grade of rationality and imagination brought to the cognitive enterprise, but also on the contingent powers and the contingent circumstances of the knower. This idea is evident in our own situation. Our view of the world would have been poorer and much more error-prone had we possessed no hands, or had we lived at the bottom of a murky sea, unable to glimpse the stars. It is a happy circumstance that the experience of the brilliant night sky guides our reason and our imagination to a more accurate conception of our place in the universe; without it, we might have remained trapped in a superstitious, Earth-centered view. To assume ideal rationality and imagination is not to assume omnipotence and omnipresence. It is not surprising, therefore, that ideal rational belief can fail to coincide with truth.

Minimal realism—that is, the distinctness of truth from ideal rational belief—is an immediate consequence of the possibility of familiar skeptical scenarios. If there is an evil demon deceiving us, then our conception of the world is fundamentally mistaken but the rationality of our beliefs is not impugned. This remains true, furthermore, irrespective of how perfect our reason and our imagination are supposed to be. Hence, if it is possible that there is an evil demon bent on deception, then it is possible that ideal rational belief is false.[27] Other skeptical scenarios—for example, the brain-in-a-vat scenario—can be used to generate parallel arguments for the same conclusion.

26. In *Realism and Reason*, Putnam characterizes metaphysical realism as "the view that truth outruns even idealized justification" (p. 85). This is not the only (or the predominant) characterization of metaphysical realism in Putnam's writings. However, even when Putnam offers alternative characterizations, he often takes the denial of metaphysical realism to imply the denial of the idea that truth outruns idealized justification.

27. This argument is merely an illustration of the point made in the preceding paragraph. If there is an evil demon bent on deception, then our contingent epistemic circumstances are the most unfortunate. We can be diligent in fulfilling all our epistemic duties and yet end up with an erroneous view.

Minimal realism has been denied by some philosophers. The principal motivation for the denial comes from epistemology and can be traced to the propositional given. We have seen that, under the propositional given, the skeptical scenarios thin out the contribution of experience, and as a result, the rationality of our commonsense view is called into question.[28] Thus arises the philosophical impulse to rule skeptical scenarios as impossible or meaningless. And the idea that truth is ideal rational belief provides a means to do so. There is a standing temptation in philosophy to

28. There are also some less serious variants of the skeptical worry. (i) It is sometimes thought that the mere possibility of, e.g., the evil-demon scenario, all by itself, casts doubt on our knowledge claims. But this is to misunderstand the nature of the possibility in question. The sense in which the evil-demon scenario is possible is not that the scenario is *consistent* with what we *know*. We do know that there is no evil demon, and hence it is not consistent with our knowledge that there is one. In the same way, I know that I had cereal for breakfast, and it is not consistent with my knowledge that I had none. Still, I might not have had cereal for breakfast—it is a coherent supposition that I ate eggs instead. Similarly, though the evil-demon scenario does not obtain, it might have obtained. The supposition that the scenario obtains is not incoherent.

(ii) Minimal realism, it is sometimes said, implies that in order to sustain one's knowledge claims, one is under an obligation to provide a soundness proof for one's rational methods, for minimal realism imposes a gap between our rational methods and an independent reality. Hence, it is suggested, the demand arises to show that the rational methods one employs do indeed track reality. But this demand cannot be met, since we have no epistemic access to reality apart from our rational methods. It follows that minimal realism leads to skepticism.

This argument rests on a false premiss. There is no legitimate demand to supply a soundness proof. We suffer experiences, we follow our rational procedures, and we arrive at our view of the world. Further, we make knowledge claims and are prepared to offer the usual sorts of justifications for them. Our knowledge claims entail no rational obligation to provide a *prior* soundness proof for our procedures, i.e., a soundness proof that is independent of our view. Indeed, the very notion of such a proof makes little sense. The question of soundness arises only when a view is in play, i.e., when we have a conception of ourselves and our place in the world. Now we can explore the relationship between our methods and the world as we conceive it to be. The demand for a soundness proof is now legitimate and, indeed, worrisome. A failure to supply it reveals a flaw in our overall view—a flaw that skeptics have taken delight in highlighting.

(iii) It is sometimes thought that, if the skeptical scenario is coherent, then one does not know that, e.g., there are rocks, unless one can cite some consideration that distinguishes one's situation from that of one's counterpart in the skeptical scenario. Since, by hypothesis, this cannot be done, it is held that one does not know that there are rocks. The premiss of this argument is also false; it imposes an improper demand on knowledge claims. See the discussion of skepticism in §6A.

dispose of skeptical worries by defining, or conceiving, reality in epistemic terms. Verification theories of meaning provide one type of example of this temptation; the denial of minimal realism provides another. The epistemological motivation for denying minimal realism is removed under the present proposal. We do not need to deny the coherence or the meaningfulness of the skeptical scenarios to reject the skeptical conclusion. The nonpropositional conception of the given developed in this essay enables us to embrace minimal realism while at the same time insist on the rationality of the commonsense view of the world.

Recent philosophy has provided a different kind of argument against minimal realism. This argument begins with the premiss that the reference and meaning of our terms (names, predicates, etc.) are determined by use, and moves to the conclusion that verification-transcendent truth-conditions are impossible. Putnam and Michael Dummett have offered arguments to this effect.[29] Let me briefly consider an argument that Putnam offers to show that minimal realism is "incoherent" (Putnam's term). Underlying the argument is the observation that if a theory is consistent, then its terms can be assigned referents so as to make the theory true. For instance, an interpretation exists that makes the sentence 'Socrates is a cat' true: let 'Socrates' be assigned the number 2, and the predicate 'is a cat' be assigned the set of even numbers. This example is, of course, completely trivial. But the interesting fact is that this kind of thing can be done for *any* consistent theory, irrespective of its complexity.[30] (It takes a delicate construction to ensure that choices made to render one member of a theory true do not interfere with the choices required to render other members true.) Now, it is reasonable to suppose that the ideal theory will be consistent. It follows that an interpretation exists that makes the ideal theory true. All this is straightforward. But Putnam goes further and claims that an interpretation exists that not only renders the theory true but also meets all the "operational and theoretical constraints." This interpretation, Putnam says, must be an "intended interpretation"; it cannot be deviant in the way that, in the

---

29. Davidson's argument that belief is intrinsically veridical is of the same general character, though it aims to establish a stronger conclusion (see §6C).

30. I am assuming for the duration of the argument that theories are formulated in a classical first-order language.

example above, the interpretations of 'Socrates' and 'is a cat' were deviant. Hence, the ideal theory is bound to be true under some intended interpretations. It follows that the ideal theory cannot be false *simpliciter*.[31]

This argument has received much attention in the philosophical literature.[32] Let me confine myself to a few observations about "operational and theoretical constraints." There is an ambiguity in the role they play in the argument. If they are read as constraining only the ideal theory—so that they are used to determine which sentences go into making up the theory—then we can grant that there exist interpretations of the sort claimed by Putnam: the operational and theoretical constraints are met, and the theory is rendered true. But Putnam has provided no reason to think—and indeed, there is little reason to think—that these interpretations fall among the intended interpretations of the theory. On the other hand, if the "operational and theoretical constraints" are read as constraining our procedures for determining the referents of the terms in the theory, then we can grant that anything that meets these constraints is an intended interpretation. But now we have no reason to think that an interpretation that meets the constraints will make the theory true. So, either way, the path to Putnam's desired conclusion is blocked. Note also that Putnam's argument rests on an overly simple (and syntactic) conception of "operational and theoretical constraints." It incorrectly assumes that these constraints are independent of the semantic content of the theory. The theoretical constraint of simplicity, for example, makes no sense if it is applied to uninterpreted sentences: we cannot assess whether a theory is simple if all we are given is a collection of sentences without any semantic interpretation. A similar point holds for the second reading of the "operational and theoretical constraints." The constraints on finding interpretations of the terms of a theory cannot be stated independently of the beliefs of the subjects who accept the theory. As Davidson has stressed, belief and interpretation are interdependent: attribution of belief depends

31. For fuller expositions of the argument, see Putnam's "Realism and Reason" and "Models and Reality." See also chapter 2 of his *Reason, Truth and History* and chapter 4 of *Realism and Reason*.

32. Good critical discussions include Anthony L. Brueckner's "Putnam's Model-Theoretic Argument against Metaphysical Realism," chapter 12 of Michael Devitt's *Realism and Truth*, and David Lewis's "Putnam's Paradox."

upon the interpretation of terms, and, as just noted, the latter depends upon the former. The fixing of interpretations is not a simple and direct affair, and Putnam's argument provides no reason to think that constraints on interpretation can be met and, at the same time, our terms assigned interpretations that render true the sentences we accept (or would ideally accept). Use, we can grant, fixes interpretation, but perhaps it does not always do so in a charitable way.[33] So much for the first grade of realism that is sustained by our reformed empiricism. Let us now go on to consider some other grades.

(B) *Mind Independence.* Our empiricism recognizes that there are mind-independent objects in the world. This grade of realism—which I shall simply call "mind independence"—resembles minimal realism in modesty, but should for the following reasons be clearly distinguished from it. (i) Minimal realism does not imply mind independence. Even if there are no mind-independent objects in the world—even if all objects distinct from minds are merely constructions of minds—the gap between truth and ideal rational belief can remain, for not everything about mind-dependent objects need be accessible to rational inquiry. (ii) Minimal realism makes a conceptual claim. It affirms that the concept of truth *can* diverge from that of ideal rational belief. If it is true, it is necessarily true. Mind independence, on the other hand, is not a necessary truth: it is coherent to suppose that all objects distinct from minds are mind dependent.

Minimal realism, though it does not imply mind independence, serves to protect it. The principal threat to mind independence comes from idealistic reinterpretations of the truth of the commonsense view. If this threat is warded off, as it is in the present theory, then mind independence can be accepted as the modest thesis that it is.

(C) *Commonsense Realism.* Our reformed empiricism supports what may be called "commonsense realism," the idea that the commonsense view understood in the ordinary way is rational. It is reasonable for us to think that there are, for example, rocks and planets, that there are other persons, and that the existence of these and many other objects does not depend upon our experiences,

---

33. Davidson holds that correct interpretation is bound to be charitable. I consider his argument in §6C.

thoughts, and beliefs. Caution must be exercised, however, in interpreting this grade of realism. It does not immediately yield a *metaphysics* of commonsense. It does not entitle us to favor an ontology of ordinary things—rocks, planets, and persons—over that of theoretical posits. The serious work of metaphysics does not end, as I see it, with commonsense realism but *begins* with it. Our commonsense view is rich, subtle, and open; at the same time, it is not entirely free of tensions and conflicts. It is one thing to accept, and act upon, such claims as that Fred sees the bus approaching, that Mary chose freely to wear her purple coat, and that the Internal Revenue Service office is closed on Sundays. It is another thing altogether to resolve the perplexities that such claims are apt to generate on reflection. The commonsense view is rational—at least, relative to our limited intellectual resources. But the view appears not to be entirely coherent. It is as if we had several different pictures, each useful in its own limited way but that are not easily reconciled with each other. We think of ourselves as "taking in" the world directly in perception. But we also think of perception as a highly mediated activity, depending not only on the world but also on our bodily states. We think of ourselves as autonomous decision makers, shaping and expressing our inner character and initiating changes in the world around us. But we also think of ourselves as natural beings, buffeted by environmental forces, not knowing exactly how we came to be what we are and exactly why we sometimes choose the way we do. We think of ourselves as approaching, petitioning, and fearing institutions. But, on reflection, these demipersons are apt to lose their awesome solidity and to dissolve into a confusing mass of buildings, persons, and number-crunching computers. The task—partly descriptive, partly normative—of bringing coherence, order, and clarity to our total view belongs to metaphysics.

A time-honored method in metaphysics is to declare certain kinds of entities and certain relations between them to be fundamental and to explain the rest in terms of these favored elements. Thus, a physicalist declares the fundamental constituents to be subatomic particles and the other postulates of physics, together with their properties and relations; the Platonist declares them to be minds, numbers, universals, and such; and the subjective idealist has them be minds, sense-data, and their properties and relations. Let "ontological realism with respect to X" be the claim that Xs belong among the fundamental constituents of reality. Then, the present point is that commonsense realism is not committed to ontological realism with respect to familiar kinds of entities (e.g., rocks, planets, and persons). A mathematician engaging in her exploration of numbers and sets is not doing metaphysics and takes on no ontological commitments. She is not committed to ontological realism with respect to numbers or sets. A historian trying to decipher distant events is not engaged in metaphysics and may have little to contribute to the metaphysics of time. Similarly, in merely accepting the commonsense view and acting in accordance with it, one does not suddenly become a metaphysician, one with ontological commitments and an ontological program. Metaphysics is a discipline with its own distinctive presuppositions and its own distinctive synoptic concerns. It bears on the sciences and other specialized disciplines and can be enlightened by them. But it is not subsumed or rendered otiose by them.

Commonsense realism, as I understand it, is compatible with subjective idealism.[34] It is compatible even with a rejection of metaphysics—say, on the ground that the supposed tensions within the commonsense view are merely apparent. It is compatible also with a quietism that counsels that in philosophy we should not go beyond a peaceful acceptance of the commonsense view, regardless of the tensions inherent in it. I am inclined to think that the tensions in the commonsense view are real and require a subtle and imaginative metaphysics for their resolution. But here I go beyond anything licensed by commonsense realism.

6C. The Dogma, the Dualism, and the Myth

Philosophy of the past sixty years or so has nurtured the impression that empiricism entails untenable doctrines. One hears that empiricism is irreparably compromised by its involvement with the Dogma of the Analytic–Synthetic Distinction, the Dualism of Scheme and Content, and the Myth of the Given. In a famous passage of a famous paper, Davidson wrote,

---

34. Thus, commonsense realism does not imply mind independence, when the latter is read as an ontological thesis. The considerations in this essay buttress mind independence by removing the principal, epistemological motivation for subjective idealism.

I want to urge that this . . . dualism of scheme and content, of organizing system and something waiting to be organized, . . . is itself a dogma of empiricism, the third dogma. The third, and perhaps the last, for if we give it up it is not clear that there is anything distinctive left to call empiricism.[35]

Quine had argued for the rejection of, what he called, "the two dogmas of empiricism"—namely, the Analytic-Synthetic Distinction and Reductionism—and he proposed a way of freeing empiricism from these "dogmas." (I considered Quine's proposal in §2E.) Davidson labels the Dualism of Scheme and Content "the third dogma of empiricism," and he thinks that empiricism cannot be freed from it: if the "third dogma" is abandoned, then empiricism must be abandoned also. It is a fair question what relationship the empiricism proposed in this essay bears to the Dualism of Scheme and Content, as well as to the Dogma of the Analytic-Synthetic distinction and the Myth of the Given.[36] The short answer is that the relationship is a little murky because the second items in the relationship—the Dogma, the Dualism, and the Myth—are all a little murky. Nonetheless, there is nothing in the relationship to embarrass empiricism.

THE DISTINCTION BETWEEN ANALYTIC AND SYNTHETIC sentences is traditionally explained as that between sentences that are true or false solely by virtue of the meanings of their constituent expressions and those whose truth or falsity owes in part to something outside these meanings. Examples of analytic sentences are

All men are men, some bachelors are married, and nothing can be both red and green all over;

and of synthetic,

All men are mortal, some bachelors like spinach, and the theory of plate tectonics is true.

---

35. Davidson, "On the Very Idea of a Conceptual Scheme," p. 189. Richard Rorty agrees with Davidson and thinks, furthermore, that abandoning empiricism results in substantial benefit:

> Renouncing empiricism will leave us in Wittgensteinian peace and Humean good spirits—able to walk away from the traditional epistemological problematic with a good conscience. (Rorty, *Truth and Progress*, 142n10)

36. The relationship to Quine's other dogma (i.e., Reductionism) will become plain in the course of the discussion below of the analytic-synthetic distinction.

Quine called the analytic-synthetic distinction "an unempirical dogma of empiricists, a metaphysical article of faith,"[37] and he gave, over the years, a range of arguments against the legitimacy of the distinction. His principal argument calls into question the notion of meaning and rests on a strong behaviorist assumption. Neither the argument nor the assumption has generally been accepted, and I will not take time to review them here.[38] Setting aside the argument, there is something obviously puzzling about Quine's charge: how is the analytic-synthetic distinction a dogma of *empiricism*? If the distinction is a dogma, why is it not equally a dogma of rationalism and, indeed, of common sense? As Quine himself notes, the analytic-synthetic distinction goes back to Kant and was foreshadowed in Leibniz's distinction between truths of reason and truths of fact. By no stretch of interpretation can Kant and Leibniz be counted as empiricists.

There *is* a dogma—or, better, doctrine—about the analytic and the synthetic that is specific to early twentieth-century empiricism, a doctrine that is called into question by Quine's critique, and one whose rejection does not depend upon Quine's radical skepticism about meaning. We can isolate this doctrine if we focus not on the legitimacy of the analytic-synthetic distinction but on the *use* to which the empiricists put the distinction.

Hume distinguished between "relations of ideas" and "matters of fact." The former, he held, are "discoverable by the mere operation of thought, without dependence on what is any where existent in the universe."[39] In contrast, "matters of fact," Hume held, cannot be so discovered and require the aid of experience. Reichenbach followed Hume and said that it is an "empiricist principle" that "reason cannot make other than analytic contributions to knowledge."[40] Reason, according to Reichenbach's "empiricist principle," has no insight to impart to us about the structure of reality. Its contribution is only to unpack concepts, to spell out meanings, and to draw out that which is implicitly contained in given premises. Now, let us represent the natural thought that our

---

37. Quine, "Two Dogmas of Empiricism," p. 37.
38. Quine's argument occurs in chapter 2 of *Word and Object*, and it has spawned a vast critical literature.
39. Hume, *Enquiry*, 4.1.
40. Reichenbach, "Rationalism and Empiricism," pp. 342–43.

knowledge is built from the materials supplied by reason and experience as the equation

> Our knowledge = the contribution of reason + the contribution of experience.

We have seen that the contribution of experience, according to traditional empiricism, is propositional in form. We can represent this idea thus:

> The contribution of experience = the propositional given.

Then, Reichenbach's "empiricist principle,"

> The contribution of reason = the analytic,

yields the following characterization of the domain of the analytic:

> (1) The analytic = our knowledge – the propositional given.[41]

Since the propositional given is thin, it follows that the domain of the analytic must be large. That is, the notion of meaning must bridge the large gap between our knowledge and the propositional given. Thus arises the empiricist attraction to phenomenalism, the idea that the *meaning* of physical-object sentences can be spelled out in terms of sense-data.[42] (This is essentially what Quine called "the second dogma of empiricism.")

It is interesting that in Quine's empiricism there is also a significant remainder when the sensory input is "subtracted" from our knowledge. Quine says

> we can investigate the world, and man as a part of it, and thus find out what cues he could have of what goes on around him. Subtracting his cues from his world view, we get man's net contribution as the difference.[43]

---

41. For the purposes of this exposition, let us take the three terms in this equation to denote sets of sentences.

42. I should note that Reichenbach himself did not subscribe to phenomenalism. He offered instead an antirealist picture of empirical knowledge. He proposed that the propositions of empirical science should not be asserted with the claim of truth, but only in what he called "the sense of posit." This means roughly that it is advantageous to act as if these propositions are true.

43. Quine, *Word and Object*, p. 5.

This "net contribution" turns out to be large indeed and leads Quine to some radical conclusions. He writes, "Our ontology, like grammar, is part of our own conceptual contribution to our theory of the world"[44] and "the furniture of our world, the people and sticks and stones along with the electrons and molecules, have dwindled to manners of speaking."[45] Already in "Two Dogmas," he speaks of our knowledge as a "man-made fabric." Quine's predicament is thus similar to that of his opponents. One central difference between them is that Quine, unlike his opponents, refuses to invoke the notion of meaning to bridge the gap between knowledge and experiential input.

I suggest that equation (1) provides a good reading of the Dogma of the Analytic-Synthetic Distinction. Under this reading, the Dogma makes a strong claim about the analytic and the synthetic, namely, that the analytic side of the divide is heavy and the synthetic side light. It thus captures what is distinctive about early twentieth-century empiricists: they expected the notion of meaning to do heavy philosophical work.[46] They invoked meaning to underwrite a broad range of truths—from those of mathematics to those linking physical objects to experience. To reject this invocation, it is not necessary to show that the notion of meaning is illegitimate, only that it cannot serve the desired function. We can therefore separate the radical strands in Quine's attack on the analytic-synthetic distinction from those that call into question the empiricist use of the distinction. (I myself wish to reject the former, but I see great value in the latter.) In summary, then, under the proposed reading, we obtain a doctrine—dogma, if you insist—specifically of early twentieth-century empiricism, one to which rationalism and commonsense owe no allegiance, and

44. Quine, *Pursuit of Truth*, p. 36.

45. Quine, "Reply to Stroud," p. 474. This is not all that far from the Carnap of 1950. Carnap wrote in "Empiricism, Semantics, and Ontology" that "to accept the thing world [as opposed to a 'phenomenal' world] means nothing more than to accept a certain form of language" (§2).

46. Their expectation was fueled in part by the logicisms of Frege and Russell, which greatly impressed them. They took Frege's and Russell's work to show that all mathematical truth is analytic, i.e., that all of mathematics can be seen as arising from the fountainhead of meaning.

one that can be rejected on the basis of a moderate critique of meaning.[47]

I hope it is now plain that objections to the Dogma of the Analytic-Synthetic Distinction are not a threat to the empiricism proposed here. Our empiricism does not call upon the notion of meaning to do any heavy-duty philosophical work. This is possible because, in the first place, our empiricism is built upon a richer conception of the contribution of experience. The manifest gap between knowledge and experience that one finds in classical empiricism is simply avoided in the present account. In the second place, as noted above, our empiricism assigns a more robust role to reason: reason demarcates the views that are acceptable starting points of revision from those that are not. We can recognize that reason has no insight into the structure of reality. But it does not follow that its contribution is confined to the analytic. The total contribution of reason, like that of experience, is not propositional in form; it cannot be captured by a collection of sentences or propositions. Reason contributes to our knowledge by serving experience. It helps ensure that experience is not muffled, that in the course of arriving at our view of the world, we do our part in letting experience speak in a full and clear voice.

DAVIDSON CLAIMS THAT THE DUALISM OF SCHEME AND Content undermines empiricism. He thus implies that empiricism requires a separation of something called 'scheme' from something called 'content' and—since the separation is characterized as a "dualism"—this separation is wrong or undesirable. What is Davidson talking about when he speaks of "scheme" and "content"? He writes

> The scheme may be thought of as an ideology, a set of concepts . . . or the scheme may be a language. . . . The contents of

---

47. Under this reading, Quine's "second dogma" can be seen as arising from conjoining the "first dogma" with the thesis that empirical content can be distributed sentence by sentence. The "first dogma" becomes more fundamental. It can be held while the second is denied, say, on the basis of verification holism.

I should stress that, in proposing (1) as a reading of the "first dogma," I am not offering an interpretation of Quine's texts. Quine's intentions are obviously more radical.

the scheme may be . . . sense data, percepts, impressions, sensations, or appearances. . . .[48]

A little further on Davidson adds, "World view and cues, theory
and data; these are the scheme and content of which I have been
speaking."[49]

We are offered here several pairings of scheme and content,
including ideology and sense-data, language and impressions,
world views and cues, and theory and data. One question that
arises immediately is why these pairs count as instances of a *dualism*.
Why is it wrong or undesirable to separate, for example, language
from impressions, and world view from cues? The two are about as
distinct as things get and, it would appear, *ought* to be separated.[50]

We shall understand Davidson better, I think, if we set aside the
terminology of 'dualism' and focus directly on the features of
empiricism that Davidson finds objectionable. The following extract provides a useful hint:

Although sensation plays a crucial role in the causal process that
connects beliefs with the world, it is a mistake to think that it
plays an epistemological role in determining the contents of
those beliefs. In accepting this conclusion, we abandon the key
dogma of traditional empiricism, what I have called the third
dogma of empiricism. But that is to be expected: empiricism is
the view that the subjective ('experience') is the foundation of
objective empirical knowledge.[51]

Here we learn that it is not the mere separation of sensation from
belief that constitutes the "third dogma of empiricism," but the
idea that sensation "plays an epistemological role in determining
the contents of [the] beliefs." Davidson suggests that this idea is
implied by empiricism, which he characterizes as the view that

---

48. Davidson, "The Myth of the Subjective," p. 41.

49. Ibid., p. 42. See also his characterization of the scheme-content contrast on
pp. 189–91 of *Truth and Interpretation*.

50. McDowell interprets the scheme-content contrast to be that between
concepts considered "in abstraction from any connection with the deliverances of
the senses" and sensory intake considered in abstraction from concepts ("Scheme-
Content Dualism and Empiricism," p. 88). This separation may be regarded as a
genuine dualism. But it does not help Davidson, since, as McDowell himself argues,
empiricism does not imply that this kind of separation is legitimate.

51. Davidson, *Subjective, Intersubjective, Objective*, p. 46.

"the subjective ('experience') is the foundation of objective empirical knowledge." Davidson's conception of empiricism is clarified in his "Reply to John McDowell":

> What the senses "deliver" (i.e., cause) in perception is perceptual beliefs, and these do have an ultimate evidential role. If this is what it takes to be an empiricist, I'm an empiricist. An empiricist, however, in the "pallid" sense, since I postulate no epistemic intermediaries between reality and perceptual beliefs about reality.[52]

So, as Davidson understands it, "nonpallid" empiricism is a view that posits epistemic intermediaries between reality and perceptual beliefs. The intermediaries may be experiences, impressions, sensory stimulations, and other such things. What Davidson finds objectionable in empiricism[53] is that it assigns these intermediaries an *epistemic* role; it treats them as constituting the epistemic foundation of empirical knowledge. (Davidson's own view is that there are no epistemic intermediaries: experience, sensation, etc., have only a causal role in sustaining belief.) The "third dogma" as recently characterized is, then, a consequence of empiricism. It states that the intermediaries play "an epistemological role" in determining the contents of beliefs.

What is wrong, according to Davidson, with epistemic intermediaries? Three different arguments can be recovered from Davidson's writings. First, the intermediaries lead to skepticism. Second, they are of the wrong logical type to justify beliefs. Only something propositional can justify a belief, but sense-data and sensory stimulations, for instance, have no propositional content.[54] Third, these intermediaries are useless. Davidson argues that belief is by its very nature veridical and that all systems of belief are intertranslatable. If this is right, then all need for an external rational constraint—and thus for epistemic intermediaries—evaporates.

About this final argument I will confine myself to only one critical observation. Davidson argues for the veridicality of belief on

---

52. Davidson, "Reply to John McDowell," p. 106.
53. In the "nonpallid" sense. Henceforth, I omit this qualification since I shall be concerned only with "nonpallid" empiricism.
54. See, e.g., *Subjective, Intersubjective, Objective*, pp. 42–43 and 142–46. See also "Reply to John McDowell."

the basis of his theory of radical interpretation.[55] Crudely, the idea is that when interpreting the speech of another, it is necessary to construct simultaneously an account of the other's beliefs and also of the meanings of the other's utterances. One cannot first figure out meanings and then arrive at beliefs, nor can one first arrive at beliefs and then use these to figure out meanings. Belief and meaning are interdependent. Davidson concludes that the only way to deal with this interdependence is to assume *Charity*, that is, to assume that there is agreement between our beliefs and those of the other. (A further argument—which I shall skip—leads from Charity to the intrinsic veridicality of belief.) The observation I wish to make is that Davidson's argument rests on an improper treatment of interdependence. When dealing with interdependence, one should not favor any one hypothesis. One should work with arbitrary hypotheses and let the interdependence guide one to those that are the best. Davidson proposes one hypothesis—Charity—and then treats the hypothesis as the right one. This is illegitimate. Here is Davidson's formulation of the crux of his argument:

> We cannot take even a first step toward interpretation without knowing or assuming a great deal about the speaker's beliefs. Since knowledge of beliefs comes only with the ability to interpret words, the only possibility at the start is to assume general agreement on beliefs.[56]

The transition here is plainly invalid. There is not just one possibility "at the start." There are numerous possibilities: we can assume a general disagreement on beliefs; we can assume agreement on beliefs acquired during the day and disagreement on those acquired during the night; we can, in short, *assume* anything. Interdependence does not bestow any special status on Charity— either absolutely or "at the start." Davidson's final argument thus rests on a premiss that not only has little intrinsic credibility but that is not rendered the least bit plausible by considerations brought forward by him.[57] Let us set this argument aside.

55. See *Truth and Interpretation*, especially essays 9 and 13.

56. Davidson, *Truth and Interpretation*, p. 196.

57. Another argument for Charity, found in Davidson, rests on the premiss that "disagreement and agreement alike are intelligible only against a background of massive agreement" (*Truth and Interpretation*, p. 137). But this argument plainly begs the question; its premiss is no less doubtful than its conclusion.

Davidson's first two arguments are good, I think, when directed to specific choices of intermediaries. If the intermediaries are subjective entities (sense-data, etc.), then Davidson's first argument applies: skepticism is inevitable. If the intermediaries are sensory stimulations, as Quine takes them to be, then Davidson's second argument applies: the stimulations are not of the right logical type to be the epistemic foundations of our knowledge. Davidson is perfectly right in observing that Quine's empiricism involves a confusion of the causal with the rational. Sensory stimulations are at best the causal ground of our empirical knowledge, not its rational ground.

Davidson's arguments do not show, however, that *all* epistemic intermediaries are unacceptable. Davidson shares an assumption with the empiricists he criticizes: that the epistemic intermediaries must carry propositional content. He writes, "The relation between a sensation and a belief cannot be logical, since sensations are not beliefs or other propositional attitudes."[58] But, as we have seen, from the fact that something—e.g., experience—is not a propositional attitude, it does not follow that its relation to belief cannot be logical. At best, Davidson's arguments show that epistemic intermediaries that are propositional are unacceptable. They leave untouched the conception of experience I propose here. Experience, when conceived of as yielding a hypothetical given, can bear logical relations to beliefs. Indeed, its logical force may be powerful enough to sweep aside skepticism.

We can treat experience as an epistemic intermediary, and we can allow that "it plays an epistemological role in determining the contents of beliefs."[59] That is, we can embrace the Dualism of

---

Yet another argument for Charity can be extracted from Davidson's writings. It rests on the idea that a theory of meaning for a language is a Davidsonian theory of truth for it. And a theory of truth for another's language can be confirmed, the argument goes, only if the other's assents are taken as indicative of truth and his dissents are taken as indicative of falsehood. But this last step can be challenged: if the theory of truth is embedded in a broader psychological theory of the subject, then confirmation is possible without any presumption of Charity. And, of course, the equation of the theory of meaning with a Davidsonian theory of truth can be— and has been—reasonably challenged.

58. Davidson, *Subjective, Intersubjective, Objective*, p. 143.

59. Note that this idea does not commit one to a verificationist account of content. To say that experience helps determine content is not to say that experience constitutes content. Nor is it to say that content is fixed by verification or falsification conditions.

Scheme and Content in one of its readings. I have argued that in this reading the Dualism is a reasonable doctrine, not one that Davidson has refuted or rendered dubious.

CONCERNING THE MYTH OF THE GIVEN, I CAN BE BRIEF IN light of the earlier discussions (see especially §5B). If 'the given' is understood broadly to include all rational contribution of experience, irrespective of form, then empiricism is definitely committed to the existence of the given. However, so understood, the given is not a myth. To deny it is to deny that experience makes any rational contribution to knowledge, and this extreme position has little to recommend it. On the other hand, if 'the given' is understood narrowly and encompasses only such things as ideas, impressions, and sense data, then the given may be deemed a myth.[60] But under this reading, the given represents a commitment only of classical empiricism, not of empiricism in general. We can uphold the idea that the rational contribution of experience is large—we can even insist that experience is the supreme epistemic authority—while forswearing entirely the Cartesian conception of experience and the accompanying impressions, sense-data, and the like. Indeed, the principal goal of the theory offered here is none other than to sustain this idea.

Philosophers who would use the Dogma of the Analytic-Synthetic Distinction, the Dualism of Scheme and Content, or the Myth of the Given to kill empiricism will do well not only to sharpen their weapons but to aim more carefully at their target. Thus, they may score a hit against the Hume of 1739, or the Russell of 1912, or the Quine of 1969. Otherwise, they merely swing blunt metal in a fog of their own creation.

---

60. It is not completely clear how Sellars himself understands the Myth of the Given. One finds several nonequivalent formulations of the Myth in his *Empiricism and the Philosophy of Mind*. (On one formulation, that which occurs at the beginning of §32 of Sellars's book, even a classical empiricist can reject the Myth.) The ambiguity in the Myth is reflected in the divergent opinions of commentators on the question whether Sellars's aim is to dismantle empiricism or only to reform it. See chapter 5, fn. 30.

◌◌◌

SEVEN

REMOVING IDEALIZATION

◌◌◌ The picture of empirical knowledge I have painted is highly idealized, and this raises a legitimate question: does the picture have any application to our actual epistemic situation? We are not ideal, solitary beings that passively contemplate experience. We are active, and our choices affect our experiences; on occasion, we can even cause our experience to follow a particular course. Furthermore, we cannot run through the entire course of our past experience, with different conceptions in mind, looking for points of convergence. Our reason and our imagination are highly limited, and our memory is so weak that we can vividly recall only a few of our past experiences. (Indeed, it is our view that helps us to gain some inkling of what many of our past experiences must have been like.) It follows that we cannot arrive at, or justify, our conception of the world via a revision process of the sort described above. How, then, can any of us claim our conception of the world to be rational? Does the picture painted above retain any validity if we set aside idealization and turn to our actual situation?

I shall consider below the effects of recognizing that the resources available to the cognitive subject are limited (§7A), that the subject's actions affect her experiences (§7B), and that the subject is not solitary but a member of a society of knowledge seekers (§7C). In each of these cases, I shall argue, the removal of idealization actually strengthens and confirms the theory proposed above.[1]

7A. Limitation of Resources

It is true that the picture I have painted is highly idealized, but this is so in part because the picture is of an *ideal*, the ideal of rationality. An account of an ideal does not purport to be an account of our practices or of our achievements. It is obvious that we do not—and cannot—arrive at our view through a revision process. We *inherit* the greatest part of our view from our parents, our teachers, and our friends. It is also obvious that we do not achieve the ideal of convergence. Our view is a rich and profound inheritance, but it is not perfectly coherent. It seems to be a collage of conflicting pictures that are difficult to reconcile (e.g., the scientific image and what Wilfrid Sellars called the "manifest" image). And it contains both empirical anomalies and conceptual paradoxes. Hence, our view does not meet even the ideal of coherence, let alone that of convergence. None of this casts any doubt on the present proposal. An account of empirical rationality is to be assessed not by whether it deems us successful in reaching the ideal but by the guidance it provides to our empirical inquiries and by the sense it makes of our epistemic practices.

Consider a creature much like us that has limited resources: a limited memory to recall past experiences, a limited power of deduction, a limited ability to conceive alternatives, and so on. How might such a creature conduct itself if its aim is empirical rationality? The answer depends, of course, on the creature's conception of empirical rationality. If the conception were simple coherence, the creature would devote its efforts to seeking out points of incoherence in its view and to rectifying them; experience would play little or no role. If the conception were a foundationalist one, the creature would devote its efforts to drawing up lists of basic propositions ("axioms") and to logically linking its beliefs—even perceptual beliefs—to these propositions. Plainly, the creature's behavior in either case has very little in common with our own. It is true that we

---

1. The issues that arise here are large and complex. In this chapter, I merely take a peek behind the veil of idealization.

attempt to remove points of incoherence from our view, but this concern does not eclipse all others: we continue to experiment, to explore, and to build on experience. Further, while we seek justification for many of our beliefs, we rarely attempt to cast our entire view into a foundationalist mold. We devote little effort to founding, for example, perceptual beliefs on more basic propositions.

If the creature were a nihilist and rejected entirely the ideal of empirical rationality, then assessments of evidence and reasonableness would play no role in its practices. The creature would speak of "cause," "power," and "force," not of "reason," "evidence," and "persuasion." Again, this is far removed from our own empirical practices.

Suppose the creature's conception of empirical rationality is convergence in light of experience. How will the creature behave now? The creature cannot run through the entire course of its experience: its memory is too weak. It cannot consider all possible views: it has no antecedent grasp of all possibilities; its sense of possibility evolves with inquiry. What, then, will the creature do? Well, in the first place, the creature will consider, as far as it is in its power, alternative views. A perfect being, a raimex, having achieved convergence, might rest content with its uniquely perfect view. Not so with our imperfect creature, no matter how impressed it is with the view bequeathed to it and no matter how free the view is from empirical anomaly. Second, the creature will set aside alternative views such as solipsism that are self-perpetuating, that constitute epistemic traps. It will also attempt to weed out elements in its own view that promote epistemic entrapment. Third, the creature will set aside views that it already knows by past experience not to be viable. It will not take on the burden of seeking convergence with all views; it needs to conserve its resources. Fourth, and most crucially, the creature will appeal to experience to bring about convergence among the alternatives that remain. It is as if each view represents a person, and the creature tries to so expose it to experience that it is transformed in the desired way. (Of course, sometimes the effect will be to transform the creature itself, not the competitor.) Fifth, and finally, the creature will repeat the above four-stage process as its sense of possibility expands and its own view is enriched by criticism and experience. All this is a fairly good reflection of our own best conduct. The ideal of convergence is visible in our epistemic practices once we factor in limitation of resources. Experience is the oracle we consult—and should consult—to settle the most profound differences. But appeals to the oracle are not free, and we consult it mindful of our limited resources.

Let us say that a view is *reasonable (for us)* iff it meets the ideal of empirical rationality as far as our resources allow.[2] And let us say that a perceptual judgment is *reasonable* iff it is a product of a reasonable view.[3] Then, neither our view nor our perceptual judgments are reasonable if the ideal of empirical rationality is simply coherence or empiricist foundationalism. We simply do not devote our resources in the manner dictated by these ideals—nor do we think it worthwhile to do so. On the other hand, if the ideal of epistemic rationality is convergence in light of experience, then it is plausible to claim that our view is reasonable, at least in its main features if not in all the details.[4] Hence, it is plausible to claim also that our perceptual judgments are largely reasonable.

Limitation of resources renders it vital to draw a distinction between *reasonable* and (*absolutely*) *justifiable*, where the justifiable is that for which one can prove entitlement.[5] Suppose our creature puts its resources to the best possible use and arrives at length at a view. The creature's view is, by definition, reasonable. Now, let us press the creature for a justification for its view; let us press it to establish entitlement. What will we gain except some amusement at the creature's expense? The creature cannot recount its entire epistemic history. It can recall at best a few episodes and still fewer experiences. The creature can say that it has diligently sought the epistemic ideal, but it will be unable to back up its claim with sufficient instances. Here is another illustration of the same point: A forgetful mathematician constructs a proof, carefully following

---

2. This is really a definition schema, not a particular definition; different specifications of "available resources" yield different notions of reasonableness. For my purposes here, the schematic definition suffices.

3. More precisely, a perceptual judgment P is reasonable for us *in light of an experience e* iff there is a view v such that v is reasonable for us and $P \in \Gamma_e(v)$.

4. I take the main features to include not only such broad ideas as that we have bodies and that we can move about from place to place, but more specific ones as well, e.g., that we have eyes and that white things look yellow to us in certain circumstances.

Note that the presence of incoherence does not refute the claim that our view is reasonable. Limitations in resources may render it impossible for us to eliminate all incoherence.

5. This is a philosophical notion of justifiable, not the ordinary one.

sound logic. But by the time he reaches the end, he cannot remember the beginning of his proof! The mathematician is reasonable in asserting his theorem, though he cannot now provide a justification for it.

What if someone challenges us for the justification of our view or for the justification of the claim that our view is reasonable? There is little we can say in direct response. But this is no cause for embarrassment, for the challenge is empty. Failure to meet the challenge costs us nothing: we are not required to change any element of our view, nor is the reasonableness of our view undermined. It is a false picture that creates a contrary impression: the picture of a self-sufficient, limitless knower whose entire past is available to present consciousness. It is this picture that leads one to confuse diachronic reasonableness with the synchronic ability to establish entitlement (or, if the two are distinguished, to undervalue diachronic reasonableness). The synchronic ability is highly demanding of our epistemic resources; we simply cannot afford it.

In some areas of inquiry—parts of mathematics being paradigm examples—the resources needed to discover the truth of a claim are large. But the resources needed to establish entitlement, once the discovery is made, are trivial. Desargues's theorem requires genius for discovery. But after Desargues, even a dunce can establish full entitlement by reproducing Desargues's proof. To establish entitlement, one does not need to rehearse the historical complexities of how the proof was discovered, or might be discovered. In other areas of inquiry, however, to establish full entitlement, one has in effect to retrace the history of the discovery. For instance, one may have arrived at an empirical claim by an extended rational reflection on a long series of experiments. To fully establish entitlement, one would simply need to go over that long history—something that may be beyond one's limited powers. A failure to *establish* entitlement here does not show lack of entitlement.

The epistemic ideal that has one always ready with a proof of entitlement is of highly limited value. The ideal is harmful in most areas of inquiry. (It fails to be useful even in all parts of mathematics.) The ideal can easily distort our view of our ordinary epistemic practices, including the practice of giving and asking for justification. These practices, it is important to remember, serve to further *our* epistemic goals, the goals of beings with highly limited resources. Their function is not the absurd one of letting us mimic an epistemic god.

Bald challenges to our entitlement to our view are worthless. There is a different kind of challenge, however, that is often of great value. Here the challenge is specific. The challenge may be, for example, that some element of our view is incoherent in a hitherto unsuspected way, or that we have not considered a particular alternative, or that we have not conducted some inquiry in an optimal way. These challenges test our view and can help us to improve it. We value such challenges, and we prize the ability to meet them. This points to a third epistemic notion, different from reasonableness and justification. Let us say that a position P of a person X is *dialectically viable* iff X can meet specific challenges (of a certain kind) to P.[6] Then, X's position P may be reasonable but may neither be justifiable (because of limitation of resources) nor be dialectically viable (because, e.g., the position becomes unstable when some evidence beyond the ken of X is considered). Furthermore, X's position P may be dialectically viable but may be neither justifiable nor reasonable. (X may have arrived at P by a fallacious argument and there may be no sound way for X to reach P within the bounds of available resources.)[7] Our own view is unjustifiable, and its dialectical viability is limited. It is achievement enough if it is reasonable.

7B. Actions and Experiences

The most significant idealization in the picture painted above is the neglect of action. It is obvious that our experiences depend on our actions. I turn my head to the right and the yellow coaster comes into view. The resulting visual experience obviously depends on my action; had I turned my head to the left, my experience would have been different. This simple fact of the dependence of experience on action raises an important epistemological problem. It implies that experience depends also on view: views substantially

6. I put in the parenthetical condition to record that dialectical viability comes in degrees. A comparative notion of dialectical viability is useful and is easily defined.

7. In some contexts, the distinction between the three notions—justifiability, reasonableness, and dialectical viability—may in effect collapse. One establishes one's entitlement to Desargues's theorem by producing a proof of it from accepted axioms. The same proof establishes the reasonableness of one's claim and enables one to meet all dialectical challenges.

affect courses of actions ("lifestyles"), and these in turn affect a subject's experiences. Hence, a view exercises a considerable influence on the experiences that are called on to assess it: the judged plays an important role in the selection of the jury. Isn't this dependence of the jury on the judged vicious? Doesn't it cast doubt on the epistemic authority of experience?

The dependence *can* be vicious, as can be seen in the following examples. (1) A community accepts a chauvinist view that denigrates outsiders and forbids interaction with them. The chauvinist attitude so narrows the life of the community that its experiences provide no rational incentive for a change in view. The community's view ends up being stable, but this stability is of little epistemic value. The judged has now thoroughly corrupted the jury. (2) A community accepts a mystical view that takes ordinary experience to be nearly worthless in gaining a true account of reality. A true account can be gained, the view holds, exclusively through certain rare and extraordinary experiences that occur only when a prescribed course of austerities is followed with great diligence. The view thus sends its devotees off in a vain search for extraordinary experiences. Again, the view so limits experience that any stability it possesses is of little value. (3) A drug addict holds the view that he is most perceptive when he is "high"; he thinks that by leading his drugged lifestyle he best fulfills his epistemic obligations. The addict's experiences may confirm his view. Indeed, the drugs may so corrupt his cognitive mechanism that he may, in fact, be the most perceptive when he is "high." Nonetheless, there is something sick in his lifestyle and in the view that leads to it.[8]

The dependence of experience on action points to the necessity of distinguishing two components in the notion of epistemic rationality.[9] The first component is "rationality of a view relative to a sequence of experience $\mathscr{E}$," a notion discussed in chapter 4. The second component is "epistemic rationality of $\mathscr{E}$" or, more

---

8. A related example is a view that may promise confirmation but only *after* a devotee fully accepts the view. (In a variant example, the view promises confirmation but only after a devotee is dead!) And full acceptance may be possible only via such corruption of one's rationality that subsequent experiences have little rational force. E.g., one so damages the rational mechanism that one finds confirmation of the view in every possible experience.

9. The same holds for reasonableness.

accurately, "epistemic rationality of actions that result in $\mathscr{E}$." These two components correspond to two different types of epistemic criticism. An individual is open to the first type of criticism if the view he accepts is not warranted by his experiences. An individual is open to the second type of criticism if his experiences are a product of actions that are not epistemically appropriate. In example (1), a community member may be immune from the first sort of criticism. Assuming he is blameless in accepting the community view, the member may be right not to have shifted his view in light of his actual experiences. Nonetheless, he may be open to the second type of criticism: it can be argued that he should have exposed himself to broader experience, that he should have interacted with the outsiders. Full epistemic rationality requires not only that the subject's view be rational in light of her experiences; it requires that the experiences result from actions that are rational from the epistemic viewpoint. In short, a subject's view is fully rational iff it is rational relative to a *rational* course of experience.

A full assessment of a subject's epistemic rationality requires, then, an assessment of the subject's actions. It follows that the assessment of epistemic rationality (and reasonableness) needs to be made in the context of an assessment of rationality in general. Pure epistemic rationality may demand that we perform a series of experiments, but it may be foolish or immoral to do so. Epistemic values are not the only ones that concern us when we choose between actions. We have other concerns—we want to live and we wish to respect others, for example—and sometimes it is rational for us to let these other concerns override epistemic values.[10] Suppose the mystical view considered in example (2) was put to us as a challenge. Should we seek convergence with respect to it? Should we go through the prescribed course of austerities and seek extraordinary experiences posited in the mystical view? If we had no other concerns—no body to feed, no children to care for, and so on—epistemic concerns might render it rational for us to abandon our ordinary life for a life of austerity. But, under normal circumstances, it would be foolish for us to do so. (And this is so even if as a matter of fact the mystical view is correct.)

---

10. It is a delicate question, when we should let other concerns override epistemic values, for our conception of values is itself affected by our view of the self and the world. Hence, our interest in arriving at a correct view is great.

The dependence of experience on action and view brings to light a new kind of epistemic entrapment. The solipsist view considered above (§5E) entraps by weakening the logical power of perceptual judgments: the solipsist perceptual judgments are unable to bring the view into alignment with the world. Irrespective of how the world is, a person who subscribes to the solipsist view is trapped within it. His perceptual judgments have no power to guide him out of his error.[11] In the new kind of entrapment, the view is again self-perpetuating, but it invokes a different mechanism for this effect. Now it does not reduce the logical power of perceptual judgments. Instead, it perpetuates itself by (epistemically) debilitating the subject, as example (3) vividly illustrates. Here, the view leads the addict to so weaken his cognitive system (and perhaps his will) that he is unable to overthrow the view. Example (2) exhibits a more subtle instance of the same phenomenon. The mystical view guides the subject to waste valuable epistemic resources and so renders him incapable of escaping the trap that the view sets for him. Example (1) is not an instance of epistemic entrapment, I think. The subject's epistemic horizon is narrowed here also, but one can seek convergence with the chauvinist view without being trapped within it.

The mystical and the addict views are not rigid, and they are not inadmissible. A godlike being with large resources may well be able to bring about convergence with them: it can undertake a series of experiments that radically transforms these views into its own. Still, the mystical and addict views are *inadmissible for* creatures like us—creatures with limited powers and with needs that leave scant resources for purely epistemic ends. To meet the challenge posed by these views, we should not attempt to bring about convergence—that would be foolish. We can meet the challenge simply by observing that these views are epistemic traps for us. Our view is reasonable if it is the point of convergence of views that are admissible *for us*.

The epistemic situation of a finite creature determines the views that are admissible for it; the more powerful the creature, the wider the range of admissible views. Hence, a view that is reasonable for one creature can be unreasonable for another, even though the two suffer subjectively the same experiences.

---

11. I am setting aside the power of imagination.

It is rational for a finite creature to avoid epistemic traps, but there is no guarantee that it will be successful in doing so. The views that a creature deems admissible are determined by its antecedent view. And the antecedent view, though reasonable, can steer the creative away from fruitful lines of inquiry—lines of inquiry that might radically reshape its conception of admissibility. For example, the belief that a particular drug greatly harms cognitive power may be reasonable for a particular creature. But the belief may be false. The drug may actually enhance cognitive power, as the creature would discover if it would throw caution to the wind and just try the drug.

The danger of epistemic traps comes with our finite situation, and nothing we can do will guarantee security from it. Some consoling thoughts can, nonetheless, be offered. First, the danger shows the importance of freedom and tolerance—tolerance even of certain kinds of irrationality. An eccentric individual who follows a crazy lifestyle at great risk to himself can show us out of a trap when all rational calculation will keep us confined. Second, even if our view is an epistemic trap, it may be sufficient for our practical needs; it may be adequate to feed and shelter ourselves and our children. Third, epistemic traps are more realistic, but they are no more a threat to our rationality than are such skeptical hypotheses as the evil demon.

The dependence of experience on action and view is a source not only of epistemic danger but also of epistemic opportunity. Let us notice, to begin with, that the dependence does not preclude the *epistemological* autonomy and integrity of experience. An experience may be a product of some actions, which in turn may be prompted by a view. Nevertheless, the experience can undermine the view to which it owes its existence (see §4C). The jurors, though selected by the judged, can rule against him. Notice next that sometimes the dependence of experience on action actually enhances our rational confidence in a view. My confidence in the belief that almost all crows are black is enhanced when my experiences of black crows are the results of my own actions and choices: I choose to visit such and such crow habitats to test the belief. If I had been wheeled to the same locations by some alien force, then my confidence in the belief would be lower even though my visual experiences were subjectively the same. (I would want some positive reason to think that the alien force had no bias in favor of habitats where crows are black.) Finally, let us notice that the dependence enables us to overcome some limitations of resources. Presented with two theories of mechanics, we may find it difficult to render a decision in the face of passive experiences. The objects experienced may exhibit behavior that is much too complex for our poor abilities. But if we could construct our own experiment, the decision might be easy.

In short, by recognizing the dependence of experience on action, we recognize that our epistemic situation is complex. However, the dependence does not threaten the epistemic authority of experience. Nor does it threaten the account of the authority offered here. In fact, by bringing to light a new kind of epistemic trap, the dependence enables us to reject a wider range of views as inadmissible and thus it strengthens the present account.

7C. Society

One approach to a society of knowers—an approach not without some usefulness—is to treat the society as a unitary cognitive subject. In this approach, we allow ourselves to speak of such things as the "societal view" (a collage constructed somehow from the views cf the members) and of the "experiences of the society" (as if the society were a leviathan with billions of eyes and ears). We can then go on to consider epistemological questions such as whether the societal view is rational or reasonable, given societal experiences. Of course, this particular question poses no new problems once we accept the underlying abstractions. But a more demanding epistemological problem lurks in the neighborhood. Suppose that the societal view is rendered rational by societal experiences. Now, it appears that typically these experiences will render rational a far richer view than any that is rendered rational by the experiences of an individual member. The experiences of an individual are a minute sliver of the experiences of the society as a whole. And it is precisely because the wider experience of society teaches more that we pursue inquiry cooperatively, not in isolation. But this fact creates a problem. Empiricism seems to say that a subject is (epistemically) irrational if he accepts anything that is not rendered rational by his own experiences. Hence, if the subject accepts anything novel that societal experiences teach, then the subject is being irrational. This makes it seem as though education, by enriching the view of a subject, does not promote but rather undermines individual rationality.

We can put the problem as a dilemma. Either the societal experiences render more claims rational than the experiences of an individual (say, Z), or they do not. In the latter case, the societal experiences promote, by hypothesis, no epistemic gain for Z. In the former case, the societal experiences render rational some claims not known to Z, but this is useless for Z. For it remains irrational for Z to accept any of these claims. Hence, in either case, the wider experience of society is of no epistemic value for Z.

An obvious response to this argument is to say that it equivocates on 'renders rational'. In one sense of this phrase, societal experiences typically do render rational a wider body of claims than do the experiences of an individual Z. For example, societal experiences may render rational the claim that almost all crows are black, but Z's experiences, consisting of only a few observations of crows, may fail to do so. Here the sense of 'renders rational' is something like "renders rational directly." To determine whether Z's experiences render a claim rational in this sense, we ignore things Z has read in books and has heard from his teachers. The other sense of 'renders rational' is broader and takes into account all of Z's experiences, including reading and listening experiences. In this sense, Z's experiences can render rational the claim that almost all crows are black, even though Z has seen relatively few crows.

The response is helpful but does not dissolve the real problem. Let us set aside the first sense of 'renders rational'—we shall not be concerned with it any longer—and focus on the second, broader sense. The response has it that Z's experiences can render rational claims that are rendered rational by societal experiences. But how can this be? Through his reading, Z may have acquired much of the far-ranging societal view. How can Z's narrow experiences render rational a far-ranging societal view? What magic has language wrought that the rational power of far-flung and extensive societal experience can be concentrated in the tiny sliver of experience that is Z's?

This problem is one of many thorns in the side of classical empiricism. Even if classical empiricists can work themselves out of their solipsist beginnings into the world of everyday objects, and even if they can come to see some of the inhabitants of the world as persons, and even if they can attach meanings to the sounds that these persons produce—and each of these steps presents classical empiricists with overwhelming difficulties—even after all that, the present problem remains to pester them. How do they gain entitlement to the claim that the inhabitants are reliable, that their utterances are mostly true? If the degree of entitlement is given by the degree to which one has independently checked that the utterances are true, then the entitlement is feeble indeed. What, then, is the source of the entitlement? The question is urgent for classical empiricists because without an answer to it, they are unable to explain how an individual gains entitlement to the greater part of her view.

An alternative approach to the problem reverses the order of explanation found in classical empiricism. Instead of beginning with the internal and the individual, we now take the external and the societal to be primary. We begin by explaining rationality at the societal level, making free use of external factors (e.g., reliability). We then go on to explain rationality at the individual level, jettisoning any elements of the internal and the subjective that escape our net. The program is refreshing, but as far as I can see, it is no more viable than classical empiricism. For how do we get around the obvious fact that the reasonableness of the societal view requires that the relevant perceptual judgments of individual members be reasonable (for the most part)? How are we to explain societal rationality without some reliance on the notion of individual rationality? Davidson tried to gain societal rationality solely on the basis of holistic considerations. He argued that the very interpretation of language requires that the principle of charity must be respected, and this ensures, according to Davidson, the veridicality of belief. We have already seen, however, that this optimistic picture rests on an improper treatment of interdependence (§6C).

The rationality and reasonableness of an individual's view should not be closely tied to the rationality and reasonableness of the societal view. The societal view may be irrational and unreasonable, yet the individual's subscription to that view may be perfectly reasonable. A child is no less reasonable when she swallows "intelligent design" at school as when her counterpart takes in Darwin. The epistemic positions of the two children are similar. They both arrive at their beliefs on the basis of what they encounter: books of impressive thickness, realistic pictures, and so on.

It is immaterial that the former's textbook contains shoddy science, for the child is in no position to know this.[12]

The mismatch between reasonableness at the societal and individual levels has one of its roots in the mismatch of available resources at the two levels. Intelligent design is an unreasonable societal view for it cannot meet certain routine paleontological challenges. Nevertheless, the doctrine can be reasonable for the child to accept because the paleontological challenges are inappropriate in light of her resources, her epistemic position, and her needs. Much of a layman's acceptance of science has the same character. The acceptance is reasonable because, in part, the challenges it must meet are minimal. A wise layman realizes this and seeks the safety of skeptical neutrality in an encounter with an expert challenger.

An individual's far-flung view is not, I suggest, rendered rational by her experiences. Rationality—or, at any rate, full rationality—demands convergence over *all* admissible views, and an individual's experiences are too meager to ensure such wide convergence. Still, the experience can render the view *reasonable*: there can be convergence enough, given the individual's resources and needs. Ideally, the individual's view would be rendered rational by the experiences of the society as a whole. In our own case, even this is too much to hope for; the resources of our society are limited, and the demands on them numerous. There is gain nonetheless because societal experiences render the view more robust: they ensure convergence over a wider domain. Thus, even though an individual cannot meet a challenge on the basis of her own experiences, she may meet it indirectly, by deferring to others and their experiences.

Let me stress that by suggesting that an individual's view may not be rendered rational by her experiences, I am not abandoning empiricism. The empiricism I have defended is not psychological or sociological in character. This empiricism does not claim, for example, that experience is the primary force shaping human belief. Nor does it claim, to take another example, that our societal

---

12. For another example, the reasonableness of my belief in plate tectonics is not affected even if, as a matter of fact, the evidence for the theory is doctored; and even if the whole science enterprise, unbeknownst to me, is a giant conspiracy; and even if I am deluded by an evil demon into thinking that there is an external world.

mechanisms enable us to conduct inquiry in a rational or reasonable way. Such psychological and sociological claims are empirical and should be settled by an empirical inquiry, not by philosophy. The empiricism defended here makes a normative claim, namely, that we should consult experience to settle claims about the world, that experience is the supreme epistemic authority. This normative thesis is challenged by the skeptical argument that experience is unfit to serve this role because its pronouncements are confined to the subjective. I traced the skeptical argument to a logical premiss—that the given in experience is propositional—and I argued that we should reject this premiss. I buttressed the normative claim with an alternative account of the given and with a *logical* thesis: experience, under the proposed given, *can* dictate a specific view about the self and the world; indeed, it can dictate a view very much like our commonsense view. It is thus that I tried to defend the normative claim from the skeptical challenge. Plainly, the defense does not depend upon psychological and sociological theses of the sort mentioned above.

Returning to the dilemma, I suggest that we respond to it by distinguishing two senses of 'epistemic value'. In one sense, something has epistemic value iff it affects what it is reasonable for a subject to accept. In this sense, societal experiences do not have any epistemic value over and above the subject's experiences. Nor should they be expected to have any such value, for what is reasonable for a subject to accept is determined by her own experiences. In the other sense of 'epistemic value', something has epistemic value iff it affects epistemic assessments of the subject's beliefs and practices—assessments such as whether the subject's beliefs are true and whether her practices are reliable. In this sense, societal experiences plainly have epistemic value over and above the subject's experiences. Under the former reading, the dilemma is a sound argument for an unremarkable conclusion. Under the latter, both horns of the dilemma are fallacious.

EIGHT

☾◉☽

CONCLUDING REMARKS

☾◉☽ The idea around which the argument of this book is built is that of the interdependence of perceptual judgments and view. The rationality of our view depends upon the rationality of our perceptual judgments, and the rationality of our perceptual judgments depends in turn upon the rationality of our view. This interdependence is not a threat, I have argued, to the unconditional rationality of our view and perceptual judgments.[1] Far from it! It provides the best route to understanding this rationality. The interdependence dictates that the given in an experience is hypothetical, not propositional. The epistemological function of an experience is not to reveal little facts to us; it is to reveal empirical rational links that emanate from a view—*any* view. So, an experience, taken in isolation, does not impose any categorical rational obligations on us. However, a sequence of experiences can impose such obligations. A sequence of experiences induces a rational dynamics on all views, and if the dynamics displays convergence, we gain absolute rationality of view and perceptual judgment. Just as the dynamics of our Earth ensures its stability even in the absence of material support, similarly the revision

---

1. I revert here to the idealization and so speak of rationality and not of reasonableness.

dynamics of empirical knowledge ensures its rationality even in the absence of sensory, propositional foundations.

The present proposal respects both the Multiple-Factorizability of Experience and the Insight of Empiricism (chapter 1). By acknowledging the invariable interdependence of perceptual judgments and view, it respects the idea of Multiple-Factorizability (see §2F). By recognizing experience to be the force behind the rational dynamics of views, it accommodates the Insight of Empiricism.

The present proposal improves on classical models of epistemic rationality. We can accept the classical-empiricist idea that the rationality of our view is rooted in experience, but we dispense with the mythical pure datum that classical empiricism posits in experience. We thus evade the forces that push classical empiricism toward skepticism and idealism (see chapters 2 and 6). The proposal improves on rationalist models because we do not ossify any part of our view as a priori. Even broad features of our conception of the world (e.g., the existence of external objects and the structure of space-time) remain malleable; they are changeable in light of experience.

The proposed model of rationality is abstract, but it conforms with—and makes sense of—our best epistemic practices. We subscribe to the ideal of rationality in our epistemic practices, including the practice of making perceptual judgments. Our commitment to the ideal remains strong even though we cannot break free of the interdependence of perceptual judgments and view. Any attempt we make to provide empirical justification presupposes the rationality of something, of a part of our view or of some perceptual judgments; we never reach presuppositionless ground. The proposed model makes sense of this. It shows that the ideal of epistemic rationality does not require us to break free of the interdependence. In accepting the ideal, we do not take on a commitment to build empirical knowledge on the basis of a pure datum. Nor do we take on a commitment to provide an a priori argument for any substantial part of our view. As the skeptics have repeatedly pointed out, these commitments are impossible to meet. But this fact casts no doubt on the ideal of rationality or on our commitment to it.

According to the proposed model, the commitment we take on in accepting the ideal of rationality is quite different. The commitment is to the ideal of *convergence in light of experience*. This entails not only the familiar commitment to modifying our view in light of experience. It entails also a commitment to openness to alternative views and to meeting challenges posed by them. We fail to live up to the ideal of epistemic rationality not only when we are insensitive to experience or blind to logical implications but also when we are oblivious to alternative views. Failures of imagination, no less than failures of perception and reason, are failures of epistemic rationality.

We can meet challenges posed by alternative views in a variety of ways. One familiar way is logical: we can try to bring out an incoherence in the alternative view. Another method, more powerful and satisfying, is through experience: the alternative view so evolves under the force of its own perceptual judgments that it converges with our view. These two methods are insufficient, however, to meet the challenges posed by all views. Certain views loved by the skeptics—for instance, solipsism—are neither incoherent nor convergent. The present model provides a new tool for dealing with these troublesome views. The model shows that the dynamical behavior of a view can provide a reason for rejecting it. For instance, we may rule out solipsism because it is a rigid view and because experience provides no positive reason in its favor (§5E).[2]

In short, a commitment to encourage and meet challenges posed by alternative views is a part of our best epistemic practice. This commitment makes perfect sense under the proposed model. Indeed, according to the model, this commitment is the practical core of the ideal of epistemic rationality.

---

2. I believe the present proposal improves here on traditional models of epistemic rationality. Traditional models invoke *conservativeness* to rule out troublesome views. But, in my opinion, conservativeness is not an epistemic virtue. The mere fact that we accept a view does not render it more rational than other views. Suppose we are faced with a view that has all the other epistemic virtues as the view that we hold. We cannot claim that our view is epistemically superior simply on the ground that we accept it. For if we could, then by parity, a person who accepts the alternative view could equally well claim that it is his view that is epistemically superior. We have a stand off, and epistemic rationality demands that we suspend judgment. Of course, there may be strong practical reasons for persisting with our acceptance of the original view. But this shows only that conservativeness may be a practical necessity, not that it is an epistemic virtue.

The present proposal throws light on another aspect of our epistemic practice. In our empirical inquiries, *ordinary* perceptual judgments play a critical role: it is these judgments that guide us to enrich and, sometimes, to radically reshape our view. But ordinary perceptual judgments typically implicate a view and are liable to error. For example, judgments such as the following can be perceptual:

1. The straight distance between city X and city Y is 3,000 stadia.
2. The broken lamp is up above the stove.
3. The pain is in my tooth.

But these judgments can carry false implications. Judgment (1) can implicate an erroneous conception of "straight distance"; judgment (2), an erroneous conception of "up above"; judgment (3), an erroneous conception of "pain" and "in," and perhaps even "my." In the present model, this situation does not call for logical rectification. We do not need to seek error-free grounds for empirical knowledge; we can accept the situation as is. The fundamental logical process in empirical inquiry, according to the present model, does not take us from truth to truth, but from error to truth. Erroneous perceptual judgment can have the power to guide us to the truth about reality.

The distinction between empirical and a priori inquiries is a useful part of our ordinary epistemic practice. And the proposed model preserves the distinction while avoiding traditional distortions. The tradition understands the distinction in terms of the idea of the propositional given. An inquiry is empirical iff its characteristic knowledge claims are empirical. And a knowledge claim is empirical iff its justification is indispensably grounded in one or more propositions in the given in experience. In the traditional picture, each knowledge claim sits on top of a pyramidlike structure of justification. If some of the propositions in the base of this structure belong to the given in experience, then the knowledge claim is empirical; if not, then the knowledge claim is a priori. In the former case, the justification of the knowledge claim is rooted in experience; in the latter case, the justification is independent of experience.

The traditional explanation imposes a sharp and absolute division on our inquiries, and therefore raises a puzzle. Under which head does philosophy fall? Philosophy has little to offer that is empirically novel, and its a priori arguments are dwarfed by the most elementary mathematics. What, then, is the role of philosophy in our epistemic practice? Should we think of philosophy as concerned with concepts and with the elucidation of meaning (and thus as being a priori after all)? Or should we think of it as an assistant to the empirical sciences, helping them to smooth out ontology (e.g., enabling them to dispense with the quantity of temperature in favor of ordered pairs and, as a bonus, ordered pairs in favor of sets)? Neither account seems to fit what is best in philosophy.

The present model rejects as fictional the idea of a propositional given and the concomitant idea of a pyramidlike structure of justification. Still, the model allows for a realistic distinction between empirical and a priori inquiries. The distinction can be drawn not in terms of *justification* but in terms of *methodology*. An inquiry is empirical (a priori) iff its characteristic questions are empirical (a priori). And a question is empirical (a priori) iff our methods for arriving at a rational answer to it require an appeal (no appeal) to experience. Geography is empirical because our methods for arriving at rational answers to its questions—for example, "is Lake Michigan at least 900 feet deep at some point?"—require appeals to experience. Arithmetic is a priori because rational answers to its questions—for example, "is there a prime number between 1,000 and 1,010?"—can be gained independently of experience. One can shut out one's senses completely and still come to know that there is a prime number between 1,000 and 1,010 (assuming one's memory for numbers is good).

The distinction thus made between empirical and a priori inquiries is not sharp, and more important, fails to be absolute. The distinction makes reference to *our* methods of rationally settling questions and hence it has validity only for us, not for all rational beings. Given our capacities and our knowledge of the world, the rational method for us to determine the depth of Lake Michigan at its deep points is to follow certain well-understood empirical procedures involving sonar and such. For other rational beings, the method may be quite different. Some beings may have the capacity to estimate depths simply by looking, somewhat the way we can estimate heights of men. It is even conceivable that some beings come to know that they have perfectly reliable intuitions about depths—perhaps a god has stamped information about depths in their minds. For such beings, questions about depths would be a priori. (The example is far-fetched, but a similar view has been held for properties of space.) In any case, the point is that our methods for answering questions depend upon our view.[3] Hence, under the above elucidation, the distinction between the empirical and the a priori is not independent of view. This should not count against the elucidation, for the functions allocated to the distinction in ordinary practice do not require absoluteness.

The proposed elucidation yields an intuitive sorting of disciplines and their inquiries into the categories of the empirical and the a priori. Some disciplines (e.g., physics) turn out to be heterogeneous, consisting of some inquiries that are empirical and others that are a priori. What about philosophy? Is it empirical, or a priori, or heterogeneous? The question does not seem to be apt. Philosophical questions—for example, "do external objects exist?" "are any of our choices genuinely free?" "are moral values real?"— cannot be answered by a course of experimentation. One can raise one's hand, look at it, and pronounce "here is a hand," but one leaves the question of the external world completely untouched, and matters are not improved by more complex experimentation. Nor do we know of any a priori course of inquiry that would settle these questions. There is, in fact, no available *method* for answering philosophical questions. All attempts to bring method into philosophy—to turn philosophy scientific—have been dismal failures. None of this reflects badly on philosophy and its concerns,

---

3. The same holds for the broad methodological injunction of empiricism to explore and experiment. This, too, is not independent of view. Had we accepted a different view about ourselves and the world, we might have had reason to reject the injunction.

Observe that the injunction is logically distinct from the empiricist thesis that the rationality of a view is rooted in experience: that it is convergence in light of experience that renders a view rational. A view may imply a rejection of the empiricist injunction, yet the rationality of that very view may be rooted in experience. Equally, it is possible to reject the empiricist thesis about rationality but accept the injunction. This would be the position of one who accepts the present scientific view with its methodological stress on experience but sees the rationality of the view as coming in part from substantive truths of reason.

A full defense of the insight of empiricism thus consists of two separate parts. One part contains a defense of the idea that experience is the supreme epistemic authority. The argument here rests on the thesis that the rationality of a view is rooted in experience. This argument is general and does not refer to the details of our actual view. The other part contains the defense of the methodological injunction. The argument here is specific and appeals to the detailed elements of our view. In this book I have focused on the first part of the defense, which is the one of greater philosophical interest.

only on attempts to force the subject into the empirical/a priori mold.

The desire to force philosophy into the empirical/a priori mold arises from much too simple a picture of our epistemic situation—a picture I hope to have undermined. The methods that have come down to us for seeking knowledge are rich and profound. But they are not universal—they do not cover all domains—and they are not founded on a crystal-clear, error-free view. We can pursue our arithmetical inquiries while remaining fundamentally unclear about the nature of number and about its role in our thought. Our conception of space and time can be flawed, and yet it can guide us to a better conception. And we can study human cognition while remaining confused about the logical structure of empirical knowledge. The edifice of knowledge that has been bequeathed to us is magnificent. Still, the skeptics are not without a point when they draw attention to structural defects in it. Any searching examination in any area of our inquiry reveals lacunae and, worse, paradox. The early pages of a textbook, whether on logic or geology or some other subject, have to be passed over uncritically if one is to make progress—and these are the pages that deal with the most fundamental questions about the subject. This should not be surprising. Our view of the self and the world is rich, but it is also flawed in fundamental ways. We do not understand fully our own rationality, our own agency, and our own values. We do not understand how these essential aspects of our being fit into the world we inhabit. These flaws do not hinder our substantive inquiries except occasionally when science encounters revolutionary problems. And it is then that science seeks the counsel of philosophy.

Philosophy aims neither to spell out meanings nor to sweep up debris left by the sciences. Philosophy does not dictate to the sciences, nor is it subservient to them. Philosophy begins with a recognition of fundamental problems in our view of the self and the world, and it aims to respond to these problems with clarity, with imagination, and with a full cognizance of the actual human situation.

SUPPLEMENT ON 'EXPERIENCE'

I intend my use of 'experience' to be in accord with the way the term is used in philosophy and, in particular, epistemology. This latter use is, in turn, in accord with a range of uses of the term in ordinary speech. But there are multiple ambiguities in the philosophical and ordinary uses of 'experience', and I should specify how I understand the term in this essay.

To begin with, let us notice what may be called the *thick* use of 'experience'. We encounter this use when, for example, we hear a friend talk about his "experiences in Nepal," when we see an advertisement boasting "twenty years' experience repairing sewing machines," and when we read an announcement for the documentary *The American Experience*. What does the friend talk about when he narrates his experiences in Nepal? He talks about such things as his hikes in the mountains, his visits to the temples, and his encounters with aging hippies.[1] These are activities and happenings that are extended in time—over several hours, days, or perhaps even weeks. The experience of repairing sewing machines extends, the advertisement says, over twenty years, and this may well not be a lie. The documentary is not violating linguistic usage if it takes "the American experience" to encompass the whole of American history. Experiences in the thick sense

---

1. The friend may include even his sleep among his remarkable experiences in Nepal: "For the first time in a long while, I enjoyed peaceful, dreamless sleep."

are rich and complex; they typically involve interactions of the experiencing subjects with a range of things and persons. An account of a thick experience can sometimes fill a thick book.

Thick experiences are not subjective entities or events, though they have a subjective dimension. There is a "what it is like" aspect to them. The friend may be telling us what it was like for him in Nepal when he tells us about his experiences there. We can ask the repairman what it was like for him repairing sewing machines over those long years. The documentary is not living up to its title if it narrates American happenings from an objective viewpoint, as an entomologist might narrate the activities in a beehive. To be an account of the American experience, it must inform us what it was like for Americans as they dealt with the events in their history. Let us notice that the subjective aspect of thick experience is not private or hidden: the friend's wife may well be able to tell us what it was like for him in Nepal; an English historian may be the most skillful in informing us about what it was like for Americans during, for example, the Civil War. The subjective aspect does exhibit a distinctive characteristic, namely, mismatch with the objective. Subjectively, the hikes in the mountains might have been peaceful and worry-free for the friend. But objectively, the friend might have been in a fool's paradise, escaping great dangers by sheer good luck.

Thick experiences are of undeniable importance to epistemology. When we speak about the testing of a theory against experience, the sense of 'experience' in play is almost invariably the thick one. The empirical testing of a theory typically involves complex interactions between an individual and the environment (e.g., when a lab assistant sets up an apparatus for a chemical experiment). Often it involves complex and cooperative exchanges between persons (e.g., when an experiment demands a long voyage to a particular place on the globe). Sometimes empirical testing demands such large resources that cooperation between nations is required (e.g., in the construction of particle accelerators). And it is not inconceivable that an empirical test be so extended in time that it requires generations of humans to complete it (compare our talk of "the American experience"). Thick experiences—even *very* thick experiences—can plainly bear on the rational acceptance of a theory. And no epistemology can be adequate that fails to accord with this fact.

It is also plain, however, that the epistemology of thick experiences—their rational bearing on knowledge—is highly complex. We cannot hope to understand it unless we are clear on the epistemology of simple experiences. The visual experience of an apparatus can enable one to know that the mercury column is thirty inches high; one smells something and judges "that is asafetida"; and one hears a voice and knows that the lab assistant is saying that the meter reading is three volts. The experiences in these examples are relatively simple, but they make a crucial contribution to the rationality of the ensuing perceptual judgments. The first step in understanding the epistemology of thick experiences is to understand the epistemology of such simple, *thin*, experiences. We need to understand the rational contribution of thin experiences to knowledge. This is the principal concern of this book. Hence, for much of the book, I use 'experience' to talk about thin experiences: experiences that are relatively short in duration and that occur in (but not only in) our simple, everyday perceptions of the world. I look at the yellow coaster and then I glance at the orange one nearby. Here I have two visual experiences, each lasting a few seconds.[2] Both experiences are relatively simple, and an ordinary narration of them will hardly fill a page, much less a book. (Though reflections on their epistemology can easily fill several books!)

'Experience' is sometimes used to refer to universals, and sometimes to particulars. 'Experience of the yellow coaster', for instance, can be used to refer to a universal: something that can be instantiated in several persons as they look at the coaster, perhaps at the same time or perhaps at different times. 'Experience of the yellow coaster' can also be used to refer to a particular: an event, process, or state of affairs that involves a particular person at a particular time. In this book, I take experiences to be particulars. Furthermore, I take them to be so individuated that one can recover from a particular experience such elements as its subject and the time period of its occurrence. This individuation is merely a terminological convenience; nothing metaphysical turns on it. It allows me to speak about "the rational contribution of experience *e*," while omitting, for example, the subject to whose knowledge *e* makes the rational contribution.

I understand by 'experience' *conscious* experience, and thus exclude phenomena such as blindsight.[3] A blindsighted person can make

---

2. I look at the figure of the duck-rabbit. First I see it as a duck and then as a rabbit. Here, too, I have two different visual experiences.

3. Otherwise, I understand 'experience' broadly. Consciousness of any of the following counts as experience: sounds, shapes, odors, tastes, tactile feelings (e.g., of touching the keyboard), pain, hunger, sense of the body, pushes and pulls on one's body, mental images, one's actions and thoughts, flashes before one's mind, etc.

reliable guesses about, for instance, the orientation of the lines before her, but she has no conscious visual experience of the lines. Information about the orientation of the lines is somehow present in the subject's visual system and shapes her guesses. Still, she has no experience, as I understand the term, of the lines. The presence of information in the visual system and the occurrence of a visual experience must plainly be distinguished. The latter contributes to the rationality of perceptual judgments in a way that the former does not. In the present example, our subject is not being irrational when she denies the existence of any lines in her field of vision. A blindsighted person may, of course, come to know that under certain conditions, her dispositions to make guesses are reliable and thus may become aware of the existence and orientation of the lines. But this is different from knowledge gained on the basis of the visual experience of the lines, for the knowledge of the blindsighted person is based on an awareness of her internal states (namely, her dispositions).

It is important to distinguish, at least nominally, *experience* and *perception*.[4] When I look at the yellow coaster, I have a perception of the yellow coaster; I see that a yellow coaster is before me. A seeing is a knowing: if I see that a yellow coaster is before me, then I *know* that a yellow coaster is before me. It is reasonable to say, therefore, that the rational contribution of my perception—my seeing that a yellow coaster is before me—includes the proposition that a yellow coaster is before me. But this simple observation does not address the fundamental epistemological problem about perception, which is to understand how it can be rational in a perceptual situation to take the world to be thus-and-so—to take it, for instance, that there is a yellow coaster before one. The question "what is the rational contribution of experience to a subject's knowledge?" aims to elicit a solution to this fundamental problem. Hence, it must be sharply distinguished from the question "what is the rational contribution of a perception to a subject's knowledge?" The latter might have an easy, commonsensical answer; the former does not.

Experiences can occur outside of perceptions. An experience *subjectively identical* to the one I had when I saw the yellow coaster may occur when I am not seeing a yellow coaster. Indeed, it may occur even when I am not seeing anything at all—for instance, when I am

---

4. Here and below, I am concerned only with *thin* experiences.

hallucinating. The notion of subjective identity plays a critical role in the epistemological problem of perception. It occurs in skeptical argumentation, ancient and modern. It plays an indispensable role both in the Argument from Illusion and in my reconstruction of the argument for Cartesian conceptions of experience (§§2B and 2C). Further, it is an essential constituent of the constraints within which I seek to construct a theory of experience (in particular, the Equivalence constraint of §2B). Now, it is important to recognize that this notion of subjective identity has considerable intuitive content and also that it is not without its problems.

First, intuitive content: There are many instances in which the notion of subjective identity has clear application. One does not need to be a connoisseur to be aware of a subjective difference between the experience of smelling cumin and that of smelling asafetida. Two successive glimpses of the yellow coaster may well produce in me visual experiences that I easily (and correctly) judge to be subjectively identical. And such examples can be multiplied indefinitely. There is another route to appreciating the intuitive content of "subjective identity." The notion is a limiting case of a richer, comparative notion of *subjective similarity*, which also has considerable intuitive content. It is easy to tell, for instance, that the ordinary visual experience of seeing red is subjectively more similar to that of seeing pink than to that of seeing yellow. Now, subjective identity is definable as perfect subjective similarity. More precisely, two experiences are subjectively identical when no possible experience is more similar to one than the two are to each other. Let us notice also that the notion of subjective identity gains some content through its linkage to the notion of the total internal state of a person: there cannot be subjectively distinct experiences where the total internal states are identical.

Second, problems: There are instances in which the application of the notion of subjective identity is not at all clear. Consider the phenomenon of inattentional blindness, investigated by Daniel Simons and Christopher Chabris, among others. In one of their famous experiments, Simons and Chabris showed subjects a short video of a ball game. The game has two teams, and members of each team pass a basketball back and forth to one another. Simons and Chabris asked their subjects to count the number of consecutive passes between the members of one of the teams. At one point in the video, a woman dressed in a gorilla suit walks through the play, stops briefly in the center of the picture, faces the camera, thumps her chest, and then walks off.[5] Simons and Chabris found that about half their subjects, when queried about the gorilla antics, turned out to be entirely oblivious of them. Let *e* be the visual experience of one such subject as she was busily counting, say, the sixth pass of the ball and the woman dressed as a gorilla was thumping her chest. Now, what visual experiences are subjectively identical to *e*? Suppose the subject performs the same task of counting consecutive passes while she is shown a video exactly like the one that Simons and Chabris showed her except that the gorilla character is absent from it. Is her new visual experience as she counts the sixth pass subjectively identical to *e*? What determines subjective identity? The subject's judgment of identity and difference, or the nature of the experiences? One may be tempted to say that two experiences are subjectively identical iff a consciousness that perfectly recalls both would judge them to be subjectively identical.[6] But this only highlights the problems. How do we understand perfect recall without a prior understanding of subjective identity? Furthermore, how do we make sense of subjective identity of experiences suffered by *different* individuals? In particular, what sense can we attach to the notion of a consciousness recalling an experience suffered by a distinct consciousness?

The problems with the notion of subjective identity make it tempting to dismiss the notion entirely and, with it, the whole epistemological problem of perception. But this easy way out is a mistake. The fact that a notion has unclear content and problematic applications should not lead us to conclude that the notion is useless; otherwise, we shall have to condemn most of our empirical notions. The notion of subjective identity *is* unclear and problematic, but it is clear enough to indicate a substantial problem in understanding the rationality of our perceptual judgments. Straightforward, unproblematic applications of the notion help establish the falsity of the naive epistemological idea that the given in an experience consists of ordinary judgments of perception. There is little difficulty in applying the notion of subjective identity when, for instance, the total internal states, conscious and unconscious, of a subject are perfectly similar (assuming physicalism: when total brain states are perfectly similar). Now, it is *possible* that even though no yellow coaster is before me, I am in an internal state that is perfectly similar to the one I was in a

---

5. The video was available over the internet. Readers wishing to view it may be able to find it there.

6. See Sydney Shoemaker, *Identity, Cause, and Mind*, p. 179.

moment ago when I experienced the yellow coaster. If this is so, then it is possible that I have an experience subjectively identical to my perception of the yellow coaster, even though I am not perceiving a yellow coaster. It follows that my perceptual judgment that a yellow coaster is before me does not belong to the given in my experience (see §§2B and 2C).

Let me stress that the positive theory of experience defended in this book is not hostage to the notion of subjective identity. The theory can be accepted by those who reject this notion and the Equivalence constraint within which it figures. Indeed, the theory can be accepted even by those who reject all four constraints within whose bounds I have chosen to work. The role of the constraints and the notion of subjective identity in the present theory is twofold. First, they help to make clear that there is an epistemological problem about perception. Second, they help to show that the challenge posed by classical empiricism can be met while respecting almost all of the underlying intuitions that motivate that seductive doctrine.

I COUNT IT AS AN IMPORTANT VIRTUE OF THE PRESENT PROPOSAL that it separates the epistemological question of the given in experience from the metaphysical question of the nature of experience. Just as we do not first need to analyze the chemistry of the ink used to print a book in order to understand the logical structure of its argument, similarly we do not first need to become clear about the nature of experience in order to understand the logical character of its rational contribution. What experience is and what the subjective identity of experiences comes to are things that we can better understand only through an empirical study of the world and of ourselves. We are equipped with no special insight into the nature of experience or into the metaphysical basis of subjectivity. If I wish to understand my experience of the yellow coaster, or if I wish to understand what makes it subjectively identical to another of my experiences, I do not get very far if I merely contemplate the experience in isolation. I cannot understand my nature—what I am—solely by inner contemplation. How, then, can I understand the nature of my experience by mere contemplation?[7] The only way for me to gain an understanding of myself and of my

---

7. If the proper method of understanding (the subjective character of) an experience is contemplation, how do I understand (the subjective character of) a fleeting experience I have when I am being inattentive?

experience is not to "bracket" the account of the world but to fully embrace it.

It is a feature of classical empiricism that it ties firmly together the epistemology and the metaphysics of experience. In contemporary philosophy, classical empiricism is in low repute, yet the linkage between epistemology and metaphysics persists, and several a prioristic metaphysical ideas about experience have gained prominence. I do not wish to—or need to—argue against these ideas here. For my purposes, it suffices to observe the neutrality of the present proposal with respect to them. Let me highlight some dimensions of this neutrality.

(a) *The act-object analysis of conscious experience.* This analysis, which is fundamental to many varieties of classical empiricism, takes experience to be an act of consciousness that is in itself perfectly transparent and that is directed to an object (or objects). The analysis thus takes the subjective character of an experience to issue from the object (or objects)[8] to which consciousness is directed. My experience of the yellow coaster, for example, has a certain subjective character: a yellow diamond seems to be present in my consciousness. According to the act-object analysis, this subjective character is not to be located in the act, which is transparent, but in the object of consciousness: my consciousness is directed to a yellow diamond.[9] In its most natural and simple version, the act-object theory takes the object of consciousness to have all *and only* those attributes that contribute to the subjective character of the experience. In this version, the subjective identity of experiences is explained in terms of the qualities (and relations) of the objects of the experiences.[10] For example, an experience is subjectively

---

8. I will sometimes suppress the parenthetical qualification and speak as if experience is directed to just one object.

9. Another example: there is a subjective difference in the visual experiences of the second hand when the clock is working and when the clock is stopped. The act-object analysis takes this difference to issue from a difference in the qualities of the object of experience: in one case, the object has the property of movement (or phenomenal movement); in the other, it does not. Hence, the act-object analysis is not committed to taking the objects of experience to be instantaneous sense-data. Indeed, it must not be so committed if it is to be adequate to the phenomenology of experience. It must allow that the objects of experience may well be extended in time (or at least in "phenomenal" time).

10. A more complex version makes a distinction between sensory and nonsensory attributes, and allows the object of consciousness to have nonsensory attributes that do not contribute to the subjective character of experience. In this version, two experiences are subjectively identical iff their objects have the same *sensory* attributes.

identical to my experience of the yellow coaster iff its object is a yellow diamond and has no other properties. Thus, we have the idea that not only is our sensory knowledge of the objects of consciousness error-proof, but that the objects are fully revealed in consciousness. (See the quote from Hume's *Treatise* in §2A.)

I want to allow that, in a broad sense of 'might', the act-object analysis might be—or might have turned out to be—the right account of the nature of experience: consciousness might have been a meta-physically primitive act directed to some special objects and qualities. (As things are, this is not so.) Furthermore, I want to allow that the act-object analysis, whether it is metaphysically correct or not, may well provide a good scheme for constructing phenomenologically apt descriptions of experiences (or some kinds of experiences). A phenomenologically apt account of subjective similarities and differences between visual experiences, for example, may well follow the act-object analysis and locate them in the objects of consciousness. Such an account will undoubtedly invoke some funny Meinongian objects in its description of experience, but as I have indicated, this invocation is completely legitimate (see §5C). What must be resisted is the temptation to invest the picture of experience as transparent, with metaphysical or epistemological significance. Phenomenologically, there is in experience a transparent directedness to objects and, as I have noted in §5D, this transparency is of great practical importance. But one cannot read the metaphysics of experience from the phenomenology. Two experiences may be subjectively identical—they may be associated with the same phenomenology—and yet may have entirely different natures. My recent experience of the yellow coaster is perhaps best identified with my recent *seeing* of the yellow coaster. If so, then the recent experience involves the yellow coaster I saw. But a hallucination that is subjectively identical to my experience will not involve the yellow coaster: same phenomenology, but different meta-physical natures. A parallel point holds about the epistemological significance of transparency. In experience, one seems to be trans-parently taking in facts. But, as I have argued at length, experience does not entitle one to any propositions. And it does not establish any privileged semantic relations between terms and objects, or between terms and properties (§5D).

The above viewpoint has a noteworthy consequence for our talk of *qualia*. Qualia are typically understood as having a double charac-ter. They are features of the objects of experience that, at the same time, contribute to the subjective character of experience. The quale yellow, for instance, is a feature of the object of my visual experience, and by being, as they say, "present in my consciousness," it is responsible for some aspects of the subjective character of my experience. Again, I want to allow that talk of "the quale yellow" and such is logically legitimate. However, it is an error to suppose that the expression 'the quale yellow' must pick out a genuine property, as it would if the transparency conception of experience were metaphysically correct.[11]

(b) *The act-content analysis of conscious experience.* The act-object analysis of conscious experience, once predominant, is now out of favor. The predominant analysis these days is the act-content analysis. According to this analysis, experience has propositional content: content of the form "such-and-such things are thus and so." The precise nature of this content has provoked debate: it has been debated whether the content is conceptual, or nonconceptual, or part conceptual and part nonconceptual.[12] The precise mechanism by which experience gains content has also provoked debate: it has been debated whether the gain occurs through an exercise of concepts, or through some naturalistic indication relations, or through some combination of the two. There seems to be an alignment of positions in the two debates (although this is not inevitable). Those who think that experience involves an exercise of concepts favor the idea that the content of experience is conceptual. Those who incline to naturalistic indication relations favor the idea that the content is nonconceptual.[13]

I need engage in these debates only to this extent: to observe that the content at issue is *not* the given in experience; the content cannot be the rational contribution of experience to knowledge. Having made this point, I can remain a mere kibitzer in these voluminous

---

11. Imagine that it seems to you that you are looking at two instances of a new color, one that you have not so far experienced. You assign a name to the color. Does the name pick out a determinate property? If it does, how do we figure out which property this is?

Now consider the possibility that your experience is a hallucination. Is the name bound to pick out a determinate property now? If so, how do we figure out which property this is? If the transparency conception is metaphysically correct, these questions have an easy answer. If it is not correct, the language-world relations of the new name will likely be complex.

12. It has also been debated what precisely it means to affirm, or deny, that the content is "conceptual."

13. See the works reprinted in *Essays on Nonconceptual Content*, edited by York H. Gunther.

debates. Experience may or may not have propositional content; it may or may not involve an exercise of concepts. None of this matters for my epistemological concerns. Nevertheless, a few incidental points are worth making.

First, the empiricism I have defended does not require any notion of *pure* experience, experience unsullied by views and concepts. I have noted above that experience *is* affected by concepts, beliefs, and views. And while this fact poses a danger to our knowledge of the world, it does nothing to undermine the epistemic authority of experience (see §§4C and 7B). The source of a contrary appearance lies in the notion of the propositional given.

Second, the idea that experience has content is entirely theoretical; it cannot be read off from the phenomenology of experience.[14] Hence, the idea must be judged solely by the effectiveness with which it fulfills its antecedent theoretical function. The argument of this essay, if sound, undermines one theoretical motivation for the idea, namely, that of understanding the rational constraint that experience exercises on knowledge. But there are other theoretical motivations, and these are left untouched by my argument.

Third, a notion of propositional content can be recovered quite easily from the account of the given I have proposed: let the *perceptual content* of *e* be the totality of perceptual judgments $\Gamma_e(v)$, where *v* is the view that the subject of *e* accepts at the time of *e*'s occurrence. I doubt, however, whether this notion can be identified with any of the notions in play in the debates over content. For perceptual content is undefined when the subject fails to accept a unique view; not so for the notions in play in the debates over content. Furthermore, there is little reason to take perceptual content to be a feature of *experience*, as opposed to, say, a feature of the entire person. To attribute perceptual

14. The phenomenology favors, if anything, the act-object analysis. Sellars, who was one of the early philosophers to embrace the idea of propositional content, felt the need to bring in something distinct from it to capture the phenomenology of experience. He calls this something else "impression"; sometimes he calls it "descriptive content" (*Empiricism and the Philosophy of Mind*, §22). There is, however, an important movement in contemporary philosophy that dispenses with Sellarsian impressions. Here, an attempt is made to explain the subjective character of experience entirely in terms of content. But the attempt remains controversial. For an account of the controversy, see William Lycan's "Representational Theories of Consciousness." See also Susanna Siegel's "The Contents of Perception," which provides a fine overview of theories of perceptual content.

content to experience is a little like attributing the number 3 to a machine that calculates square roots. This number is best attributed not to the machine but to the machine-cum-input-9; what corresponds to the machine is the square-root function. Similarly, perceptual content is best attributed not merely to experience but to experience-cum-view; what corresponds to an experience is the function Γ_e.

(c) *The adverbial analysis of conscious experience.* This analysis arose as a challenger to the act-object analysis. Here, experience is viewed as having neither an object nor a content, but as being an act of consciousness that is performed in a particular manner. Experience, in this analysis, is an *act*, and the world merely affects *how* this act is done. An example often used to motivate the analysis is this. To dance the waltz is not to perform a dance that has a particular relation to a special object, "waltz," but to dance "waltzily."[15] So, in the phrase 'to dance the waltz', 'waltz' designates a manner of dancing, not an object. Similarly, according to the adverbial analysis, to have an experience of a yellow diamond is not to have an experience with a special object but to have a particular species of experience. 'Yellow diamond' characterizes not the object of the experience, but the manner of *experiencing*. So, 'I am experiencing yellow-diamond-ly' is a more perspicuous representation of the experience than 'I am experiencing a yellow diamond'.

Again, it is plain that the theory I have proposed is neutral on whether the adverbial analysis captures the correct metaphysics of experience, and also on whether it provides a good way of talking about experiences. Furthermore, whereas the adverbial analysis takes seriously the description of experiences as *acts*, the theory I have proposed is entirely neutral on the ontological category of experiences. It leaves open whether experiences belong to the category of states, events, processes, acts, or something else altogether different. The theory is neutral also on whether the subjective identity of experiences is to be explained by the commonality of properties among experienc*ings*, or among the objects of experiences, or among contents, or in some other way. To repeat: I insist on keeping the metaphysics of experience separate from its epistemology.

A FINAL OBSERVATION: I AM NOT ASSUMING THAT 'EXPERIENCE' and 'subjective identity' are privileged expressions, which are assured

---

15. The example is due to C. J. Ducasse, the originator of the adverbial analysis.

of having tidy, unproblematic semantical links to the world.[16] These expressions are like any other expressions; their language-world relations depend upon our conceptions and, of course, on the world as it turns out to be. Our conceptions of experience and of subjective identity enjoy no special privilege. Far from it: we are liable to have the greatest misconceptions about that which is most intimate. Empirical inquiry can reveal our errors here as much as it does elsewhere.

Consider the example of dreams. The ordinary, naive conception of dreams is somewhat as follows. "Dreams are experiences that are quite like perceptions. When a person has a visually vivid dream about, say, the yellow coaster, his internal state is similar to the one he is in when he sees the yellow coaster or vividly imagines the yellow coaster (from a particular point of view). A dream can be subjectively identical to a veridical perception, and this subjective identity is grounded in some sort of similarity among the internal states of the subject when dreaming and when enjoying veridical perceptions."

This simple conception may, as a matter of fact, be right. But it is not empirically incorrigible. Suppose neurological studies reveal that there is little brain activity that is shared by states described as that of dreaming and those described as that of seeing and of visually imagining. The latter two, let us suppose, are found to have similar neurological correlates, but no such correlates are discovered for dream states. The correlates for dream states, let us imagine, are all purely linguistic— indeed, they are the very ones involved in storytelling. We can even imagine that these correlates occur in an order that does not reflect the supposed dream sequence, but in a distinct linguistic order.[17] Such neurological discoveries are possible from an epistemological point of view. And were they to be made, they would shake up our simple conceptions of experience, dream, and subjective identity. In particular, they would call into question the idea that dreams can be subjectively identical to visual experiences.

We have no incorrigible insights into the nature of experience or of subjective identity. "Experience" and "subjective identity" are not immutable concepts, somehow delivered to us in their complete

16. See chapter 5, fn. 3, for an explanation of 'privilege'.

17. A more radical supposition is that even linguistic correlates fail to exist for dreams. In so-called dreams, the subject merely acquires a disposition to tell a story. The shape of the story is fixed not by anything going on in the subject while she is asleep but by what the subject experiences on waking up.

perfection. These concepts are as open to improvement as are our other concepts. It may even turn out that these concepts are highly defective and serve a limited function in a limited environment (like the concepts "up above" and "celestial sphere"). The path to discovering whether or not this is so lies through experience: not reason, not intuition, and certainly not armchair speculation.

Summary: The notions of experience and subjective identity with which I work in this essay are not novel; they are ordinary and familiar. Furthermore, I do not assume any particular metaphysical account of these notions. I stay neutral on such philosophical theories as the act-object and the act-content analyses discussed above. Finally, I do not assume that the notions of experience and subjective identity are perfectly clear. I recognize that these notions are murkier than many empirical notions. And like them, they can be improved only through a systematic empirical inquiry. The empiricism I wish to defend does not need to be—and is not—dogmatic about the nature of experience.

REFERENCES

Alston, William P. *Epistemic Justification: Essays in the Theory of Knowledge*. Ithaca, NY: Cornell University Press, 1989.

Annas, Julia, and Barnes, Jonathan. *The Modes of Scepticism: Ancient Texts and Modern Interpretations*. Cambridge, UK: Cambridge University Press, 1985.

Audi, Robert. "Contemporary Foundationalism." In *The Theory of Knowledge: Classical and Contemporary Readings*, 2d ed., edited by Louis P. Pojman, Belmont, CA: Wadsworth, 1999, pp. 204–211.

Aune, Bruce. "Sellars, Wilfrid Stalker." In *The Encyclopedia of Philosophy Supplement*, edited by Donald M. Borchert, New York: Macmillan Reference, 1996, pp. 527–528.

Austin, J. L. *Sense and Sensibilia*. Reconstructed by G. J. Warnock. Oxford: Clarendon Press, 1962.

Ayer, A. J. *The Foundations of Empirical Knowledge*. London: Macmillan, 1940.

Ayer, A. J. *The Problem of Knowledge*. London: Macmillan, 1956.

Ayer, A. J. *The Central Questions of Philosophy*. London: Weidenfeld and Nicolson, 1973.

Bach, Kent. "A Rationale for Reliabilism." Reprinted in *Knowledge: Readings in Contemporary Epistemology*, edited by Sven Bernecker and Fred Dretske, Oxford: Oxford University Press, 2000, pp. 199–213. Originally published in 1985.

Belnap, Nuel D. "Grammatical Propaedeutic." In *The Logical Enterprise*, edited by Alan Ross Anderson, Ruth Barcan Marcus, and R. M. Martin, New Haven, CT: Yale University Press, 1975, pp. 143–165.

Bergmann, Michael. "A Dilemma for Internalism." In *Knowledge and Reality: Essays in Honor of Alvin Plantinga*, edited by Thomas Crisp, Matthew Davidson, and David Vander Laan, Berlin: Springer, forthcoming.

Berkeley, George. *A Treatise Concerning the Principles of Human Knowledge*. Edited by Jonathan Dancy. Oxford: Oxford University Press, 1998. Originally published in 1710 and reprinted in the classic edition of Berkeley's works by A. A. Luce and T. E. Jessop.

Berkeley, George. *Three Dialogues between Hylas and Philonous*. Edited by Jonathan Dancy. Oxford: Oxford University Press, 1998. Originally published in 1713 and reprinted in the classic edition of Berkeley's works by A. A. Luce and T. E. Jessop.

BonJour, Laurence. "Externalist Theories of Empirical Knowledge." Reprinted in *Epistemology: Internalism and Externalism*, edited by Hilary Kornblith, Oxford: Blackwell, 2001, pp. 10–35. Originally published in 1980.

BonJour, Laurence. *The Structure of Empirical Knowledge*. Cambridge, MA: Harvard University Press, 1985.

Brandom, Robert B. *Making It Explicit: Reasoning, Representing, and Discursive Commitment*. Cambridge, MA: Harvard University Press, 1994.

Brandom, Robert B. Study Guide to *Empiricism and the Philosophy of Mind*, by Wilfrid Sellars. Cambridge, MA: Harvard University Press, 1997, pp. 119–181.

Brewer, Bill. *Perception and Reason*. Oxford: Clarendon Press, 1999.

Broad, C. D. "Some Elementary Reflexions on Sense-Perception." Reprinted in *Perceiving, Sensing, and Knowing: A Book of Readings from Twentieth-Century Sources in the Philosophy of Perception*, edited by Robert J. Swartz, Berkeley: University of California Press, 1965, pp. 29–48. Originally published in 1952.

Brueckner, Anthony L. "Putnam's Model-Theoretic Argument against Metaphysical Realism." *Analysis* 44 (1984), 134–140.

Camp, Joseph L., Jr. *Confusion: A Study in the Theory of Knowledge*. Cambridge, MA: Harvard University Press, 2002.

Carnap, Rudolf. *The Logical Structure of the World and Pseudoproblems in Philosophy*. Translated by Rolf A. George. Berkeley: University of California Press, 1967. Originally published in 1928.

Carnap, Rudolf. "Empiricism, Semantics, and Ontology." Reprinted in *Semantics and the Philosophy of Language: A Collection of Readings*, edited by Leonard Linsky, Urbana: University of Illinois Press, 1952, pp. 208–228. Originally published in 1950.

Chapuis, André. "Rationality and Circularity." In *Circularity, Defini-tion and Truth*, edited by André Chapuis and Anil Gupta, New Delhi: Indian Council of Philosophical Research, 2000 [distributed outside India by Ridgeview Publishing Company, Atascadero, CA], pp. 49–78.

Chisholm, Roderick M. "The Problem of Empiricism." Reprinted in *Perceiving, Sensing, and Knowing: A Book of Readings from Twentieth-Century Sources in the Philosophy of Perception,* edited by Robert J. Swartz, Berkeley: University of California Press, 1965, pp. 347–354. Originally published in 1948.

Cicero, Marcus Tullius. *Academica.* Translated by H. Rackham in Loeb Classical Library, vol. 268. Cambridge, MA: Harvard University Press, 1933. Originally written in 45 B.C.E.

Clarke, Romane. "The Sensuous Content of Perception." In *Action Knowledge and Reality: Critical Studies in Honor of Wilfrid Sellars,* edited by Hector-Neri Castañeda, Indianapolis, IN: Bobbs-Merrill, 1975, pp. 109–127.

Cohen, Stewart. "How to Be a Fallibilist." *Philosophical Perspectives* 2 (1988), 91–123.

Conee, Earl, and Feldman, Richard. "Internalism Defended." In *Epistemology: Internalism and Externalism,* edited by Hilary Korn-blith, Oxford: Blackwell, 2001, pp. 231–260.

Davidson, Donald. "On the Very Idea of a Conceptual Scheme." Reprinted in Davidson's *Inquiries into Truth and Interpretation,* Oxford: Clarendon Press, 1984, pp. 183–198. Originally published in 1974.

Davidson, Donald. "A Coherence Theory of Truth and Knowledge." Reprinted in Davidson's *Subjective, Intersubjective, Objective,* Oxford: Clarendon Press, 2001, pp. 137–157. Originally published in 1983.

Davidson, Donald. *Inquiries into Truth and Interpretation.* Oxford: Clarendon Press, 1984.

Davidson, Donald. "The Myth of the Subjective." Reprinted in Davidson's *Subjective, Intersubjective, Objective,* Oxford: Clarendon Press, 2001, pp. 39–52. Originally published in 1988.

Davidson, Donald. "Reply to John McDowell." In *The Philosophy of Donald Davidson,* edited by Lewis Edwin Hahn, Chicago: Open Court, 1999, pp. 105–108.

Davidson, Donald. *Subjective, Intersubjective, Objective.* Oxford: Clar-endon Press, 2001.

Demopoulos, William. "On the Rational Reconstruction of Our Theoretical Knowledge." *British Journal for the Philosophy of Science* 54 (2003), 371–403.

DeRose, Keith, and Warfield, Ted A., eds. *Skepticism: A Contemporary Reader.* Oxford: Oxford University Press, 1999.

Descartes, René. *Meditations on First Philosophy.* In *The Philosophical Writings of Descartes*, vol. 2, translated by John Cottingham, Robert Stoothoff, and Dugald Murdoch, Cambridge, UK: Cambridge University Press, 1984, pp. 1-62. Originally published in 1641 and reprinted in the classic edition of Descartes's works by C. Adam and P. Tannery.

Devitt, Michael. *Realism and Truth*, 2d ed. Oxford: Blackwell, 1991.

Earman, John. *Bayes or Bust? A Critical Examination of Bayesian Confirmation Theory.* Cambridge, MA: MIT Press, 1992.

Fales, Evan. *A Defense of the Given.* Lanham, MD: Rowman and Littlefield, 1996.

Field, Hartry. *Truth and the Absence of Fact.* Oxford: Clarendon Press, 2001.

Fine, Kit. *Reasoning with Arbitrary Objects.* Oxford: Basil Blackwell, 1985.

Foley, Richard. "What Am I to Believe?" Reprinted in *Epistemology: Internalism and Externalism,* edited by Hilary Kornblith, Oxford: Blackwell, 2001, pp. 163–179. Originally published in 1993.

Friedman, Michael. *Reconsidering Logical Positivism.* Cambridge, UK: Cambridge University Press, 1999.

Fumerton, Richard A. *Metaphysical and Epistemological Problems of Perception.* Lincoln: University of Nebraska Press, 1985.

Ginet, Carl. *Knowledge, Perception, and Memory.* Dordrecht: D. Reidel, 1975.

Goldman, Alan H. "The Given." In *A Companion to Epistemology,* edited by Jonathan Dancy and Ernest Sosa, Oxford: Blackwell, 1992, pp. 159–162.

Goldman, Alvin. "Internalism Exposed." Reprinted in *Epistemology: Internalism and Externalism,* edited by Hilary Kornblith, Oxford: Blackwell, 2001, pp. 207–230. Originally published in 1999.

Grover, Dorothy. *A Prosentential Theory of Truth.* Princeton, NJ: Princeton University Press, 1992.

Gunther, York H., ed. *Essays on Nonconceptual Content.* Cambridge, MA: MIT Press, 2003.

Gupta, Anil. *The Logic of Common Nouns: An Investigation in Quantified Modal Logic.* New Haven, CT: Yale University Press, 1980.

Gupta, Anil. "Remarks on Definitions and the Concept of Truth." *Proceedings of the Aristotelian Society* 89 (1988–89), 227–246.

Gupta, Anil. "A Critique of Deflationism." In *Truth,* edited by Simon Blackburn and Keith Simmons, Oxford: Oxford University Press, 1999, pp. 282–307. Originally published in 1993.

Gupta, Anil. "Meaning and Misconceptions." In *Language, Logic, and Concepts: Essays in Memory of John Macnamara*, edited by Ray Jackendoff, Paul Bloom, and Karen Wynn, Cambridge, MA: MIT Press, 1999, pp. 15–41.

Gupta, Anil. "On Circular Concepts." In *Circularity, Definition and Truth*, edited by André Chapuis and Anil Gupta, New Delhi: Indian Council of Philosophical Research, 2000 [distributed outside India by Ridgeview Publishing Company, Atascadero, CA], pp. 123–153.

Gupta, Anil. "Truth." In *The Blackwell Guide to Philosophical Logic*, edited by Lou Goble, Oxford: Blackwell, 2001, pp. 90–114.

Gupta, Anil. "Experience and Knowledge." In *Perceptual Experience*, edited by Tamar Szabó Gendler and John Hawthorne, Oxford: Clarendon Press, 2006, pp. 181–204.

Gupta, Anil. "Finite Circular Definitions." In *Self-Reference*, edited by Thomas Bolander, Vincent F. Hendricks, and Stig Andur Pedersen, Stanford: CSLI Publications, 2006, pp. 53–67.

Gupta, Anil. "Remarks on Christopher Hill's *Thought and World*." *Philosophy and Phenomenological Research*, forthcoming.

Gupta, Anil, and Belnap, Nuel. *The Revision Theory of Truth*. Cambridge, MA: MIT Press, 1993.

Hardy, James. *Instantial Reasoning, Arbitrary Objects, and Holey Propositions*. Ph.D. dissertation, Indiana University, 1998.

Heath, Thomas L. *Greek Astronomy*. New York: Dover, 1991. Originally published in 1932.

Hill, Christopher S. *Thought and World: An Austere Portrayal of Truth, Reference, and Semantic Correspondence*. Cambridge, UK: Cambridge University Press, 2002.

Hinton, J. M. "Experiences." *Philosophical Quarterly* 17 (1967), 1–13.

Horwich, Paul. *Truth*, 2d ed. Oxford: Clarendon Press, 1998.

Hume, David. *A Treatise of Human Nature*. Edited by David Fate Norton and Mary J. Norton. Oxford: Oxford University Press, 2000. Originally published in 1739–1740.

Hume, David. *An Enquiry concerning Human Understanding*. Edited by Tom L. Beauchamp. Oxford: Oxford University Press, 1999. Originally published in 1748.

Jackson, Frank. *Perception: A Representative Theory*. Cambridge, UK: Cambridge University Press, 1977.

James, William. *Essays in Radical Empiricism*. Lincoln, NE: University of Nebraska Press, 1996. Originally published in 1912.

Jaspers, Karl. *General Psychopathology*. Translated by J. Hoenig and Marian W. Hamilton. Chicago: University of Chicago Press, 1963. Originally published in 1913.

Kant, Immanuel. *Critique of Pure Reason*. Translated by Norman Kemp Smith. London: Macmillan, 1964. The first edition of Kant's book appeared in 1781, and the second in 1787. Kemp Smith's translation was originally published in 1929.

Kornblith, Hilary. "Naturalistic Epistemology and Its Critics." Reprinted in *The Theory of Knowledge: Classical and Contemporary Readings*, 2d ed., edited by Louis P. Pojman, Belmont, CA: Wadsworth, 1999, pp. 385–396. Originally published in 1995.

Kremer, Philip. "The Gupta-Belnap Systems $S^\#$ and $S^\star$ Are Not Axiomatisable." *Notre Dame Journal of Formal Logic* 34 (1993), 583–596.

Lee, Byeongdeok. "The Paradox of Belief Instability and a Revision Theory of Belief." *Pacific Philosophical Quarterly* 79 (1998), 314–328.

Lehrer, Keith. "The Coherence Theory of Knowledge." Reprinted in *Knowledge: Readings in Contemporary Epistemology,* edited by Sven Bernecker and Fred Dretske, Oxford: Oxford University Press, 2000, pp. 149–165. Originally published in 1986.

Lewis, David. "Putnam's Paradox." *Australasian Journal of Philosophy* 62 (1984), 221–236.

Locke, John. *An Essay concerning Human Understanding*. Edited by Peter H. Nidditch. Oxford: Oxford University Press, 1975. Originally published in 1689.

Long, A. A., and Sedley, D. N. *The Hellenistic Philosophers*, vol. 1. Cambridge, UK: Cambridge University Press, 1987.

Lycan, William. "Representational Theories of Consciousness." In *The Stanford Encyclopedia of Philosophy*, spring 2005 ed., edited by Edward N. Zalta. Available at http://plato.stanford.edu/archives/spr2005/entries/consciousness-representational/.

McDowell, John. "Criteria, Defeasibility, and Knowledge." Reprinted in McDowell's *Meaning, Knowledge, and Reality*, Cambridge, MA: Harvard University Press, 1998, pp. 369–394. Originally published in 1982.

McDowell, John. *Mind and World*. Cambridge, MA: Harvard University Press, 1994.

McDowell, John. "Scheme-Content Dualism and Empiricism." In *The Philosophy of Donald Davidson*, edited by Lewis Edwin Hahn, Chicago: Open Court, 1999, pp. 87–104.

McDowell, John. "Transcendental Empiricism." Unpublished manuscript. Appears in a Greek translation in *Defkalion* 21 (2003), 65–90.

McGrew, Timothy. "A Defense of Classical Foundationalism." In *The Theory of Knowledge: Classical and Contemporary Readings*, 2d ed., edited by Louis P. Pojman, Belmont: Wadsworth, 1999, pp. 224–235.

Martin, Robert L., ed. *Recent Essays on Truth and the Liar Paradox.* Oxford: Clarendon Press, 1984.

Martinez, Maricarmen. "Some Closure Properties of Finite Definitions." *Studia Logica* 68 (2001), 43–68.

Matilal, Bimal Krishna. *Perception: An Essay on Classical Indian Theories of Knowledge.* Oxford: Clarendon Press, 1986.

Montague, Richard. "The Proper Treatment of Quantification in Ordinary English." Reprinted in *Formal Philosophy: Selected Papers of Richard Montague*, edited by Richmond H. Thomason, New Haven, CT: Yale University Press, 1974, pp. 247–270. Originally published in 1973.

Moser, Paul. *Knowledge and Evidence.* Cambridge, UK: Cambridge University Press, 1989.

Neta, Ram. "Contextualism and the Problem of the External World." *Philosophy and Phenomenological Research* 66 (2003), 1–31.

Orilia, Francesco. *Predication, Analysis and Reference.* Bologna: Cooperativa Libraria Universitaria Editrice Bologna, 1999.

Orilia, Francesco. "Property Theory and the Revision Theory of Definitions." *Journal of Symbolic Logic* 65 (2000), 212–246.

Parsons, Terence. *Nonexistent Objects.* New Haven, CT: Yale University Press, 1980.

Peirce, Charles Sanders. "How to Make Our Ideas Clear." Reprinted in *The Essential Peirce: Selected Philosophical Writings*, vol. 1, edited by Nathan Houser and Christian Kloesel, Bloomington: Indiana University Press, 1992, pp. 124–141. Originally published in 1878.

Plantinga, Alvin. *Warrant: The Current Debate.* Oxford: Oxford University Press, 1993.

Pollock, John. "A Plethora of Epistemological Theories." In *Justification and Knowledge: New Studies in Epistemology*, edited by George S. Pappas, Dordrecht: D. Reidel, 1979, pp. 93–113.

Popkin Richard H. "The High Road to Pyrrhonism." *American Philosophical Quarterly* 2 (1965), 18–32.

Price, H. H. *Perception.* London: Methuen, 1932.

Pryor, James. "Highlights of Recent Epistemology." *British Journal for the Philosophy of Science* 52 (2001), 95–124.

Putnam, Hilary. "Realism and Reason." Reprinted in Putnam's *Meaning and the Moral Sciences*, London: Routledge and Kegan Paul, 1978, pp. 123–140. Originally published in 1977.

Putnam, Hilary. "Models and Reality." Reprinted in Putnam's *Realism and Reason: Philosophical Papers*, vol. 3, Cambridge, UK: Cambridge University Press, 1983, pp. 1–25. Originally published in 1980.

Putnam, Hilary. *Reason, Truth and History*. Cambridge, UK: Cambridge University Press, 1981.

Putnam, Hilary. *Realism and Reason: Philosophical Papers*, vol. 3. Cambridge, UK: Cambridge University Press, 1983.

Quine, Willard Van Orman. "Two Dogmas of Empiricism." Reprinted in Quine's *From a Logical Point of View: 9 Logico-Philosophical Essays,* Cambridge, MA: Harvard University Press, 1953, pp. 20–46. Originally published in 1951.

Quine, Willard Van Orman. *Word and Object*. Cambridge, MA: MIT Press, 1960.

Quine, Willard Van Orman. "Epistemology Naturalized." In Quine's *Ontological Relativity and Other Essays*, New York: Columbia University Press, 1969, pp. 69–90.

Quine, Willard Van Orman. "Reply to Stroud." *Midwest Studies in Philosophy* 6 (1981), 473–475.

Quine, Willard Van Orman. *Pursuit of Truth: Revised Edition*. Cambridge, MA: Harvard University Press, 1992.

Quine, Willard Van Orman. *From Stimulus to Science*. Cambridge, MA: Harvard University Press, 1995.

Reichenbach, Hans. "Rationalism and Empiricism: An Inquiry into the Roots of Philosophical Error." *Philosophical Review* 57 (1948), 330–346.

Rescher, Nicholas. *The Coherence Theory of Truth*. Oxford: Oxford University Press, 1973.

Richardson, Alan W. "Conceiving, Experiencing, and Conceiving Experiencing: Neo-Kantianism and the History of the Concept of Experience." *Topoi* 22 (2003), 55–67.

Robinson, Howard. *Perception*. London: Routledge, 1994.

Rorty, Richard. "Realism, Antirealism, and Pragmatism: Comments on Alston, Chisholm, Davidson, Harman, and Searle." In *Realism/Antirealism and Epistemology*, edited by Christopher B. Kulp, Lanham, MD: Rowman and Littlefield, 1997, pp. 149–171.

Rorty, Richard. *Truth and Progress: Philosophical Papers*, vol. 3. Cambridge, UK: Cambridge University Press, 1998.

Russell, Bertrand. *The Problems of Philosophy*. Oxford: Oxford University Press, 1959. Originally published in 1912.

Russell, Bertrand. *The Philosophy of Logical Atomism*. Chicago: Open Court, 1985. Originally published in 1918.

Russell, Bertrand. *An Inquiry into Meaning and Truth*. London: George Allen and Unwin, 1940.

Sauer, Werner. "On the Kantian Background of Neopositivism." *Topoi* 8 (1989), 111–119.

Sellars, Wilfrid. "Some Reflections on Language Games." Reprinted in Sellars's *Science, Perception and Reality*, London: Routledge and Kegan Paul, 1963, pp. 321–358. Originally published in 1954.

Sellars, Wilfrid. *Empiricism and the Philosophy of Mind*. Cambridge, MA: Harvard University Press, 1997. Originally published in 1956.

Sellars, Wilfrid. "Phenomenalism." In Sellars's *Science, Perception and Reality*, London: Routledge and Kegan Paul, 1963, pp. 60–105.

Sellars, Wilfrid. *Science, Perception and Reality*. London: Routledge and Kegan Paul, 1963.

Sellars, Wilfrid. "The Structure of Knowledge." In *Action Knowledge and Reality: Critical Studies in Honor of Wilfrid Sellars*, edited by Hector-Neri Castañeda, Indianapolis, IN: Bobbs-Merrill, 1975, pp. 295–347.

Sextus Empiricus. *Outlines of Scepticism*. Translated by Julia Annas and Jonathan Barnes. Cambridge, UK: Cambridge University Press, 2000. The original work probably dates from second century C.E.

Shoemaker, Sydney. *Identity, Cause, and Mind: Philosophical Essays*. Cambridge, UK: Cambridge University Press, 1984.

Siegel, Susanna. "The Contents of Perception." In *The Stanford Encyclopedia of Philosophy*, summer 2005 ed., edited by Edward N. Zalta. Available at http://plato.stanford.edu/archives/sum2005/entries/perception-contents/.

Smith, A. D. *The Problem of Perception*. Cambridge, MA: Harvard University Press, 2002.

Snowdon, Paul. "The Objects of Perceptual Experience." *Proceedings of the Aristotelian Society,* suppl. vol. 64 (1990), 121–150.

Soames, Scott. *Understanding Truth*. Oxford: Oxford University Press, 1999.

Sosa, Ernest. "The Raft and the Pyramid: Coherence Versus Foundations in the Theory of Knowledge." Reprinted in *The Theory of Knowledge: Classical and Contemporary Readings*, 2d ed., edited by Louis P. Pojman, Belmont, CA: Wadsworth, 1999, pp. 251–266. Originally published in 1980.

Sosa, Ernest. "The Mythology of the Given." *History of Philosophy Quarterly* 14 (1997), 275–286.

Stine, Gail. "Skepticism, Relevant Alternatives, and Deductive Closure." Reprinted in *Skepticism: A Contemporary Reader*, edited by Keith DeRose and Ted A. Warfield, Oxford: Oxford University Press, 1999, pp. 145–155. Originally published in 1976.

Strawson, P. F. "Perception and Its Objects." Reprinted in *Perceptual Knowledge*, edited by Jonathan Dancy, Oxford: Oxford University Press, 1988, pp. 92–112. Originally published in 1979.

Stroud, Barry. "Transcendental Arguments." Reprinted in Stroud's *Understanding Human Knowledge: Philosophical Essays*, Oxford: Oxford University Press, 2000, pp. 9–25. Originally published in 1968.

Stroud, Barry. *Understanding Human Knowledge: Philosophical Essays*. Oxford: Oxford University Press, 2000.

Swartz, Robert J. *Perceiving, Sensing, and Knowing: A Book of Readings from Twentieth-Century Sources in the Philosophy of Perception*. Berkeley: University of California Press, 1965.

Tarski, Alfred. *Logic, Semantics, Metamathematics: Papers from 1923 to 1938*. Translated by J. H. Woodger. Oxford: Clarendon Press, 1956.

Thomason, Richmond H. "Introduction." In *Formal Philosophy: Selected Papers of Richard Montague*, edited by Richmond H. Thomason, New Haven, CT: Yale University Press, 1974, pp. 1–69.

Unger, Peter. *Ignorance: A Case for Scepticism*. Oxford: Clarendon Press, 1975.

van Fraassen, Bas C. *The Empirical Stance*. New Haven, CT: Yale University Press, 2002.

Williams, Michael. "Epistemological Realism and the Basis of Scepticism." *Mind* 97 (1988), 415–439.

Wilson, Mark. "Predicate Meets Property." *Philosophical Review* 91 (1982), 549–589.

Wilson, Mark. "Inference and Correlational Truth." In *Circularity, Definition and Truth*, edited by André Chapuis and Anil Gupta, New Delhi: Indian Council of Philosophical Research, 2000 [distributed outside India by Ridgeview Publishing Company, Atascadero, CA], pp. 371–95.

Wilson, Mark. *Wandering Significance: An Essay on Conceptual Behavior*. Oxford: Clarendon Press, 2006.

Wittgenstein, Ludwig. *Philosophical Investigations*. Translated by G. E. M. Anscombe. New York: Macmillan, 1953.

Wittgenstein, Ludwig. *The Blue and Brown Books: Preliminary Studies for the 'Philosophical Investigations'*. New York: Harper and Row, 1958.

Zalta, Edward N. *Intensional Logic and Metaphysics of Intensionality*. Cambridge, MA: MIT Press, 1988.

INDEX